D0975336

TRIPLE CROSS

TRIPLE CROSS

by Louis Toscano

A Birch Lane Press Book
Published by Carol Publishing Group

Copyright © 1990 by Louis Toscano

A Birch Lane Press Book
Published by Carol Publishing Group

Editorial Offices
600 Madison Avenue
New York, NY 10022

Sales & Distribution Offices
120 Enterprise Avenue
Secaucus, NJ 07094

In Canada: Musson Book Company
A division of General Publishing Co. Limited
Don Mills, Ontario

All rights reserved. No part of this book
may be reproduced in any form, except by
a newspaper or magazine reviewer who wishes
to quote brief passages in connection
with a review.

Queries regarding rights and permissions
should be addressed to: Carol Publishing Group,
600 Madison Avenue, New York, NY 10022

Manufactured in the United States of America

Library of Congress Cataloging-in-Publication Data

Toscano, Louis.
        Triple cross / by Louis Toscano.
            p.   cm.
        "A Birch Lane Press book."
        Includes index.
        ISBN 1-55972-028-x : $19.95
        1. Israel--Military policy. 2. Vanunu, Mordechai. 3. Nuclear
weapons--Israel. 4. Defense information, Classified--Israel.
5. Treason--Israel. 6. Sunday times (London, England : 1981).
I. Title.
UA853.I8T67   1990
355.8'25119'095694--dc20   90-2048
                                                      CIP

For my parents, for Ellyn, and for Mark

Acknowledgments

This book could not have been written without the cooperation of more than 120 people who contributed their recollections about the Mordechai Vanunu affair. It is impossible to thank each of them individually in this space, but several must be singled out for special mention.

I am indebted to the Israeli intelligence and government sources who helped fill in the gaps in a fascinating story of international intrigue. For personal and professional reasons, they cannot be thanked by name. They offered their cooperation in the belief that I was intent upon writing a balanced and accurate account of the story. For their confidence, I am grateful.

Current and former editors and reporters at the London *Sunday Times*—in particular, Peter Hounam, the principal reporter on the team that pieced together the Vanunu story—graciously permitted me to interview them at length about the events of 1986.

Meir Vanunu put aside reservations about the project to trace the story of his brother and of his family. Mordechai Vanunu's attorneys, Avigdor Feldman and Amnon Zichroni, were extremely helpful within the confines of legal restrictions imposed upon them by their government.

Daniel Kirtchuk and Nancie Katz provided invaluable research assistance in Israel and helped me navigate the often murky waters of the Israeli government and society.

In London, Simon Freeman generously offered his hospitality and sound advice, as well as a book title, and Sue Baker was a constant source of encouragement. In Jerusalem, William Ries helped me through the reporting process and opened his home to a journalist on a tight budget. In Rome, Brendan Murphy pointed me in the right direction. And in Washington, D.C., Jeff Stein provided his professional help and personal support throughout the writing process.

Three former colleagues at United Press International also deserve many thanks: Kim Willenson and Jay Ross, who assigned me to Israel for UPI, and Sylvana Foa, who gave me my first overseas posting.

Hillel Black, my editor, guided a first-time author through the writing process with much sensitivity, skill and good humor. Rollene Saal, my agent, maintained an unflagging optimism about the project, and has my deepest gratitude.

I must thank Bob McHugh and Joan Cavaluzzo, who cannot know how much their close friendship, encouragement and advice have meant to me over the years.

There are no words to adequately express my gratitude to my oldest friends, Norman Reimer and Linda Abrams Reimer, for two decades of love, unqualified support and simply being there. Their contribution to this book, and to my life, is immeasurable.

Finally, I want to thank Valerie Strauss, who edited each draft of the manuscript and contributed enormously to virtually every aspect of the book. More importantly, her love and understanding in the face of innumerable sacrifices have been a constant source of inspiration. None of this would have been possible without her.

Contents

TRIPLE CROSS

PART I

Betrayal

Prologue

Late on a torrid September afternoon in 1985, a battered blue-and-white Volvo bus honked its way through the heavy traffic on the edge of the Israeli city of Beersheba and rumbled onto a two-lane asphalt highway that knifed through the Negev desert all the way to Sodom. A thin film of grime swirled through the open windows as the bus picked up speed past the city limits and swayed down the road, ferrying thirty-odd men and women to work on the 3:30 p.m.-to-12 a.m. shift at the Negev Nuclear Research Center, a half hour away.

The bus rattled through the desert, a parched ocean of centuries-old bleached rock, sand, and barren hills interrupted only occasionally by signs of life: clumps of shrivelled green vegetation fading under the savage sun, groups of Bedouin children playing soccer in the dust using scraps of rusting metal as goalposts. It was depressingly familiar terrain to the passengers who made the trip daily, and they dozed or read or chatted quietly with friends to pass the time. A bored security guard clutching an automatic rifle sat up front. Another gun lay on the floor under the driver's seat.

A man wearing blue jeans and a work shirt sat alone in a seat near the rear, with a worn knapsack planted on his lap. He was short, but a wiry, muscular build made him seem much bigger. He had close-cropped black hair that was beginning to thin on top, and dark, diffident eyes that accented a swarthy complexion. He was only thirty years old, but there was about him an aura of frustrated sorrow more appropriate to someone much older. His name was Mordechai Vanunu.

The bus sped past the turnoff for the town of Dimona, a dreary, working-class community of squat concrete-block apartment houses, then rolled up a slight rise in the highway. Suddenly, in the distance off to the right, the nuclear research center popped into view. The giant silver dome housing the nuclear reactor shimmered in the heat. Several smaller buildings, a few towers and some trees made up the rest of the complex.

There were no highway signs identifying the center, commonly referred to as "the Dimona plant," but it was readily apparent that a serious business was conducted there. An electrified perimeter fence surrounded the complex at a distance of about three miles. Attached to the fence were white metal signs with red and black lettering in both Hebrew and English reading, "No Entry! It is prohibited to take photographs. Trespassers will be punished." Soldiers in trucks and helicopters patrolled the perimeter, and sentries were posted in observation towers that rose from the tops of nearby hills. The sand inside the fence was swept smooth so the footprints of intruders could be easily spotted.

What was not visible was even more ominous. The complex was guarded by several Hawk and Chapperelle ground-to-air missile batteries under standing orders to shoot down any aircraft that approached the plant. This applied to everybody. An Israeli Air Force pilot who accidentally flew over the complex in 1967 was knocked out of the sky.

There was, of course, a reason for all the security. The Negev Nuclear Research Center, "Kirya-le-Mehekar Gariny" in Hebrew, is where Israel builds its nuclear weapons.

The bus left the highway at a break in the fence marked off by a "No Access" sign and concrete-packed oil drums painted black and white. It drove slowly through two army checkpoints before braking to a stop in a parking lot outside the employee cafeteria in the heart of the complex.

Vanunu had barely stirred as the bus passed through the security gates. A control room technician, he had worked at the plant for just over eight years. He was used to the routine.

And he was tired of it. He had made up his mind four months earlier that he would quit his job. A growing disillusionment with the policies of the Israeli government—the 1982 invasion of Lebanon, discrimination against Arabs, a refusal to talk peace with the Palestinians—had spilled over into his work. He no longer felt comfortable contributing to Israel's nuclear arsenal. He wanted out, out of Dimona, probably even out of Israel. But until then, he would play the game.

This afternoon was a little different. Hidden in the knapsack on the seat next to Vanunu was a Pentax MV 35mm camera and two rolls of film. On this day, Vanunu was going to take photographs of the most secret installation in Israel.

The pictures, he knew, would show that Israel was making atomic bombs in a supersecret factory buried six levels below the desert, so well hidden that not even the sophisticated spy satellites of Israel's closest ally, the United States, had ever detected it.

Vanunu wasn't sure why he was doing it. Taking the photographs, he realized, would be a major breach of security, an unthinkable crime in a country where security is a national pastime. But Vanunu wanted a record of the place where he had spent so much time.

"Partly as a souvenir," he would explain later, "and partly because it had crossed my mind two years earlier that I might tell someone what really happens at Dimona."

What he did not know was that Israel would want him to do just that.

Chapter 1

When the state of Israel was created in 1948, the Negev desert was one of the most desolate places on earth, 6,500 square miles of sand, scrub brush and low, rocky hills untouched by development and inhabited almost exclusively by nomadic tribes of Bedouin Arabs who had roamed the stark terrain for centuries. Nothing much had changed in all those years, and the Bedouin liked that pace. A story is told about a tribesman who vowed revenge after his brother was murdered by a neighbor. Twenty years later, the man walked across the road, killed the neighbor, then returned home and boasted to a friend that he had avenged his brother's death.

"What was your hurry?" the friend replied.

But David Ben-Gurion, the impatient visionary who was Israel's founding father and first prime minister, was in a rush. He wanted to build a nation, and the Negev figured prominently in his plans. Three thousand years earlier, the Jewish people had wandered out of Egypt and into the wilderness of Zin, in the central Negev, headed for the land of Canaan. That exodus began the tortuous Jewish struggle for a place in the sun. Now, Ben-Gurion wanted another group of pioneers—thousands of them, the best of the immigrants streaming into the new nation—to return to the wilderness to fulfill the dream of their ancestors.

In the desert sands he saw vast irrigation projects that would make the Negev an agricultural heaven, and factories and laboratories that would turn Israel into an enormous industrial power supplying the needs of Africa and Asia. In Ben-Gurion's eyes, the Biblical city of Beersheba, then a sleepy Arab way station for the camel caravans that crisscrossed the desert, would be transformed into the bustling, modern capital of the new Negev.

Israelis, however, overwhelmingly ignored Ben-Gurion's call. Few were willing to trade the relative comfort of life in the north for a spartan existence in the hellish heat of the desert. Many of the first Israelis had come from Europe and North America, and found life in the cities of their underdeveloped new homeland incredibly difficult. Living in the desert was almost unthinkable, no matter what the goal. When the sixty-eight-year-old prime minister, determined to lead by example, stepped aside in 1954 to spend a year working on a central Negev kibbutz, even his own wife was aghast.

In desperation, Ben-Gurion turned to the flood of late-arriving immigrants from North Africa. Despite a general lack of skills and education, their efforts met with some success. Patches of desert bloomed. Refineries and plants were built to process the copper, potash, methane gas and quartz gypsum pulled from beneath the sand. Beersheba ballooned into a city of more than 100,000 people, and a few development towns and kibbutzim sprang up to house workers and their growing families. Military outposts dotted the landscape, forming a first line of defense against an Egyptian attack.

But Ben-Gurion's audacious plans ultimately failed. The Negev never became the industrial gateway to the underdeveloped world, and the new Israelis never reclaimed the wilderness of Zin. And instead of a glittering desert jewel, Beersheba grew into a despairing Third World city that traveled a hopeless path from frontier boomtown to blue-collar ghetto in the wink of a decade. As the dreams of the 1960s gave way to the disenchantment of the 1970s, development ceased and unemployment rose. The middle class moved out, leaving behind a stagnant pool of the uneducated and unskilled, most of them North African immigrants and their families. For them, there was not enough work, not enough play and nowhere to go. As the jobs dried up, crime and drug abuse flourished. The city had tried to make a deal with the desert, and lost.

In the best of times, Beersheba is a hard place seemingly on the edge of the world. Searing winds blow in from the desert, filling the scorched air with a throat-burning mist of grit, and a fierce, unforgiving sun pounds down on streets lined with cracked, peeling apartment buildings. Residents live in tiny, thin-walled concrete boxes in neighborhoods identified by letters, not names. Everywhere there is a palpable sense of confinement created by the Negev lurking on the not-so-distant horizon, visible even from the middle of town.

Mordechai Vanunu grew up in Beersheba and the experience helped shape him in a way that would one day shake his country.

Chapter 2

Vanunu was born October 13, 1954, in Marrakesh, Morocco, the second son of a middle-class family living in the Jewish quarter of the city. His father, Solomon, ran a small food store and his mother, Mazal, took in sewing to help meet expenses.

It was a comfortable existence. The European influence of Morocco's French rulers lent an air of sophistication to everyday life, even for people like the Vanunus who wore homemade clothes and moved every two years as the family grew. There were weekends spent playing in the parks, holidays in the mountains. The children attended good schools and did well: Mordechai quickly learned French and Arabic and showed an early aptitude for mathematics. And every evening there were Torah study classes. Solomon Vanunu was a pious man, so devout and learned that he was regarded as a rabbi in the Jewish community.

But Morocco was changing. The country's Berber majority had long tolerated the small Jewish enclave in their midst, and relations had even warmed slightly after the French took control of Morocco in 1912. As Morocco moved toward independence in the early 1950s, however, anti-Jewish sentiment rose. Arab mobs stoned Jews on the streets and pillaged their businesses. Mordechai's twenty-minute walk to school every morning was increasingly fraught with danger.

More than 100,000 Jews emigrated to Israel in the years following the birth of the nation. But when Morocco gained its independence from France in 1956, the exit gates slammed shut under pressure from other Arab states determined to prevent Israel from growing. Perhaps as many as another 100,000 Jews were left behind.

Israel had begun preparing for the emigration crackdown even before France freed its colony. The fledgling Israeli intelligence agency, the Mossad, had secretly built a network of agents inside Morocco to help protect the remaining Jews from Arab attacks and to eventually spirit them out of North Africa to Israel. It was often a treacherous journey. In January 1961, forty-four men, women and children died when the ship carrying them out of Morocco sank off the coast.

But by bribing Moroccan officials and playing on post-World War II guilt feelings to establish temporary relocation camps on Spanish and British territory, the Mossad managed to slip out more than 80,000 additional Jews after Morocco gained independence. The Jewish community in Marrakesh rapidly dwindled between 1955 and 1963 as families succumbed to the Zionist recruiters who went door-to-door trying to persuade Jews to emigrate.

One of Mordechai's grandfathers and almost all of his aunts, uncles and cousins had left for Israel in the first wave of emigration in 1952. But Solomon Vanunu, like many of the more affluent Moroccan Jews, steadfastly resisted the blandishments of the recruiters. His business was thriving, he argued, why give it up now? Besides, what he knew of Israel worried him. Israel sounded like a very secular society, he complained, run by God-forsaking socialists. Solomon Vanunu hated the thought. Religion was his life. He wanted no part of a country where religion was forced to take a back seat.

But as the Jewish quarter emptied, the elder Vanunu began worrying about being left alone. Like many Moroccan Jews, he could have gone to France or Canada. But ultimately the attraction of living in a land where Jews were kings was too strong to resist.

By 1963, when Mordechai was nine years old, Solomon was ready to move. He sold his business and most of the family's belongings, raising a substantial bankroll to finance the new start in Israel. It would be a wonderful life, he told his seven children. With hundreds of their neighbors, the Vanunus took a night train to Casablanca, where a large ship provided by the Israeli government was waiting to move them to a relocation camp in France.

The crossing was a nightmare. The ship was packed with Jews

from all over North Africa, lying in row after row of bunk beds crammed together below decks. It was the first sea voyage for most of the passengers and many spent the first night vomiting as the ship steamed into rough weather.

The Vanunus spent about a month in the camp outside Marseilles. Solomon, intent on making life in Israel as comfortable as possible, spent a small fortune on modern appliances. He bought a Westing-house refrigerator, a washing machine, expensive rugs, a record player and a tape recorder, even a little motor scooter. "Israel is a modern, European country," he assured his wife when she began to worry about the purchases. "Everyone has things like this. We must, too."

No one told him that in Israel blocks of ice were still being used to cool food. Or that electricity was a luxury in many areas of the country. Or that many Israelis lived cheek-to-jowl in tiny apartments, with little room for furniture. Worse, no one explained then that there would be no room for any of Solomon's acquisitions when the Vanunus set sail on the final leg of the journey to Israel. But as the family boarded the boat, emigration officials promised the appliances and furnishings would be sent along later.

The trip to Israel took about a week, with a one-day stopover in Italy. This voyage was better. The weather was fine, the food was good and the children spent much of the time swimming in the ship's pool.

On the morning of June 12,1963, the Vanunus saw Israel for the first time. It was an emotional, breathtaking experience. As they approached the coastline, heading for the northern port city of Haifa, miles of pristine Mediterranean beaches could be seen, with mountains glistening in the background. Off in the distance were fields of crops and trees. Nearer to shore, the family watched women pick through tables laden with fresh fruits and vegetables at an open-air market, and stared at the houses on the slopes of Mount Carmel, which rose sharply from the harbor.

Solomon Vanunu stood on deck and wept quietly. He had made the right decision. Here was Israel, land of the Jews. Here he could raise his family in peace. Here they would be among their own people.

Almost immediately, the Vanunus ran into trouble. The family had planned to move in with relatives living near Haifa. But the port was only the first stop for most of the 38,000 North African Jews who emigrated to Israel in 1963. The Israeli government had decided the North Africans would be well-suited to the harsher realities of life in Israel, particularly in regions like the Negev. And unlike the European Jews who rebuffed Ben-Gurion's efforts to draw them to the desert, the new arrivals would have no choice in the matter. Immigration officials ignored the Vanunus' pleas to settle near Haifa, and told them they were going to a new settlement at Beersheba. A few short hours after their ship came in, the family was packed into two taxis and sent south.

They arrived in the blistering heat of the afternoon, sweltering in their French-cut clothing and fancy straw hats. Everyone was stunned by the bleak landscape surrounding them.

"We got out of the taxi and they showed us to a small hut," Mordechai would recall later. "It was made of wood, and there was one big room inside. Outside, there was a small toilet. My father was upset. He sat in the corner of the hut, not believing this was the land of honey. He thought about green land and water, and he didn't speak with anyone. And for a couple of days we didn't understand where we were. It was like leaving the Garden of Eden and going into the desert."

Devastated, Solomon sought the advice of relatives living in Ashkelon, a town on the Mediterranean, but they told him there was nothing to be done. In Israel, you do as the government tells you.

Anger, however, emboldened the old man. "This is ridiculous," he told his wife. "It is Israel. I am a Jew. We will live where we want."

The family drove north and joined Mazal's relatives in a settlement east of Haifa. This was much more like the Israel that Solomon had envisioned—trees, green fields and a cool breeze. An empty apartment was located, and the Vanunus happily occupied it.

Six weeks later, the police turned up and ordered them back to

Beersheba. By the time they returned, the shipment from Marseilles had arrived. Some of the items were missing, stolen along the way. Most of the rest were useless. There was no electricity in their barracks-style shelter.

At the end of 1963, the Vanunus were moved to two new apartments in a huge building in a rundown, crime-ridden neighborhood. There was no room for the appliances there, either. Making matters worse was more culture shock. The neighbors were mostly Moroccan, which lent an air of familiarity to their surroundings. But the size of the multi-story housing complex was intimidating. No one in Morocco had lived in such an enormous building, and children frequently lost their way home.

The readjustment was particularly difficult for Solomon. In Morocco, he had taken care of all his family's needs, made all the decisions. But in Israel he had to rely on the state to take care of everything from education to health to employment. And he had trouble finding work. He finally was hired on as a laborer on a road crew, but long days in the 100-plus-degree heat of the desert sapped his strength. The fifty-three-year-old man tried picking peanuts but only became sicker. Physically and emotionally exhausted, he broke down and was confined to bed, unable to earn a living to support his wife and children.

The constant assault on his authority took its toll. Solomon lost his confidence and berated himself for what he perceived to be his failure. In Morocco, Vanunu had been a relatively well-to-do merchant, a religious authority, a respected community leader. In Israel, he was a common laborer pushed around by the police. And as his self-image shattered, his authority over his family crumbled.

Solomon's travails had a profound effect on young Mordechai. He was depressed and angered by his father's plight. Years later, Mordechai would cry when he recalled how the appliances Solomon bought to make life in Israel easier had sat outside in the dry desert climate and gradually deteriorated.

Chapter 3

Four more children had come along by mid-1969, and the Vanunus moved into two apartments across a tiny hall from one another in a small apartment house on Derech Avraham Avinu, a quiet residential street in the "D" neighborhood of Beersheba. The apartment looked out on a small, long-neglected backyard, strewn with garbage and overgrown with weeds. One morning, Mordechai set to work by himself clearing the lot, and eventually planted a vegetable garden.

The Vanunus were recovering from their rocky start. To make ends meet during his convalescence, Solomon had begun selling off some of the family's possessions from the floor of the city's central market. Then he discovered he could drive to Tel Aviv, buy second-hand goods and sell them back in Beersheba, where even used merchandise was at a premium. He rented a stall with a corrugated tin roof on the edge of the market and opened a new business, specializing in religious items like books, prayer shawls, menorahs and mezzuzahs. Solomon had also reestablished his reputation as a community religious leader and was once again leading synagogue services and dispensing Torah-inspired advice. He was occasionally invited to make speaking tours of Moroccan Jewish communities in the United States and other countries. But Solomon turned down the offers. He was a modest, shy man who much preferred to stay at home, enjoying a life that revolved exclusively around his work, his synagogue and his family.

As his social and economic position slowly improved, the father tried to erase any feelings of bitterness his children might have developed after their first years in Israel. "It doesn't matter what happened," he sternly lectured when they complained about their treatment. "We should kiss the land. This is Israel. We have to make it work. It is for us to take it from here."

Solomon Vanunu's willingness to work hard, his ready acceptance of the need for sacrifice, represented precisely the kind of driving spirit that Ben-Gurion had so fervently hoped would be the hallmark of the new nation. But in a perverse, haunting twist, Israel had instead quickly become a society where men with backgrounds like Solomon Vanunu could never hope to move too far ahead, no matter how hard they tried.

The North Africans, Oriental Jews known in Hebrew as Sephardim, were lured to Israel by promises of social, political and economic equality and an end to the oppression they faced from the Moslem majorities who scorned the Jews as outsiders. To their dismay, however, the Sephardim soon encountered a remarkably similar pattern of discrimination in Israel. They arrived in a country tightly controlled by a relatively educated and affluent European elite that regarded the late-arriving immigrants with unbridled contempt—illiterate, crude, primitive people, prone to violence and crime, Arab in appearance and culture. The European Jews, or Ashkenazim, created a society that was essentially European in nature, and arrogantly stamped out attempts by the Sephardim, bewildered by their alien new world, to inject aspects of their own national backgrounds into the developing Israeli culture.

The Sephardim were Jews, yes, so they had to be accepted. But not absorbed.

Other Sephardic Jews who emigrated from places like Turkey, Greece, Asia and, to an extent, South America also faced discrimination. But the problem was perhaps most acute among Jews from North Africa and Middle Eastern countries like Iraq and Iran, who bore the added burden of looking and acting like Arabs in a country threatened with extinction by Arabs.

Many Sephardim, like Solomon Vanunu, actually found conditions in Israel worse in some ways than in their homelands. Confined to their tiny enclaves in Morocco, Tunisia, Algeria, Libya, they had at least achieved a measure of economic and professional success. In Israel, however, men who had once worked as lawyers or merchants or small businessmen were relegated to only the most menial tasks, forced to take jobs as laborers or construction workers or field hands.

Moreover, the Ashkenazim were clearly uninterested in sharing any of the power they were enjoying for the first time after centuries of repression in Europe. An informal system of "protekzia" gave European Jews preferential treatment in most areas of Israeli society. Cities like Beersheba became dumping grounds for the politically powerless Sephardim who were left to wallow in poverty, often living ten to a room in rotting slums without the jobs, social services or educational programs desperately needed to prepare them for a brighter future.

Solomon Vanunu, however, was determined to help his family escape the deadly morass. He struggled to shut out the world of disillusionment in the streets just outside the front door and implored his children to study hard and rely on each other for support in their attempts at advancement. Mordechai and his brothers and sisters avoided others their age and instead played among themselves or with a small group of Romanian immigrant children whose parents shared Vanunu's ethic. The father imbued his children with a sense of superiority, a feeling that they were placed on earth to make a difference in life, no matter what the obstacles.

The Vanunu boys and girls were all well-behaved, bright achievers, but no one doubted that Mordechai was the favorite. The oldest son, Albert, had been taken out of school at age fourteen and sent to work to help support the family, and Mordechai, the second son, became the focus of his father's hopes and dreams. Motti, as the youngster was known, was in many respects an unusually compliant child. Without protest, he cared for his younger siblings, helped his mother clean the house, went shopping, did the laundry, and took care of minor repairs and other odd jobs at home. He spent his free time reading, mostly classical and religious literature. Solomon sent both Mordechai and his younger brother Meir to private religious academies, and Mordechai embraced his father's emphasis on the importance of education, spending hours studying on his own. Solomon, who harbored a hope that his second son would become a great religious figure, insisted Mordechai receive traditional Orthodox Jewish religious training, and his son unquestioningly plunged into Torah studies.

By his early teens, Mordechai was a quiet, shy boy with an unquenchable curiosity. But he rarely ventured far from home, aside from weekly pilgrimages to the Bedouin market held on the edge of town every Thursday, where he spent hours sampling food and inspecting the wares before returning home to regale the other children with his experiences.

Despite the father's efforts, however, the outside world slowly creeped into the Vanunu household. The clash between the implacably religious culture of the Sephardi immigrants and the more secular society that dominated a country largely founded by European socialists was creating conflicts that the elder Vanunus were ill-equipped to handle. On the street, the children learned that religion at best was only one option, and they began challenging their father's Biblically inspired explanations and decisions. At age sixteen Motti insisted on leaving his strict religious high school, preferring to study in a more open environment.

Solomon was upset and disappointed, but he never stopped believing he could reinvigorate his children's flagging religious beliefs. It was just a phase, he told himself, and sometimes it appeared he was right. Even after he openly broke with his father over religion, Mordechai would go out of his way to please the old man by reciting long passages of the Torah from memory.

"Look," his beaming father told him one night, "even though you've become so secular, you've got all that in you. You're going to be all right. Deep down inside, you still have the religion in you."

Chapter 4

After graduating from high school, Mordechai faced military service, which is compulsory for all Israelis at age eighteen. Vanunu was eager to serve. At seventeen, just out of school, he had volunteered for the air force in hopes of becoming a pilot. It was unusual for Moroccan Jews to be accepted in the air force in 1971, but Vanunu was permitted to take the entrance examinations on the strength of his exceptional academic record. To his disappointment, however, he didn't pass the test.

Still, when he entered the army the next year, he was quickly tapped as a squad commander and was assigned to the engineering corps. He served with distinction in the 1973 Yom Kippur war, and in 1974 spent time in the Golan Heights, blowing up army installations in advance of the return of part of the region to Syria.

Soldiers who served with him later remembered Vanunu as an indifferent or ineffective unit commander. But he progressed through the ranks to first sergeant and was highly regarded by his superiors, who urged him to consider a career in the army. Vanunu turned them down, saying he was more interested in pursuing his education. But he was very flattered.

After leaving the army, Vanunu enrolled at Tel Aviv University to study physics. Forced to work fulltime to support himself, he quickly encountered difficulties keeping up with his course work. At the end of the first year, he dropped out of school and returned to Beersheba in 1976 to look for a job.

Vanunu made the trip with little enthusiasm. His time in Tel Aviv—a European-style city on the Mediterranean with restaurants and cafes, museums, and a degree of sophistication sorely lacking in the desert—had exposed him to the possibilities of a better life.

He dreaded the prospect of going home, living again in a city bereft of intellectual stimulation. "It's like a giant labor camp," he moaned to his brother Meir. "They all get up at 6 a.m., go off to work, then scurry home to their little cells."

With no money or job prospects in Tel Aviv, however, Vanunu had little choice but to head home. For the first few months, he held a series of odd jobs, including one lengthy stint as a records clerk at the Beersheba District Court. His supervisors were impressed with his intelligence and urged him to stay, but the work was not satisfying, and Vanunu continued to search for something more fulfilling.

One day, he bumped into a friend of Meir's who worked at the Dimona nuclear reactor. The plant was hiring.

Vanunu was already interested. He had noticed help-wanted advertisements in the newspapers for jobs at Dimona that paid well, offered good benefits, and involved science and mathematics, subjects that Vanunu had excelled in and enjoyed since childhood. Vanunu rushed over to the plant's employment offices on the third floor of a building near Beersheba's central bus station and picked up an application form. A month later, after a routine interview by a woman in the security office who asked whether he had a criminal record and inquired about his political affiliations, Vanunu was notified that he had been accepted for training.

For ten weeks, his class of forty-four recruits was given a crash course in English, mathematics, physics and chemistry at a special school in the town of Dimona. In late January, the candidates were given an examination. All forty-four passed, but six students were washed out of the program anyway. No one said anything, but the other recruits were led to believe that the six had failed security checks.

A few days later, the thirty-eight survivors were taken by bus inside the Dimona complex for the first time. They were asked to sign a security form pledging not to disclose any information about their work and promising not to visit any communist or Arab country for five years after leaving their jobs. Violators faced up to fifteen years in prison. After signing the secrecy document, Vanunu was given a plant access pass, No. 9657-8, and a series of medical examinations. He and the other trainees spent two more months in school, taking courses in the rudiments of nuclear physics and chemical engineering, and studying technical English and first aid and fire prevention in a small six-classroom building within the Dimona complex. A few more students dropped out for academic reasons, and by April, after another comprehensive examination, only twenty-eight candidates remained.

The class was then split into two groups of fourteen for advanced training as radiation monitors and process controllers. Three months later, Vanunu passed his final examinations and was approved for duty by a certification board. On August 7, 1977, he went to work for the first time, his salary jumping from the $300-a-month training wage to about $500 monthly, good pay by Israeli standards at the time.

It was a heady moment for Vanunu. Before he even spent an hour on the job, he was consumed with visions of a glowing future. This entry-level job would be only the start of a climb to the top. Here was a chance to use his abilities in the natural sciences. Very few people growing up in the confines of Beersheba received an opportunity like this, or, more importantly, had the skills to exploit it.

Work hard, study hard, Vanunu told himself, and you'll go a long way.

Chapter 5

Israel claimed Dimona was a research center where work was conducted on ways to harness nuclear power for peaceful purposes, and on the surface the complex appeared to be exactly that. Along streets lined with palm trees lay ten separate production units, nine of which were in operation, including the giant domed reactor that could be seen from the highway. The classroom building where trainees received advanced instruction, a union office, an employee cafeteria, a library and a parking lot sat at one end of the complex, near the road leading out of the plant.

The operation of the plant was highly compartmentalized. Each worker was assigned a specific task in a specific unit, known as a "machon" in Hebrew, and was discouraged from asking colleagues about the nature of the activities being conducted in other units. Most employees accepted these restrictions without question. If they had suspicions about the plant's true purpose, they rarely, if ever, discussed them.

By chance, Mordechai Vanunu was assigned to Machon 2. To an outsider, the windowless, two-story concrete building next to the reactor seemed to be one of the more mundane facilities at Dimona, a warehouse, perhaps, or some kind of administrative office. But there was something odd about Machon 2. The roof was topped with an elevator tower, a curious feature for a two-story building. The walls were several feet thick, a precaution generally taken to protect a building from bomb attack or to prevent radiation leakage. Only 150 of Dimona's 2,700 workers were issued the special passes needed to enter the building, and once inside their movements, even the bathrooms they used, were strictly controlled. More so than elsewhere at Dimona, officials did not want in Machon 2 employees swapping information about their activities. And the high degree of automation made it unlikely that workers trained to perform isolated, relatively simple tasks would ever understand exactly what they were doing.

Still, new employees quickly learned the truth about their jobs: Machon 2 was Israel's supersecret nuclear weapons factory. In laboratories and work shops on six levels under the desert floor, scientists and technicians were building bombs.

The discovery excited Vanunu. Eager to advance, he was determined to learn how the unit operated, and his work assignment gave him the opportunity. Trained as a controller, or "menahel," Vanunu was placed in the main control room on Level 2. Once he learned the routine, Vanunu found the work anything but stimulating. Machon 2 was divided into at least thirty-seven smaller production units, and Vanunu would eventually work in thirty-three of them. He likened much of the work to the baking of a cake; during the actual cooking, there was little to do. Alarms would sound if any part of the process went awry. The control room technicians would then have only to check an instrument panel to determine the problem and devise a solution.

His colleagues would take advantage of the free time to relax in the canteen, shower, sleep, read or play endless rounds of canasta. But Vanunu, bored and as always insatiably curious, would wander through Machon 2, talking to other workers, asking questions, learning about the process.

Nuclear warheads are made from one of two elements—uranium 235 or plutonium. The production of weapons-grade uranium entails the use of cumbersome gaseous diffusion plants or a large number of gas centrifuges. In contrast, plutonium, a natural by-product of the nuclear reactor process, can be stripped from the reactor's spent fuel rods in a much smaller separation plant. Machon 2 was essentially a giant reprocessing plant where the plutonium was produced and then fashioned into nuclear weapons.

The two above-ground floors and the first subterranean level of the production unit were a tedious warren of offices, storerooms, workshops and power plants. But on one second-floor corridor were two elevators—one for freight and the other for passengers—that dropped into the heart of the weapons plant. Vanunu later learned the entrance to the corridor where the elevator doors were located had been routinely bricked up when American inspectors were shown the building, but the inspections had ended in 1969.

Most of Machon 2 was a mesmerizing scientific wonderland. An enormous production hall, housing the main chemical laboratory for the separation of plutonium from uranium, rose from Level 4 through Level 2. The view from Level 2 was so impressive that its "Golda Balcony," named after former Prime Minister Golda Meir, was a featured attraction on inspection tours by senior Israeli officials.

The main control room on Level 2 was a 100-foot-long maze of polished instrument panels, switches, illuminated dials, gauges and flow charts that Vanunu and his co-workers used to monitor operations throughout the production hall. Spent fuel rods from the reactor were lowered by hoist from the ground floor to Level 3 where they were stripped of their aluminum casing and dissolved in nitric acid. The corrosive, radioactive solution then moved through pipes to the various automated units where the plutonium was retrieved. Scientists assigned to laboratories on Level 3 tested the purity of the chemicals used in the plutonium-extraction process. On Level 4, a smaller control room monitored the conversion of the plutonium solution into pure metal, as well as the production of tritium, a radioactive gas used to enhance the power of atomic bombs. Level 6 housed storage tanks to hold the radioactive solutions in case of an emergency.

Only one floor—Level 5—was off-limits to Vanunu. A special key needed to open the doors to the workers' elevator on Level 5 was issued to only a few employees, and he was not one of them.

The discovery of Machon 2's true purpose did not particularly bother Vanunu. Like most Israelis, he had long believed Israel possessed a primitive nuclear arsenal, although the government repeatedly denied it. Vanunu also accepted without question the need for the strongest possible national defense. The morality of nuclear weapons and the propriety of a secret nuclear program were not issues that concerned him. He was not interested in politics. Science was the fascinating subject, and the job at Dimona involved science. It was a good position with a bright future that certainly appeared to offer him an opportunity to break the bonds of class discrimination that chained his father and so many other Sephardic Jews. Such a sensitive assignment could only mean his superiors had marked him as a candidate for advancement. Far from finding the work in Machon 2 troubling, Vanunu couldn't believe his good fortune.

In fact, Israel's efforts to shield its secret weapons program from foreign eyes were a source of great amusement to Vanunu and his co-workers. In November 1976, a group of thirteen United States senators had been denied entry to the complex. When Vanunu began work in Machon 2 a year later, he found taped to a wall a newspaper clipping about the senators' attempted visit and the government's denial that any weapons were being built at Dimona. It was always good for a laugh.

Chapter 6

Vanunu knew he would need more education to move ahead, and two years later he decided to resume his college studies. In November 1979, now twenty-five years old, he enrolled as a part-time student at Ben-Gurion University in Beersheba. The school had been founded in 1964 by a group of prominent local residents who believed it could play a leading role in efforts to develop the Negev. The university, up the road from the kibbutz where Ben-Gurion spent his year in the wilderness, was renamed for the country's founding father after his death in 1973, and soon after construction began on a new campus on the edge of the desert, just a few blocks from the neighborhood where Vanunu grew up.

About 5,000 people attend classes at Ben-Gurion. Most Israelis begin university studies after completing their military service—three years for men and two years for women—so the students are generally older, a bit more mature and perhaps a little more serious about their work than their American or European counterparts. Most of them also hold down jobs, leaving them little time for extracurricular activities.

Vanunu fit comfortably in this environment. He briefly toyed with the idea of studying engineering, but thought better of it after a week, realizing he would not have time for the grueling curriculum. Instead, he registered for economics and Greek philosophy, subjects he believed would provide him with the intellectual background needed to break out of the Sephardi career prison and into a position of status in the Ashkenazi-controlled society.

He quickly fell into an extremely structured daily regime. Vanunu would work the overnight shift, then catch the 8 a.m. bus back to the town of Dimona, where he had been living since training in an apartment complex operated by the nuclear plant. After a short nap, he took a bus to school for classes in the afternoon. Then it was home for another rest before heading back to work. The arduous schedule was eased only slightly when Vanunu bought an apartment in Beersheba in late 1980.

After two years, Vanunu was beginning to qualify for special privileges at Dimona. Workers with good records and some seniority were offered an additional $100 a month to help finance a car, and another $25 to defray the cost of a telephone. Vanunu wanted or needed neither, but he claimed the auto payment to help one of his brothers pay for a car and installed a telephone in his parents' home in Beersheba with the other money. Both were minor violations of plant regulations, but no one at Dimona ever bothered to check on how the money was being used.

The plant also offered its employees liberal vacation benefits, and in August 1980 Vanunu left on an extended tour of Europe. The trip marked the first time Vanunu had left Israel since arriving from Morocco seventeen years earlier, and he intended to make the most of it. He traveled alone to London, Amsterdam, West Germany, Scandinavia, West Berlin, Switzerland, France, Spain and Italy. In Rome, he caught a train to Athens, met a Canadian woman and spent ten days touring the Greek islands with her.

Vanunu returned home in mid-October exhausted but thrilled by his experiences. The world he had visited was so different than the society at home. Vanunu had long disliked the confinement of Beersheba, but now for the first time he began to wonder about Israel in general. The people he had met on his travels seemed at such ease with their surroundings. They faced none of the restrictions on thought and opportunity that he had encountered almost daily at home. Israel suddenly seemed just a little suffocating.

And when he returned to work, Vanunu was confronted almost immediately with new questions. He and a small group of technicians were temporarily transferred to newly constructed Unit 95 and told they would be producing a highly volatile metal called lithium-6. The project, plant officials stressed, was top-secret.

The other workers accepted their new assignment with shrugs, but Vanunu as always wanted to know more. One day, he pulled aside a supervisor and asked what the processed metal would be used for.

"Oh, the hydrogen bomb," the supervisor replied, nonchalantly breaching security.

Hydrogen bombs. The subject fascinated Vanunu. But the senior engineers in Unit 95 were not as forthcoming as the supervisor.

"Your job is to produce lithium-6 and not ask questions," Vanunu was coldly told by one engineer when he inquired further.

The rebuff angered Vanunu. They think I'm just another stupid Sephardi, he bitterly told himself.

Determined to find out on his own, Vanunu headed for the library. Hydrogen bombs, he soon learned, were thermonuclear weapons, the most powerful nuclear weapons available. And from his reading, Machon 2 appeared to be producing everything needed to build them. Even the tritium production unit on Level 4 was part of the process; the gas is used in the trigger mechanism of the hydrogen bomb.

For the first time, Vanunu began to think about the scope and the nature of the work being done at Dimona. He had believed that the plant was turning out a crude nuclear arsenal of Hiroshima-era weapons that would be used as a defensive system—Israel's Doomsday device, a force so self-destructive in a region as confined as the Middle East that Israel would deploy it only when defeat was imminent. No one, Vanunu thought, could quarrel with that.

But thermonuclear devices meant something quite different. From his reading, it appeared Israel was amassing a sophisticated, superpower-style arsenal of smaller but far more powerful warheads that could be used as offensive weapons. The technology involved in the production of hydrogen bombs could also be used to build neutron bombs, which emitted radiation that killed people but left buildings intact. To Vanunu, the Dimona program suggested that Israel might use its bombs to start a war, not defend itself against one.

But Vanunu knew little about politics and less about the geopolitical concerns of his country. Like most of his countrymen, he still

viewed the world in stark Arab-vs.-Israeli terms. In that context, he
eventually decided, perhaps the powerful nuclear stockpile being
assembled at Dimona was understandable.

Chapter 7

The bewildering discovery in Unit 95 came at a difficult time for Vanunu. By any measure, he was doing well. After working in Unit 95 for all of 1981, Vanunu received a raise, to more than $800 a month, and he purchased a $20,000 apartment in Beersheba with his savings and some loans. He was making steady progress toward a university degree, even after dropping economics in favor of geography.

But Vanunu was having trouble enjoying any of his success. Something was missing—a direction, a reason for being, the sense of purpose drummed into him at home. Vanunu had begun keeping a diary, scribbling away in cheap notebooks during the slack periods at work or on the bus ride to school, and his writings reflected a growing dissatisfaction about his life and his worry about the future.

"What have I achieved until now?" he wrote in August 1982. "Why am I not relaxed and settled, satisfied with something or enjoying something?"

"I have never been ready to take responsibility for myself," he continued. "Once I thought if you aren't ready, commit suicide and be released from the job given you, from the miseries you see in life. Release the world and your surroundings from your despairing and depressing personality. I am a failure in life. I don't want contact with anyone in society. What will be in the future? I'll continue to exist, without direction, without good or bad. Everything is the same. To run away all the time, to move from place to place."

"What is my path in life? What am I doing with myself in this world?"

His days grew longer as he tried to pack as much as possible into every waking hour. He wrote approvingly of his sacrifices, his ability to get by without sleep, to work long hours in solitude, to accomplish the goals he set for himself. More and more, he was adhering to a spartan lifestyle, and Vanunu brooked no compromises.

"When he did something, he always did it to the extreme," his brother Meir explained. A conversion to vegetarianism meant not only no meat—Vanunu refused all cooked food. An anti-materialistic philosophy did not mean merely an emphasis on the spiritual side of life—Vanunu stopped buying new clothes and sold a new $12,000 automobile just two months after he bought it because, he told his flabbergasted family, "it feels like a finely tailored suit I'm not comfortable wearing."

His compulsion for total commitment had turned even a brief fling with the stock market into an obsession. Intrigued by Meir's success in tripling a $2,000 investment, Mordechai plunged into the world of finance in the early 1980s. It was a volatile period for the Israeli economy, never stable in the best of times. The new Likud government of Menachem Begin, swept into office in 1981 on the votes of Sephardim disenchanted with the pro-Ashkenazim policies of the ruling Labor party, moved to increase consumer spending as a means of solving the country's chronic economic woes. The new prosperity meant some economic advances for the long-suffering Sephardim, but it also touched off an inflationary spiral that had the effect of devaluing bank accounts and other investments on a daily basis. To stay even, many Israelis began to play the financial markets, and a boom in bank shares soon developed.

With his brother's coaching, Mordechai became an active and successful investor, and the idea of using money to make money quickly consumed him.

"A quick exit from the house, straight to the bank," he would later write in his diary about his experience. "Face-to-face with the newspaper, the bank shares' rates. This is today's agricultural fields and orchards. It is the synagogue of our time, the god of our time. The god of ancient times has changed places with numbers and telexes from the stock exchange."

Already living on the edge, Vanunu reduced his expenses even further to scrape together money to play the market. Rather than buy a cup of coffee at the university cafeteria, he would take packets of instant coffee and sugar from the Dimona cafeteria, where they were provided free to workers, then ask for a cup of hot water at school and make his own coffee. In Israel's overheated economy, the austerity paid dividends. Vanunu's small investment was soon worth about $30,000.

In 1983, he spent the summer in the United States with a friend. While he was abroad, the stock market dropped sharply as the government reduced spending and devalued currency to deal with a twenty-one percent inflation rate. He returned home to find he had lost about $10,000. It was a substantial amount of money, even if it did not ruin him, and he quickly and bitterly gave up the investment game.

"What has broken me is the loss of my shares," he wrote after the crash. "Only now am I really able to fully digest it. . . . How can you live as if nothing happened? I've done many things for money. I've broken laws—morality. Physically, nothing mattered but the money."

Vanunu was frustrated. Once again, he had played by the prevailing rules and tried to succeed in Israeli society. Once again he had failed.

Increasingly, he turned to philosophy for answers. It was an odd course of study at Ben-Gurion. The university's emphasis was on engineering and the natural and computer sciences, departments that occupied all but one of the academic buildings set out around a sun-drenched central plaza. The philosophy department, in contrast, consisted of five professors—three of them part-time staff members—working in cramped cubbyholes on the first floor of the humanities and social science building. Ben-Gurion students, an overwhelmingly number of them from poor families, were more interested in subjects that might land them a job on graduation. A degree in philosophy, whatever its merits, was useless in the job market. As a result, enrollment in philosophy classes was well under fifty percent of capacity, and only a handful of students were actually majoring in the subject.

So Vanunu stood out. One of his professors, Chaim Marantz, remembers the quiet, intense young man who first turned up in 1981 for a course in the history of political philosophy from Plato to Sartre.

"He was searching," Marantz said. "He's one of these people who tend to study philosophy because he was looking for the meaning of life. 'What's it all about?' That sort of thing."

Vanunu was a better-than-average student whose principal virtue was a dogged determination to plow through his coursework. But several professors questioned his grasp of the material. On one level, he understood what he was learning. But he had a tendency to become so excited by new ideas that he failed to work them through. He was almost thirty, a late bloomer. At a time when many Israelis his age were beginning to think about careers and money and starting a family, he was just beginning his studies. And instead of a job, Vanunu now was driven by an inchoate desire to leave his mark on life.

He completed the work required for an undergraduate degree in philosophy, and began taking graduate-level courses while he finished the credits needed for the second degree in geography. Philosophy had become his latest obsession, and he was developing a deep commitment to basic values like truth, freedom, justice, and notions of equality. The great philosophers, Vanunu believed, were men who refused to back away from any belief, who battled the slightest falsehood, regardless of the sacrifice required. In their eyes, there was no middle ground. It was, he decided, the only way to live life.

Vanunu, though, ruefully admitted his commitment occasionally wavered.

"My weak point is that I am not consistent," he wrote in his diary. "I never continue in what I am doing or in what I believe. I change positions. Or, at a given moment, I believe in and then gamble on that moment. I'm ready to invest in everything and to hide from the past and the future. To go all the way for this moment. Complicated. But—there's always a 'but.' Until when? I am about to explode. I want to explode and release all the years and the power. To clear all the obstacles. I want to be left alone and be with myself, with my dirty mind, which then will be cleaned of all the filth which has become part of me. Clean like a motor after an overhaul, or a clock which has been repaired and is now working."

His philosophy studies were also eroding his religious faith. In his teens, Vanunu had turned his back on the Orthodox beliefs, on his father, but now he questioned the very basis of his religion.

At its core, Judaism, more so than most religions, is essentially tribal in nature. There is a sense of exclusivity, a well-founded feeling that Jews are an embattled, endangered minority that can only survive by banding together and taking on their enemies. Nowhere is this concept more pervasive than in Israel.

But Vanunu's study of science and philosophy was pulling him away from Judaism toward a more universal view of the world. Science and philosophy are non-denominational; acceptance of their universality clashes with the concept of tribalism. And Vanunu was ready to give up the roots of his upbringing.

"The only choice is to escape from under these wings of home, and go out and breathe clean air," he wrote. "To stand on one's feet. I left my moral backing at home, but it is only made of paper and of superstition. Now I need legs to stand up straight, to be something special."

Chapter 8

If philosophy provided a kind of moral code, Vanunu still needed some vehicle to turn his ideas into a force for change in the real world. He explored eastern religions, even Christianity, seeking the humanitarian values he could not find in Judaism. And eventually he turned to politics, attacking the subject with the same zeal that had marked all his intellectual endeavors.

Politics was a subject that Mordechai had largely ignored over the years. It was rarely discussed at home, and then only by his brother Meir. But now Meir was in college and becoming even more politically minded, and he was anxious to discuss some of his new ideas.

The two brothers, only two years apart, were extremely close all their lives. Meir had always admired his older brother's keen intellect, and was impressed to find Mordechai at age nineteen reading Nietzsche and the works of Kant, Sartre, and Spinoza. The brothers were the first Vanunus to attend university, and Meir had leaned on Mordechai for support as he struggled to earn a law degree at Hebrew University in Jerusalem. The two would talk for hours about literature and philosophy, and music, mathematics and science.

Meir's political views were decidedly left-wing, very much out of step with prevailing Israeli thought and practically heretical in the conservative environment in which the Vanunu children had been raised. Meir disagreed with the basic concept of a Jewish state where Judaism was the guiding force. He was appalled by Israel's treatment of the Palestinians, policies that he saw as brutally racist. He was angry and bitter about the second-class status accorded to Sephardic Jews by the Ashkenazi elite. Despite Sephardic support for Begin, the gap between Ashkenazi and Sephardi was widening. The Sephardim remained mired in the lower social and economic levels of society, and lagged far behind Ashkenazim in educational achievement. And Meir was pessimistic about the future. Nothing would change in Israel, he glumly told his brother. Nobody wanted to tackle these problems. The conflicts—secular vs. religious, Arab vs. Jew, Ashkenazi vs. Sephardi—would only worsen. There was no point in living in that kind of society.

Meir wanted a fresh start. His father had brought him to Israel, but he was not happy there. Meir saw himself straddling two cultures—one North African, the other Israeli—and did not feel he could ever belong in either. Solomon's experience was ample proof that Israel would never fully accept him. The Sephardim, Meir argued to Mordechai, are really Arab Jews. And where did that leave them in the state of Israel?

The passion of his brother's arguments provoked Mordechai. They were not unique opinions, but he had never heard them outlined so articulately, and with his antennae readjusted, he soon picked up similar signals at school and in his reading.

Vanunu's conversations with his brother left him disenchanted with Israel's attitude toward the Palestinians, and Israel's invasion of Lebanon in June 1982 for the publicly stated purpose of ending Palestinian guerrilla attacks was a watershed in his political development. The invasion shattered the national consensus on the country's military and foreign policies. Israelis had understandably seen themselves as the victims of the 1967 and 1973 Middle East wars, forced to defend their nation against Arab attackers. But many deplored the Lebanon invasion as an act of aggression, not the preemptive defensive action the government described. Vanunu was swept up in the nationwide protests that erupted.

For the first time, he tried to avoid army reserve duty, an annual task that most Israeli men and women accept as a responsibility of citizenship. Vanunu pretended to have not received his orders, but the army came looking for him a week later and ordered him to report for duty in Lebanon. The young man who had once tried to join the air force now requested to be assigned a kitchen job, saying he no longer wanted to bear arms.

Vanunu's political involvement intensified after he returned to school. He organized demonstrations in support of a variety of left-ist causes and against the government's repressive treatment of the Palestinians in the occupied West Bank and Gaza Strip. He be-friended Israeli Arab students, telling them how his Sephardic ori-gins and the discrimination his family had suffered gave him a clear understanding of their plight.

The campus, however, was not particular fertile ground for left-wing politics. Many students came from conservative backgrounds and, saddled with both their studies and full-time jobs, were not interested in demonstrations and rallies. University officials also made it difficult to organize. After a series of stormy protests against Israel's efforts to move the Bedouin off the desert to make room for military installations, political activity on campus, includ-ing lectures, rallies and meetings, was largely banned. But Vanunu and other activists continued to campaign outside the tall chain fence topped with barbed wire that runs along the entrance to the campus.

Professors and classmates vividly recall Vanunu publicly embrac-ing most leftist causes. He constantly probed the limits of the ad-ministration's tolerance, searching for a way to bring politics back to campus. Vanunu formed a student society, the Suitcase Club, that met weekly to discuss various topics under the guise of philosophy. One week the subject was censorship, another the role of a univer-sity, a third the relationship between politics and education. He founded a branch of a leftist student movement known as Campus and represented it at a 1984 international congress in Paris.

Vanunu organized a solidarity campaign for a philosophy profes-sor jailed for refusing service in Lebanon, and battled the school administration over better treatment for the small number of Arab students. The head of the Arab Students Committee recalled Vanunu as a person who "believed that we were not getting our fair share of dormitory rooms and grants. And he was willing to come out and say so publicly."

Among his Israeli classmates, however, there was far less enthu-siasm. Vanunu was a fairly well-known figure around campus, if for nothing more than his lengthening stay. "He was one of the students we called 'the founding generation,' " said one student. "It seemed as if Motti had always been here and would always be here." But his newly formed political views irritated Israeli students. Many believed Vanunu was acting more out of a longing for attention than from any firmly held convictions.

Arabs soon became the only friends Vanunu could find. "He just never seemed to fit in with the Jewish students," said one man who knew him for eight years. "Although many Sephardi Jews fill positions of responsibility here, he saw his own isolation as part of an overall system of discrimination by Ashkenazi Jews against Sephardi Jews. So he started eating with the Arab students and soon became their defender at meetings."

One student accused Vanunu of helping some Arab students cheat on an exam. An investigation into the allegations turned up nothing. A rumor also spread that Vanunu had been seeking psychiatric help from a student counseling service.

Vanunu was well aware of how alone he was. Of his turn to the left, he wrote: "What I have done—I have progressed even more politically and have reached the most extreme point possible in this area."

None of this, however, reached home. Vanunu had always maintained a close relationship to his family, and he stayed in touch even as he moved inexorably away from the policies of his country and the tenets of his religion. The sense of family had always been important in the Vanunu household and nothing had changed. Mordechai went home regularly, worked around the house, even contributed part of his Dimona salary to help his parents raise younger brothers and sisters.

Only occasionally would his new philosophies slip out.

"One time we were talking, I forget about what, and I said, 'Oh those Arabs!' " his sister, Miriam, once recalled. "And he said, 'Why? The Arabs are people, too. They also deserve good treatment.' "

His brother, Albert, by now a successful carpenter with his own shop, was also aware that Motti "spent a lot of time with Arabs. He always tried to show that words weren't enough. He tried to help them," even to the point of sharing a bed with an Arab roommate who lived in his apartment for a time.

But no one in the family, not even Meir, was aware of the extent of Mordechai's political involvement, or just how far to the left he had drifted.

Chapter 9

Vanunu's political leanings could not have been much clearer, or more publicly known, by 1984. He was elected to the Council of Students, representing left-wing and Arab groups. He took a leading role in the defense of four Arab students arrested on suspicion of carrying Palestine Liberation Organization literature. Vanunu's face even turned up in newspaper photographs taken at demonstrations in support of a Palestinian state and against former hardline defense minister Ariel Sharon, the architect of the Lebanon invasion.

It was not long before security officials at Dimona, the most secret installation in the entire country, were inundated with reports that one of their workers, Mordechai Vanunu, was a rabidly anti-Israeli, pro-Palestinian activist.

Incredibly, Vanunu's first two years of openly leftist political activity had somehow escaped the attention of the Shin Bet, Israel's internal security agency, which is responsible for security at facilities like Dimona. The omission was all the more remarkable because the Shin Bet relies on extensive networks of informers to keep tabs on Palestinians, Israeli Arabs, and even Israelis with questionable political views. Ben-Gurion was no exception. The campus was rife with informers. It was generally accepted that all left-wing groups at the university had been infiltrated by the Shin Bet, and that their leaders were under constant surveillance. A Shin Bet informant among the members of Vanunu's Campus organization diligently filed reports on the weekly meetings held in Vanunu's apartment, and after every session one of the Arab members would be picked up by police. But Vanunu himself was never questioned, leading some Campus members to briefly suspect Vanunu was a Shin Bet plant.

Still, Vanunu's only contact with security officials during his first two years of political activity came as a result of his 1983 trip to the United States. Because of the sensitive nature of their work, plant employees are required to notify the security office of any plans to travel abroad, and authorities generally offer "advice" on ways to avoid trouble. Shortly before he left, Vanunu was interviewed by a Dimona security officer and given a list of telephone numbers and names of Shin Bet agents stationed in embassies and consulates in various U.S. cities. If he became concerned about his safety, Vanunu was to contact one of the agents immediately. The security officer also instructed him to fly directly from Israel to the United States, avoiding transfers to other flights because of the threat of hijackings.

Too expensive, Vanunu thought as he left the plant. A direct flight to the States costs too much. So he stuck to his original plan—a charter via Shannon, Ireland.

The holiday was uneventful and Vanunu never had cause to contact any of the Israeli officials on his list. But two days after he returned to work, he was called in by plant security officials who angrily demanded to know why he had disregarded his instructions. Who did you see on your charter flight? they asked. Whose idea was it?

Motti tried to explain. It was only a question of money, he protested. The charter flight was cheaper.

Unmoved, the officials sternly informed Vanunu he would have to answer for his actions before a board of inquiry. But nothing more ever came of the threat.

Despite the extent and nature of Vanunu's political activities, however, the Shin Bet had never raised questions about his continued employment deep inside the country's most sensitive defense installation. For two long years, Vanunu simply slipped through a crack in Israel's carefully constructed, vigilantly maintained security superstructure.

Not until June 1984 did plant officials call him on the carpet. The session was brief. The officials, including a Shin Bet agent sent down from headquarters in Tel Aviv, asked Vanunu if he knew why he was being questioned.

"I said I did not, but they said it was because of my political activity at university," Vanunu recalled later. "They asked me about the Arabs I associated with. I tried to justify my activity. They said that I had to end my association with them. I realized that they knew all about me, and I told them that I would try to be careful about who I mixed with."

A month later, however, Vanunu flew off to Paris, representing the Campus group at the two-week-long student congress.

Vanunu was at ease with his new status as a marked man. "I met and became friendly with more Arab students," he noted matter-of-factly in his diary. "At work they picked up on my political activities. I feel it—I'm being watched. Sometimes it's real paranoia as well."

The Shin Bet was keeping an eye on him, but the agency's suspicions did not affect his position at the plant. In August, Vanunu and nine other workers were sent back to school for a two-month advanced chemistry and physics course designed to train them to become foremen.

The Shin Bet's failure to remove Vanunu from Dimona or at least Machon 2—an extraordinary oversight by an agency that routinely barred job applicants with the slightest hint of leftist political views from employment at the plant—was the result of a combination of factors. Vanunu's supervisors continually gave him good marks, and plant officials were also confident that the high degree of compartmentalization at Dimona prevented any worker, especially a control-room monitor, from learning the truth about the facility. In addition, security officials were satisfied that Vanunu's political activities were not tainting his work. They knew Vanunu went to great lengths to avoid discussing his duties in public.

The agency was also having some trouble drawing an accurate portrait of Vanunu. The detailed reports from informers on the Ben-Gurion campus and Vanunu's defiant pursuit of his political activities even after a warning were certainly worrisome; the Shin Bet even procured some of Vanunu's college philosophy essays in the belief his writings might provide a clearer understanding of his motives and beliefs.

But the Shin Bet also knew Vanunu had not turned against his country. Less than a year earlier, Vanunu had spotted an advertisement in a newspaper offering jobs with an unnamed government agency. When he answered the advertisement, he discovered the agency was the Shin Bet. Despite his political leanings, he filled out an application, which was later turned down after a background check revealed his leftist political bent.

Vanunu was given no explanation, but he saw the rejection as yet another example of discrimination against Sephardic Jews. The failure of his latest attempt to join the mainstream fueled his burgeoning anti-Israeli ideology.

Vanunu soon completed his undergraduate geography degree and turned his full attention to his graduate philosophy studies. His philosophy professor, Chaim Marantz, needed a teaching assistant and, with a dearth of graduate students, gave Vanunu the position. Vanunu was supposed to clear any second job with Dimona security officials, but he decided not to bother.

For the next year, he corrected papers and supervised examinations. On two occasions, when Marantz was in the army on reserve duty, Vanunu also taught classes. But his incomplete understanding of some of the material was a matter of some concern to the professor.

"I remember once that it became clear to me that his grasp of Marx was very poor," Marantz said. "I remember discussing an exam paper, how to mark a certain question, and his knowledge was very rudimentary. I was surprised. He hadn't read *Das Kapital*. Not that it was required reading for the course, but I think he mentioned to me that he was interested in Marx. And here he hadn't read 'Kapital.' "

In December 1984, just two months past his thirtieth birthday, Vanunu defied the warning from Dimona officials to stay out of politics and stood for re-election to the student council. A week after the balloting, he was summoned to the plant security office for another grilling. Vanunu explained he was only interested in making sure Arab students at school were properly represented. As that was accomplished, he hinted, he was willing to end his activities.

That vague promise was a lie. If anything, Vanunu was becoming more deeply involved in the Arab cause, both on and off campus. He was also growing increasingly pessimistic about the possibility of change. His commitment was waning. Vanunu was tired of the constant clashes with university officials and the seemingly fruitless struggle against racism and discrimination. He was also disillusioned by the lack of interest among most Israelis in creating a better society. The idea of leaving the country, moving abroad to live among people who shared his ideals, gradually began to take shape.

Meir had already made the decision. After an extended stay in the United States, Meir had returned to Israel to complete his legal studies. But after only a few weeks at home, he realized he could no longer tolerate life in the Jewish state. He left in January 1985, saying it was unlikely he would ever come back to live in Israel. The family was distressed, no one more so than Mordechai, who had come to rely on Meir as a sounding board for his developing political and philosophical beliefs. But Mordechai understood his brother's decision, and he envied the opportunity of starting a new life in a freer society.

Chapter 10

Only a few days after his brother left Israel, Vanunu stumbled on a new discovery that crystallized his deepening opposition to the policies of his country.

The relaxed atmosphere within Machon 2 had allowed Vanunu relatively unrestricted access to most of the unit, but one area—Level 5—remained a mystery. Vanunu had worked in one area on Level 5 during his temporary assignment to the lithium-6 project, but he had never been left alone long enough to inspect the rest of the floor. The nature of lithium-6, a key component in the construction of thermonuclear weapons, made him all the more curious, but he had been unable to obtain the special key needed to open the elevator on Level 5.

Vanunu finally found a way to breach the last remaining wall of secrecy at Dimona. To his utter amazement, he learned from other workers that a Level 5 supervisor, in a stupefying lapse of security, routinely dropped his key on a shelf in an open locker when he left for the day.

Vanunu wasted no time taking advantage of the opportunity. For the next few months, he made weekly visits to Level 5. The floor, filled with highly automated equipment, was often left unattended, particularly during overnight meal breaks and shift changes.

"It was not difficult to get in," he recalled later, "but I had to be careful on my way to and from the section."

The prying technician soon realized Level 5, the plant's metallurgy unit, was where the plutonium he processed was machined into nuclear bombs. It was an exacting operation. The plutonium metal discs that Vanunu and other workers produced on upper levels of the underground installation were moved to Level 5 and placed inside sealed glove boxes filled with argon, an inert gas—an artificial environment required because exposure to air could spontaneously ignite the highly volatile material. Using lathes and milling machines, the discs were converted into solid spheres weighing about ten pounds, then sealed inside copper shells, which were also manufactured in the metallurgy section.

Most of the functions were performed in separate rooms as a security and safety measure, and MM2, as the unit was designated, had its own tanks for the storage of radioactive waste. Lithium compounds and beryllium were also machined into weapons components in MM2. Lithium deuteride, for example, was used to build sheaths for thermonuclear weapons.

Once the work was completed, the components were moved in convoys of unmarked cars, with armed guards and doctors on hand in case of attack or accident, to a secret military airfield near Haifa where the spheres were fitted with triggering devices and other technology needed to turn them into nuclear weapons.

For Vanunu, MM2 was the final piece in the puzzle. What he saw on Level 5 erased all questions in his mind about the extent and purpose of Israel's nuclear weapons program. Vanunu was now convinced that Israel, not content with producing a few bombs for a last-ditch defense, was building a powerful offensive nuclear arsenal rivaled only by the superpowers. And the government was flatly lying about it, assuring the world that it would never be the first to introduce nuclear weapons into the Middle East.

Why else were such devastating bombs being assembled? Vanunu asked. Obviously, he believed, Israel meant to use them some day. The country was going to force its will on the Palestinians and the nations of the Middle East, and perhaps on the entire world.

And no one had asked Israelis whether they favored such a policy; in fact, all attempts to start a public debate on the subject had been squelched. Even the Israeli public, which Vanunu increasingly regarded as a collection of mindless, unquestioning drones marching in lockstep with their repressive leaders, might be appalled to learn what its government was doing under the sands of the Negev.

In his new no-compromises world of truth and justice, the existence of a secret nuclear arsenal in Israel was intolerable, but Vanunu had no idea what to do about it. Still, one thing was certain: the discovery of MM2 made it clear that he could no longer work at Dimona. To remain at the plant, manufacturing bombs, would be an untenable lapse of commitment. Vanunu also concluded that he could not continue to live in Israel, a country where duplicity and calculated lies were a way of life, where decisions affecting an entire country and perhaps the world were made in secret by cynical politicians.

By March, his mind was made up. "Now begins a new chapter," he wrote in his diary. "After the ideas were going on in my head, the journey now begins. I'm leaving for the voyage. I signed to sell the apartment and following this agreement other changes will occur. I'm leaving my job and my studies and this area where I've lived for so long. Far from my family and possibly far from Judaism. A new outlook, a new world. A life of choices, of forming opinions, of my own attempts."

His days at Dimona appeared numbered in any event. Vanunu had dropped all pretense of ending his political activities, and he was coming under increasing scrutiny from security officials. In March 1985, he was one of only a handful of Jews who attended a huge Arab demonstration near Beersheba that was monitored by camera-toting Shin Bet agents. And informants reported that Vanunu had turned up at a Communist Party membership meeting in Beersheba.

Early on the morning of May 1, Vanunu was called into the Dimona security office.

"We are taking you to Tel Aviv for questioning," he was told. "There are people there who have some evidence against you."

Plant security guards bundled Vanunu into a car and drove him to the Defense Ministry complex in Tel Aviv, where he was hustled into an empty office. A few minutes later, two men entered the room. One was a man who identified himself as Yechiel Cohen, the head of security at Dimona. The other was a senior Shin Bet agent. Both men appeared angry.

"Did you attend the demonstration in Kfar Rahat on March 30?" Cohen began.

There was no sense denying it. Vanunu knew he had been photographed at the rally, and at several others since then.

"Yes," he answered.

"Have you visited the offices of the Communist Party in Beersheba recently?" the agent demanded.

Again, Vanunu saw no point in denying it. "Yes," he replied, "but only to buy some books, to pick up some literature. Not to join the party."

"Do you realize that the Arabs with whom you associate are part of the PLO?" the agent asked coldly.

"Sure," Vanunu responded, "but that doesn't matter in this case because I don't talk to them about the PLO. We are interested only in student problems on campus."

Cohen opened a folder lying in front of him and pulled out a copy of the security agreement Vanunu had signed when he began work at Dimona. He asked Vanunu to read aloud one section, which warned that employees in top-security installations could be sent to prison for disclosing information about their work.

The questioning continued for another half hour. Then, the Shin Bet agent placed a sheet of paper in front of Vanunu and ordered him to sign it. The document was a statement in which Vanunu acknowledged that he had met with dissident Arab students and taken part in their political activities.

Vanunu shook his head. "No, I won't sign it. If I do, I'll lose my job," he told his questioners.

The Shin Bet agent slapped the table in anger. "If we want to sack you, we can do it without that paper," he shouted. "We know everything about you. Do you think we don't have anyone working for us in Beersheba, at the university? We know what you are up to at all times."

But Vanunu adamantly refused to sign the statement, and the two security officials finally gave up.

"There is one more thing," the Shin Bet agent said as Vanunu stood up to leave. "You should understand that you might be killed as a result of your political activities."

Startled, Vanunu asked, "By whom? Arabs?"

The agent shrugged. "Arabs, yes," he said. "Or Israelis, if you keep working with the Arabs at the university."

Vanunu nodded slowly. He understood the threat. "I'll try to be careful," he told the two men.

The meeting ended, and Vanunu was driven back to work at Dimona, inside Machon 2, the most secret section of the most secret installation in the state of Israel.

Chapter 11

As the summer dragged on, Vanunu began making arrangements to leave Israel in early January. He sold his apartment for $19,000 and rented a smaller flat near the university campus. With his savings and money raised from the sale of his car, a dilapidated Subaru, and some furniture and a few other possessions, he put together about $37,000 and sent it to Meir, who was now living in Boston. Vanunu planned to travel for a few months through Asia before heading to the United States, where he would find a job and continue his education, probably in Boston.

The Israeli economy was foundering again in 1985 and the Finance Ministry had ordered a sharp reduction in the number of government workers. Despite the importance of the work, Dimona was not excluded from the cuts. Plant officials were told to trim their payroll by 180 workers. Vanunu's name appeared on the list.

He was livid. It was a clear-cut case of discrimination, he raged. He was a senior employee with an unblemished work record who had been targeted for promotion to foreman. The other laid-off workers were people with alcohol problems, employees who were always late or frequently absent, or who did not get along with their supervisors. In Vanunu's mind, there was only one possible explanation: he had been singled out because he was a Sephardi with unpopular political views. Even knowing he was leaving at the end of the year, Vanunu decided to fight back. It was a matter of principle.

Vanunu turned to the workers' union, which mounted a campaign to save his job. In September, the layoff order was rescinded, but Vanunu's supervisor told him he would be transferred to Machon 6, a relatively low-security unit that produced electricity and steam power for the rest of the complex.

Vanunu complained that was equally unacceptable. He knew more about Machon 2 than many of the people working there. His expertise was needed. Why was he being sent to a service center?

His supervisor said plant officials believed he was going to leave Dimona after he earned his master's degree, and did not want to invest any more time in training him. Someone who would be staying on would move into his position in Machon 2.

But Vanunu flatly refused to transfer. The move was a slap in the face, more punishment for his background and his beliefs. He would not go, and plant officials backed down after the union protested the decision.

The dispute, however, had lent a greater sense of urgency to a plan that Vanunu had been mulling for several weeks. He wanted to take some photographs of Machon 2—souvenirs, in a way, of his career, but also an incontrovertible record of the truth about Dimona in case he ever decided to talk about it.

There could hardly be a more flagrant violation of plant regulations, or the security pledge Vanunu had signed. If he were caught, the camera would be difficult to explain. It would almost certainly be grounds for dismissal, possibly even arrest. Vanunu was well aware that simply *talking* about Dimona could land an employee in prison for fifteen years. What would a roll of snapshots cost him?

But he was not particularly worried. The guards rarely searched employees entering the plant, and were only slightly more diligent at the end of the shift. Besides, after nine years, the guards knew Vanunu, and he knew the guards—it would be late, they would be tired, bored.

And even if he were caught, the authorities were unlikely to prosecute him. The case would be hugely embarrassing. There would be an investigation, reams of reports, and at the end of the day, Vanunu's superiors might lose their jobs for allowing the security breach. A quiet dismissal and a quick coverup would be the likely response, Vanunu reasoned.

He moved on an afternoon in late September when he was working the 3:30 p.m.-to-midnight shift. The bus carrying workers to Dimona passed through the two security checkpoints and drove into the parking lot outside the employee cafeteria. The passengers clambered off, heading for their various work stations. Just as he had figured, Vanunu was not challenged as he strolled into Machon 2 with the camera hidden in a knapsack slung over his shoulder.

He went into the locker room on the first floor and stowed the knapsack. After the other workers had slipped into their work clothes and left, Vanunu drew out the camera and loaded a roll of film, then ducked through an emergency exit door that opened on a staircase leading to the roof of the building.

Vanunu darted up the steps, stepped out onto the roof and looked around. To his left, looming over him in the late-afternoon light, was the dome covering the nuclear reactor. To his right, on the other side of the street, were three other production units. In front of him were two more units, and in the distance he could see the parking lot and administrative offices and the small training school.

It was a good vantage point. From the roof, he could take photographs of virtually the entire complex. But he had to be careful. The shutter on the Pentax closed with a loud noise, which could easily attract the attention of a passing security guard. And there were more guards in watchtowers who might spot him.

Vanunu finished in fifteen minutes. He dashed back down the stairs, slipped into the locker room and placed the camera underneath several books in the knapsack. For the rest of the week, he was scheduled to work the 11:30 P.M.-to-8 A.M. shift, when only a skeleton crew was at work. With Machon 2 less crowded, it would be easier to take pictures of the inner workings of the production unit.

The next night, when the rest of the shift workers headed for the canteen and their meal break at 2 A.M., Vanunu returned to the locker room and retrieved the camera. For forty minutes, he roamed through the building, assembling his illicit scrapbook of memories. He snapped shots of the "Golda balcony" on Level 2, laboratories and control rooms on Level 3, and the production hall and plutonioum-separation equipment on Level 4.

The centerpiece of his photo spread would be MM2. But he had
to hurry—the meal break was almost over and some of the workers
might be returning to their posts. Using the supervisor's unattended
key, Vanunu crept into Level 5 and went to work. He photographed
the glove boxes where the plutonium discs were machined into
spheres, and the instrument panels that controlled the process. Several of the round copper sheaths in which the bombs would be
placed lay half-finished on workbenches in one laboratory, and he
quickly trained the lens on them. There was even a full-scale model
of a hydrogen bomb, used to show visiting Israeli leaders what was
being produced at Dimona, and Vanunu took a picture of that.

When he ran out of film he concealed the camera under his clothing and took the elevator to the locker room. Making sure he was
alone, he returned the camera to the knapsack and went back to
work. Vanunu could barely contain his excitement. He knew how to
use a camera and the rooms were well-lighted. The photographs, he
was sure, would be perfect.

During the entire operation, Vanunu had not seen another soul.

At the end of his shift, Vanunu casually walked out of the building
and boarded the bus carrying the knapsack with the camera underneath the stack of books. No one stopped him. The next night, he
carried the two rolls of film out in the pocket of his pants. Just as he
assumed, no one searched him.

But he still faced the possiblility of a surprise visit to his apartment by Shin Bet agents seeking information about his political activities. As a precaution, Vanunu had already hidden his diary and
other important papers in the attic of his brother Albert's house. A
few days after taking the photographs, Vanunu wrapped the camera
and film rolls in a plastic bag, placed them inside another knapsack
and went to see Albert. "I want to leave something else with you,"
he told his brother.

The operation had been a complete success. Over two nights,
Vanunu had taken fifty-seven photographs, a startlingly detailed record of the workings of Dimona. It was an unprecedented violation
of security in one of the world's most security-conscious nations.

Israel's best-kept secrets were in the hands of a man who had come to loathe his country.

Chapter 12

In mid-October, plant officials renewed their efforts to transfer Vanunu. Authorities at long last had concluded that the technician's political views made him an extremely poor choice for a sensitive unit like Machon 2. But even after almost three years of open political rebellion, it still took a particularly brazen act to persuade them. Not until Vanunu stood up and called for the creation of a Palestinian state during an Arab rally where a huge Palestine Liberation Organization flag was unfurled did Dimona officials decide to act.

After some initial resistance, Vanunu abandoned the fight to save his job at Machon 2. He was planning to leave the plant in December anyway, and the pressure brought to bear on him because of his politics was growing stronger. Perhaps it would be best if he quit immediately.

Through the union, Vanunu was offered a deal—instead of a transfer, he would accept a layoff. An agreement was quickly worked out under which Vanunu would receive a severance payment of about $7,500 and a letter from the plant saying he had been a good employee and had been laid off only because of budget cuts.

On Sunday, October 27, 1985, Vanunu left Dimona for the last time. As the bus pulled onto the highway and headed for Beersheba, he was angry and upset. It had been an unpleasant departure. First, he discovered that his co-workers, with whom he had never been particularly friendly, did not plan to throw a party for him, as they had done for every other laid-off employee. Then he had quarreled with a security officer, refusing to read and sign another secrecy pledge, which was required of all departing employees.

When he got home, he lay on his bed for several hours. It was over. His apartment, his car, his furniture, books—all gone. His life savings was in a Boston bank. And now he had quit one of the best jobs in the country. He was really leaving.

One other unpleasant task remained, however. Vanunu still had to tell his parents about his plans. He went to their house on Friday night, the start of the Jewish sabbath, and over dinner broke the news. He had decided to see some of the world, he explained, then he planned to study in the United States. He didn't know when he would be back.

His parents did not take it well. First Meir, now Mordechai. The family was breaking up, his mother wailed.

Vanunu was still attending classes at Ben-Gurion, but leaving his job had left him with time on his hands, and he began using it in bizarre ways. For the first time in his life, Vanunu felt liberated from the restrictions imposed by Israeli society, and his new freedom found eccentric expression.

He answered an advertisement for nude models at an arts school in Beersheba and was paid $33 for a three-hour session. Vanunu wanted to do it again, but the instructor turned him down, saying he was "too nervous and moved too much." Vanunu spent Yom Kippur, Judaism's day of atonement and the holiest of Jewish holidays, at the beach with Arab friends, angering his father, who had hoped he would attend religious services one last time before leaving. At a party on another night, Vanunu stood up and took off his clothes, explaining to the startled guests that he wanted to see if he had the nerve to do it. He returned to the Communist Party offices and picked up a membership application. Curious about how the party worked, he attended several meetings, sitting in the corner and saying nothing. In the end, he concluded the party members knew nothing about communism, and he broke off contact with them.

As he headed for the door, Vanunu was taunting Israel, breaking every taboo, flaunting every convention, in a final salvo of discontent and bitterness.

For the first time, Vanunu also became seriously involved with a woman. Nothing depressed Vanunu more than his lack of a social life. Marantz used to tease him about his shyness with women. "Why don't you ask her out? Or her? Or her?" He would say, chuckling at his young assistant's obvious unease, as they walked past female students in the hall.

In small groups, the man who could stand and speak in front of a rally became a painfully shy, uncommunicative wallflower, and he despaired of his inability to comfortably mingle with others.

"Why am I looking in the cafeteria or anywhere there are people—and especially girls—if I cannot make contact with them?" he wrote in his diary. "I feel it is preferable now to stay confined to books and writing."

And later: "Marriage and children? It seems that I won't have experiences like that. Why? I am willing to live alone in the midst of all the couples."

Shortly before he left Dimona, mutual friends—a Bedouin man and his Jewish girlfriend—introduced Vanunu to Judy Zimmet, a 31-year-old Jewish-American nurse who had come to Israel to work for a few years. She had landed a job as a midwife at Soroka Medical Center in Beersheba. Living in the desert was not her first choice, and she found the people a bit too nosy about her personal life. But despite the problems she had encountered, Judy still harbored thoughts about moving permanently to Israel.

Vanunu was immediately attracted to her. Judy appeared to be socially and politically aware, and Motti found her a good partner intellectually. She was not materialistic, not overly concerned with the way she looked or dressed. Zimmet seemed more interested in helping people. Motti especially liked that.

It was an odd relationship, borne more out of necessity than passion. Vanunu was almost desperate for a girlfriend. For Judy, a foreigner in a strange town, uncomfortable with the language, uncertain about the society, the slightly built student with the dark, brooding looks was someone to share her Israeli experience. He was very serious, intelligent, obsessed with morality and ethics, and there was a rebellious quality about him that Judy found appealing. He was an Israeli, but he was caught up in the Arab movement; it seemed the focal point of his existence. Most of his friends were Israeli Arabs or Palestinians, and he took Judy to their homes and villages, off-limits to most Jews. For a visiting American, it was exotic.

Motti and Judy began spending a great deal of time together, going for coffee, attending concerts, seeing movies, and in late November Motti moved into Judy's apartment. They talked constantly about politics and philosophy and religion. Judy served as a kind of sounding board for Motti's ideas, and gave him an American perspective on issues like discrimination, racism, and the peace movement.

Vanunu never talked about his work at Dimona. Occasionally, he would complain about working in a place that produced "things that could hurt people," but he never elaborated. Only once, a few weeks after he had left the plant, did Vanunu's frustration surface. They were driving past the turnoff to the complex when Vanunu stopped the car on the side of the highway.

"Look," he said angrily, waving in the direction of the complex. "People don't even know what's right over the hill there, what's going on in there. It's incredible that nobody knows in this country what's going on there."

By the end of the year, Vanunu began making final preparations for his fast approaching departure. In early January, he notified his professors that he was leaving school. Marantz, his philosophy advisor, was taken aback by the news, but heartily approved.

"He didn't seem to have it in him to do these things, to change. I mean, it's a big change—pick up and go, give up the job, leave," Marantz explained later. "I was very surprised when he told me this because I didn't think he had it in him. I said, 'Good-o. You may be growing up.' Actually, I thought he would be back. Take a trip to find himself, et cetera, et cetera, then he'd be back."

Marantz and Dr. Yuval Lurie, the chairman of the philosophy department, gave Vanunu letters of recommendation in case he decided to enroll in classes or find a job while he was abroad.

"He is at once intelligent and hard-working," Marantz wrote. "He can be relied upon and so anyone offering him employment will not only be doing him a favor but will himself also be a beneficiary. I hope that he will continue his further education as it is a shame if talent is not developed."

Vanunu's last few weeks in Israel were spent touring the country with Judy and her sister, who was visiting from the United States. He was talking constantly now about his trip, about seeing the world. Judy had decided to return to the United States in June to attend graduate school in Boston, and Motti planned to try living with Judy there, to see whether they belonged together.

The sightseeing swing through Israel quickly came to resemble a farewell tour. Vanunu was taking one last look at his homeland, and, oddly, he seemed sad about it. For twenty-two years, it had been home, no matter how hard that was for him to admit.

One of the last stops was Mount Tabor, in northern Israel, not far from the little town where Solomon Vanunu had hoped to settle when he first arrived in Israel. "One of my favorite places on earth," Motti told Judy and her sister as they drove into the Arab village of Dabburiya, which clings to the side of the mountain, to visit one of Motti's friends from school.

Mount Tabor is a far cry from the desert. The peak is thick with foliage, and a cool breeze blows across it, even at the height of summer. The view is spectacular—fertile farmland stretches for miles and in the distance the Sea of Galilee shimmers in the haze.

The mountain was a strange "favorite place" for an Israeli Jew. It is a regular stop on Christian pilgrimages, the site of Jesus Christ's transfiguration. On the peak, reached by a narrow, bumpy path that zigzags its way to the top, is a Roman Catholic monastery, built on the ruins of a Crusader abbey. A statue of Pope Paul VI sits in the garden. And there is a plaque in the ruins, reading: "The hour of transfiguration came to Jesus at the moment when he was ready to go into the night of death. As members of his body, we can only receive the grace of transfiguration which he has earned for us by the same way, of humiliation and purging."

"Humiliation and purging." It was an approach that Vanunu could readily embrace.

Before he left the country, Vanunu had one final piece of business with the government. All Israelis in reserve units must have the approval of the military before traveling abroad, primarily to make sure they will not miss their mandatory annual duty. Vanunu was not scheduled to be called up for another three months, so the army had no objection to his travel plans, and on January 14, 1986, Vanunu received permission to leave.

Vanunu bid a tearful farewell to his family. Before he left, he asked Albert to store a few more items for him, and handed him a Hebrew-language copy of the Koran, the Moslem holy book. Vanunu urged Albert to read it. "You'll find it very interesting," he told his puzzled brother.

On January 19, Vanunu said goodbye to Judy and took the bus to Haifa to catch the ferry to Athens. The bus dropped him about 6 P.M. at the Haifa port passenger terminal and he walked inside, passing the armed guards on duty and the coils of barbed wire out front. He was traveling light: a knapsack filled with three shirts, three pairs of pants, a sleeping bag, some books, $4,000 in cash, a camera—and the two undeveloped rolls of film taken inside Dimona. Concerned that he might be searched on his way out of the country, Vanunu had placed one of the rolls inside the camera and put the other in a film box to make them appear unused.

Vanunu still had no idea what he was going to do with the film. Despite his obsession with the truth and his hatred for Israel's policies, he was uncomfortable with the idea of going public. But the conflict was much on his mind as he shuffled through security without a search and boarded the ferry.

He stood on deck as the boat steamed out of Haifa harbor and thought sadly about that day in 1963 when the Vanunu family had first laid eyes on Israel, eagerly anticipating a new life in the land of Jews. There had been so much promise, so much anticipation. They were proud to be Israelis, eager to help build their new country. Now, as the sun set over the Mediterranean, Solomon Vanunu's second son was going the other way.

PART II

Calculated Risk

Chapter 13

The Dimona photographs preoccupied Vanunu from the moment the ferry steamed out of Haifa harbor. On the voyage to Athens, he struck up a conversation with a Canadian travel writer and soon poured out the story of his career. The writer tried unsuccessfully to introduce Vanunu to a *Newsweek* magazine reporter in Athens, then suggested the young Israeli contact the Soviet Embassy to discuss his work. But Vanunu was not interested; he feared the Soviets would take him to Moscow and never release him.

He wound up in the Soviet Union anyway. After five days of sightseeing in Greece, Vanunu left for Thailand on an Aeroflot flight that included a one-hour stop in Sofia, Bulgaria, and an overnight stay in Moscow. The plane arrived in Moscow in the early evening, and the passengers were thoroughly searched before being bused to a hotel inside the airport complex that served passengers in transit. It snowed all night. The next afternoon, the airline provided passengers with a bus tour of the city to pass the time before the flight continued on to Bangkok later that night.

The stopover in Moscow marked the second time Vanunu had violated the secrecy pledge he signed when he went to work at Dimona. Employees who left the plant were barred from visiting a communist or Arab country for five years. Now, only three months gone, Vanunu was standing in front of the Kremlin.

Vanunu arrived in Bangkok on January 29. He stayed about six weeks, spending time in a Buddhist ashram, traveling south to the Cambodian border and then into the "Golden Triangle," the lush opium-growing region that straddles Laos, Burma and Thailand. He loved the area. "I like this country and it is different from the West," he wrote in a postcard to Judy Zimmet in early February. "It is good to come here. It is easy to be here, and cheap."

On March 12, he flew to Burma where he met the daughter of a British television reporter. Vanunu and the woman toured the country together, then moved on to Nepal on March 19. Desperate for some advice about his dilemma, and hoping the intrigue would make him more attractive to the woman, Vanunu once again spilled the Dimona story to a stranger and asked whether she could arrange a meeting with her father. But the woman was not interested and brushed him aside.

Following a trek into the Himalayas, Vanunu returned alone to Katmandu a few weeks later. He had hoped to arrange a trip to India, but a visa was not available. Instead, he flew back to Bangkok on May 5 where he obtained a tourist visa for Australia and New Zealand. Fifteen days later, Vanunu arrived in Sydney, Australia.

Sydney provided a striking contrast to the stifling desert expanses of Beersheba. It is a beautiful, hilly city split in half by a huge harbor that is never far from view. Hundreds of inlets and coves knife into a stunning shoreline engulfed in green foliage. The city is blessed with a comfortable climate much like southern California's, although the seasons are turned upside down in Australia, where Christmas day falls in midsummer.

An extreme strain of puritanism suffocated Australia for much of the 20th century. "Wowsers," as Australians called their bluenoses, strangled nightlife, kept bikinis off beaches, and even forced the closing of playgrounds on Sundays. But the wraps came off in the 1960s, and the society rapidly assumed a gently hedonistic hue. The Kings Cross district of Sydney was one of the results.

Until the Vietnam War, Kings Cross was a relatively quiet, somewhat bohemian neighborhood of restaurants and inexpensive housing. But the influx of American servicemen on leave quickly turned the area into Sydney's version of a red-light district, a kind of tame Times Square. There is little violent crime, although prostitutes, both men and women, troll the corners, and illegal drugs are on sale in narrow alleys just off the street. But packed into the space of one neon-lighted square mile are restaurants, cafes, night clubs, strip joints, peep shows, and massage parlors where sidewalk barkers and "hostesses" shouting from open windows vie for the attention of the sailors, drunken businessmen and curious teenagers who flock to the district after dark. The Cross opens late and often does not close until just before dawn.

Not all of the business in the Cross is sleazy. There are fine hotels and restaurants along Darlinghurst Road and Macleay Street, and an elegant, floodlit fountain stands in the middle of the district. But signs advertising "Australia's largest bed" and massage parlor "menus" capture the prevailing spirit of the area. Kings Cross was about as far from Israel as Mordechai Vanunu could get.

Vanunu immediately felt comfortable in Sydney. He had planned to fly to the United States in early summer, after short visits to New Zealand and Tahiti. But a week in Australia persuaded him to extend his stay by a few months.

"Here now is starting the winter, not very cold, something like in Israel," he wrote in a May 28, 1986, letter to Judy Zimmet. "I'll try to find some job. Most of the tourists work and it is easy to find work, especially if you can speak English very well. Here it is expensive like the U.S. and the town is like in the U.S. or England. The people are friendly. They drink a lot of beer."

Vanunu took a room in an inexpensive youth hostel on the fringes of Kings Cross and found temporary work as a dishwasher in a hotel kitchen. Ten days later, he was hired in a Greek restaurant and began training to become a taxi driver.

The relaxed atmosphere of Sydney exhilarated Vanunu. The trip through Asia had been fascinating, but he was growing weary of the solitude. Still struggling with a decision about the secrets in his knapsack, he longed to share his experiences with someone.

And so it came to pass that Vanunu wandered into the open arms of the Reverend John McKnight of the St. John's Anglican church.

McKnight was a minister who had carved a vocation out of taking in strays. At St. John's, he had created a safe haven for the drifters and runaways that poured into Kings Cross, a sanctuary for losers on the edge. McKnight firmly believed the church should be a place where religion and real life bumped heads, and he made sure the doors to St. John's were always open.

Attracted by the blazing lights, Vanunu wandered into the church on a Friday night at the end of May. He told McKnight he was an Israeli on holiday in Australia and began asking questions about the church. Pleasantly surprised by such an expression of interest by a Jew, McKnight invited Vanunu to sit down and talk.

The Sydney diocese of the Church of England had a reputation for being among the most conservative in the world, but McKnight was determined to channel the church's cold, stern form of evangelism into a driving force for social change. Talking about religion was not enough, he would tell his congregation. A true Christian, McKnight maintained, is devoted to helping his neighbor. To the minister, that meant tackling the problems that plagued society.

McKnight was a conservative man, the kind of fellow who wore pullover sweaters in the summer, and he vigorously emphasized the church's austere nature. But the reverend still managed to cut a distinctive figure even in his simple black cleric's suit with the white collar. He sported long thick sideburns and a bushy walrus mustache that drew attention away from his balding pate. And, far from being a small-time minister, he moved in wide circles, taking public positions on issues like treatment for drug addicts. He was cagy, adept at politics and public relations.

The church tolerated McKnight's penchant for publicity. He was doing a good job at St. John's, creating a close-knit parish with a strong sense of social commitment.

Vanunu quickly became a member of McKnight's "family." He was befriended by the two other Anglican clerics assigned to the church, Stephen Grey and David Smith, as well as several of the parishioners who were delighted to find the morose Israeli was a sincere, intelligent man with a wry sense of humor who enjoyed talking about philosophy and religion and listening to classical music.

At McKnight's suggestion, Vanunu moved into an apartment on Darlinghurst Road, across the street from both the church and the minister's home. William Kinbacher, who shared the apartment with Vanunu, remembered his roommate as a voracious reader who seemed well-informed on a wide range of topics and talked freely, in his halting but improving English, about his life in Israel. There was no mention of Dimona, but Vanunu did discuss his military service. "I don't think he liked aggression," Kinbacher recalled.

Vanunu could also be embarrassingly candid about his loneliness and his difficulty in developing relationships with women. "I've never had sex with a woman," he blurted out to a startled Kinbacher one afternoon.

In his fragile emotional state, Vanunu was simply overwhelmed by the outpouring of unqualified friendship from the strangers at St. John's. Dazed by his good fortune, he eagerly reached out to cement his new relationship. Vanunu spent virtually all his free time at the church or with parishioners. He changed the way he spelled his nickname—"Motti" became "Mordy," which sounded more like what his new friends had taken to calling him—and seriously considered remaining in Australia permanently.

The church's earnest involvement in social issues gave the experience an even more significant luster. To Vanunu, it appeared to provide an opportunity to solve his dilemma about the Dimona secrets.

By the time he arrived in Australia, Vanunu's six-month personal struggle over the nuclear issue had developed into another obsession. He had reached a point where he could not rest or relax as a result of his quandary over an appropriate moral response to Israeli nuclear policy. Even more perplexing was the absolute certainty with which most of his new friends at St. John's seemed to approach the topic of nuclear weapons.

The nuclear issue is a sensitive subject in Australia, which lies near the French atomic testing site in the South Pacific. The country's uranium deposits and the presence in Sydney of several plants manufacturing equipment for nuclear reactors brought the controversy even closer to home. In the oddest of coincidences, Vanunu had turned up shortly before the St. John's congregation began a series of discussions on social justice and nuclear arms, built around the premise that Christians must actively oppose nuclear weapons.

As he listened to the discussions, Vanunu gradually came to the conclusion that he must make known the story of his involvement in Israel's nuclear program. He approached McKnight and offered to lead a session on peace and disarmament. The talk would include a discussion about his work at Dimona. And, he added, there might be a slide show.

The minister was thrilled by the proposal. But some of his flock did not know what to make of it. "He was very casual about it," one recalled. "I mean, the idea of us having a slide show about his work in Israel now seems rather comical. He was very casual about it, and he did say this is a secret plant which he worked at. I guess I took that with a grain of salt, really, at the time."

Vanunu, however, was wracked by doubt about his decision, and he quickly shelved the idea of sharing his still-undeveloped photographs with the St. John's congregation. For the moment, he was only interested in discussing his anguish. Talking about Dimona could ease the burden; Vanunu was by no means sure he wanted to do anything more than that.

But the secret was out. Before he arrived in Sydney, Vanunu had mentioned the photographs to only two people, and both times his disclosure was greeted with relative indifference. Now the circle had widened to include an Anglican minister with a craving for causes and dozens of members of his congregation.

It was not long before the news buzzed out the doors of St. John's and came to the attention of a peculiar little man who was busy painting the church.

Chapter 14

There was something vaguely disreputable about Oscar Edmondo Guerrero. He was thirty-six years old, a short, chubby man who spoke in bursts of excited, shrill squeaks and walked with a swagger that seemed contrived. But he conveyed a slightly sinister quality, which was embellished by a churlish manner and the jaded expression on his dark, pockmarked face. Guerrero could be friendly, even fawning. But he was a hard man to nail down, and that much harder to trust.

Guerrero claimed to be a freelance journalist, a native Colombian who left his country in 1977 because of a lack of press freedom and headed for Europe. There, he said, his work had appeared in a variety of publications, most of them in Spain and Portugal. Guerrero boasted of having broken exclusive stories about the Irish Republican Army, the international terrorist know as "Carlos the Jackal," even about the attempted assassination of Pope John Paul II. As evidence of his journalistic credentials, he would rattle off a list of well-known journalists with whom he said he was friendly, and he carried a file folder of pictures showing him with various world figures, including Polish labor leader Lech Walesa, Argentine President Raul Alfonsin, and Israeli Prime Minister Shimon Peres.

It was an extremely impressive biography. British, Spanish and Portuguese journalists who dealt with him, however, told a different story. To them, the Colombian was an inveterate liar, a rather inept hustler who survived by concocting "exclusives" and pawning them off on editors who either did not suspect or did not much care that the stories were frauds. In September 1981, he sold the Lisbon newspaper *O Jornal* a set of photographs and a dubious story, datelined Belfast, that purported to describe life inside an IRA training camp. Seven months later, he unloaded an article and picture about a massacre in Timor. Readers quickly identified the photograph as a sloppily doctored print of a picture taken in Vietnam by Larry Burrows, the prize-winning magazine photographer. *O Jornal* considered legal action, but abandoned the idea after learning Guerrero had left the country.

Guerrero's account of his groundbreaking work on the pope's shooting was another story with a gaping hole. As he frequently told the tale, he fled Colombia in 1977 because police were thwarting his investigation into Ali Agca, the pontiff's unsuccessful assassin. The shooting in St. Peter's Square, however, did not occur until 1981.

Even Guerrero's world-leaders file was questionable. In several of the photographs, the Colombian was depicted in awkward positions that led to suspicions that he had superimposed his image next to the others.

"His professional qualifications were dubious to those who only knew him in Portugal," reported the Lisbon newspaper *Expresso* in a story about Guerrero after the Timor fraud was uncovered. "He had the air of a 'marginal,' always nervous and agitated, never giving details of his movements to anyone."

One of Guerrero's favorite stories dealt with his interview with Dr. Issam Sartawi, a Palestine Liberation Organization moderate who was assassinated in the lobby of his hotel during a Socialist International conference in Albufeira, Portugal, in April 1983.

There was no question that Guerrero had attended the meeting. His curious behavior had attracted the attention of journalists and security officials. He appeared exceedingly nervous and jumpy throughout the conference, and bragged loudly about his alleged achievements. Yet nobody had ever heard of Guerrero. Most people who met him were not even sure he was a Colombian. Although he spoke fluent Spanish, he could just as easily have been of Middle Eastern extraction—Lebanese, perhaps, or even Israeli. And he never seemed to be working. Guerrero would disappear for hours at a time. It was almost as if he had something else to do.

Even more puzzling was Guerrero's reaction to Sartawi's slaying. The news sent him into paroxysms of delight. As he literally jumped with joy, Guerrero crowed that he had conducted the last interview with the slain PLO official and would certainly sell it for a huge amount of money.

A British and two Portuguese journalists who attended the conference recall that police quickly detained Guerrero for questioning about the murder, but released him without charges a few hours later, and he hurriedly left town. *O Jornal* picked up his "last interview" with Sartawi, despite concerns about its provenance.

It was not the first time Guerrero had run afoul of the law. Interpol records show Guerrero was arrested at least three times, in three different countries, in 1982 alone. On June 9, he was taken off a train traveling between Lisbon and Madrid and charged with threatening behavior. On September 14, he was picked up in Hamburg, West Germany, for pickpocketing and assaulting a policeman. And in December, he was detained by Swiss authorities for involvement in a money-changing scam.

"You must be careful of this man," *O Jornal* deputy editor Manuel Marias once said of Guerrero.

Vanunu, however, knew none of this when he ran into the Colombian in July 1986. Guerrero and another man named Roland Saluitis were painting the St. John's church building under a government jobs program. Guerrero told Vanunu that Australia had granted him political refugee status because of his anti-government writings about Colombia.

Not long after, Guerrero heard about the Dimona films, and Vanunu's plans to discuss his work with the people of St. John's parish. He smelled money.

The Israeli was still not sure what to do with the photographs, and he shared his ambivalence with his new friends. One day, he confided to Saluitis that at times he felt like burning the film to rid himself of the problem.

The prospect horrified Guerrero, and he pressured Vanunu to have the pictures developed, if for no other reason than to see what he had. On July 29, Vanunu walked down to the Kings Cross One-

Hour Photo Shop and had the film processed. A few hours later, he showed them to Guerrero and Saluitis.

The photographs were every bit as good as Vanunu had hoped—a clear, comprehensive record of the inner workings of the plutonium-processing plant where Israel built its secret nuclear arsenal. Guerrero was beside himself with elation. "These are gold," he shouted as he flipped through the prints. "We are going to be rich."

Vanunu stared at him in bewilderment. The possibility of making money with the pictures had never crossed his mind. That was not the point. His interest was only in telling the world about Israel's duplicity. That was the only reason he would even consider making the photographs public, he firmly told Guerrero.

But the shy Israeli, always grateful for friends, was no match for a shark like Guerrero. The Colombian coaxed Vanunu with arguments about the public service he would be performing by revealing the secrets. He promised to make sure the photographs and Vanunu's story wound up in the hands of a reputable news organization—*Le Monde, The New York Times, Der Spiegel, Newsweek,* the *London Sunday Times.* And if the editors wanted to offer some money for the story—well, what would be so wrong with that? The photographs would probably fetch $500,000, maybe as much as $1 million, if the sale was handled properly, Guerrero insisted.

Guerrero was consumed by the prospect of the windfall. One day, as he painted the church spire, he became so excited that he fell off a ladder and injured his leg.

The more Oscar talked, the better the plan sounded to Vanunu. Oscar knew the news business. He had friends everywhere. He could place the pictures where they would do the most good. Vanunu was swept along by the strength of Guerrero's personality until finally he succumbed.

Guerrero and Saluitis wasted little time in claiming a share of the potential wealth. The story was Vanunu's, so most of the money should go to him, the two men conceded. But they would act as brokers for small fees—maybe $25,000 for Oscar and $10,000 or $20,000 for Roland.

Nothing was signed. It was a gentlemen's agreement.

There was still the chance Vanunu might back out of the arrangement, however, and Guerrero was not about to take chances. He wangled prints of seven of the photographs, telling Vanunu he needed something to show the newspapers.

Guerrero moved quickly. A few days after the pictures were developed, he contacted Carl Robinson, a *Newsweek* correspondent based in Sydney. Introducing himself as "Alberto Brava," Guerrero showed up at Robinson's house saying he could provide *Newsweek* with the secret story of Israel's nuclear program. In return, Guerrero wanted money and a byline.

Robinson turned him down. Guerrero rubbed him the wrong way, and he was skeptical about the deal. "It's not the sort of story you expect to land on your head in Sydney, Australia," he recalled later. But Robinson did agree to talk to Guerrero's source, a man the Colombian identified only as "David."

Vanunu met with the journalist for about three hours, but he was not particularly forthcoming. He still harbored doubts about his actions, and refused to reveal his real name or allow Robinson to see his passport or papers that would prove he ever worked at Dimona.

Robinson found Vanunu flustered, but sincere. "He struck me as a confused young man who had been a rebel all his life, and this was the ultimate act of rebellion," Robinson said.

"It is good for the world to know what Israel is doing," "David" told Robinson. "I'm doing it for peace."

The few technical details about the plant that Vanunu did offer appeared genuine, and Newsweek was interested in pursuing the story. But several days after the interview, Vanunu called Robinson to say he was no longer interested in an article about his work. He was frightened, thought he was being followed. And again he was having misgivings. Perhaps going public was not the right thing to do. Without Vanunu's cooperation, *Newsweek* abandoned the story.

Guerrero was beside himself with anger. He had scored on his very first try. Robinson might have balked initially, but *Newsweek's* editors would certainly have come up with some cash once Vanunu told all he knew and showed them the complete set of photographs.

You have wasted a great opportunity, Guerrero bitterly told the Israeli.

Chapter 15

In the thrall of his new environment, Vanunu's disdain for Judaism had deepened. He was convinced that his religion was the root cause of all that was wrong and immoral in Israeli society, and he was increasingly determined to renounce it. The beliefs and attitudes of his new friends at St. John's offered an enormously attractive alternative to addressing the world's problems, and a set of well-defined answers to the questions of philosophy and ethics that preyed on his mind. In his frequent conversations with McKnight, he began to explore the possibility of becoming a Christian.

The minister was genuinely fond of Vanunu—and not unmindful of the remarkable achievement that converting a Jew to Christianity would represent. If the young Israeli wanted to join the flock, McKnight was only too happy to oblige.

Viewed in a strictly religious context, Vanunu's interest in conversion was baffling. Aside from enrolling in a few courses at Ben-Gurion and a youthful fascination with church music, he had never evinced much of an interest in Christianity, certainly nothing strong enough to trigger such an important move in the space of a few months. But it was not the religion that had seduced him. Vanunu was inexorably drawn to the community that had embraced him without reservation—a welcome departure from what he viewed as the myopic, selfish world of Israel and Judaism—and offered a daily affirmation of his own developing moral philosophies.

In early August, barely two months after he walked into St. John's, Mordechai Vanunu was baptized in the Church of England, taking the name "John."

His letters to family members and to Judy Zimmet never mentioned the conversion. But there were hints that he had changed.

Shortly after arriving in Australia, he had written to Judy expressing his continued interest in joining her at the end of his trip. "I saw many places and I met different people, but I am the same person with the same ideas," he wrote.

Only a month later, his tone was more somber and less optimistic about a future together. "You don't have to come here . . ." he wrote. "I think you have to try to do what you want, like take your tests and try to study or find the place you want to work. And after I will come and we will live together."

"I am not the same man that you know from Israel, here or in the U.S. . . . I am going to have a simple life, doing simple work. I am not going to study, maybe for a few years. So you may not like all these problems. That is the point. . . ."

A few days after the aborted contact with *Newsweek*, Guerrero convinced Vanunu to try again. He would take some of the pictures to Europe and show them to friends in the newspaper business there. Vanunu gave Guerrero five more pictures to sweeten his sales pitch, and on August 14 the "broker" left on his marketing tour. The first stop would be Madrid.

Vanunu was relieved to see Guerrero go. His uncertainty and ambivalence were becoming more than he could bear. He wanted to go on with his life. It was easiest to simply let Guerrero take care of the matter.

Predictably, however, the Colombian had not been completely honest with his "client." He would peddle the pictures in Europe, but he was not about to take a chance on Vanunu developing another case of cold feet. The *Newsweek* debacle had been frustrating. Guerrero needed the money, and he wanted it now. The longer the delay, the more likely it was that Vanunu would back out again.

Guerrero realized he needed some insurance and, just before he left, he bought some. He picked up the telephone and dialed the number of the Israeli consulate in Sydney.

Chapter 16

Avi Kliman, the intelligence officer who fielded the call at the consulate on York Street, knew all about men like Oscar Guerrero. Like many of the operators on the fringes of journalism, Guerrero was always willing to shop an unpublishable story or an unprintable picture to the intelligence community. Like their counterparts the world over, the Israelis were always in the market. But Kliman had been around long enough to know most of the information that came over the transom was worthless.

Guerrero, though, was adamant. "I've got something very important for you," he told Kliman. "Let's meet."

Out of curiosity, and kicking himself for it, Kliman agreed to sit down with the Colombian at a cafe on Martin Place, a crowded pedestrian mall in the heart of Sydney. Guerrero was waiting when the Israeli arrived. Kliman introduced himself as "Joseph Dar." There was no point taking chances.

"Joseph, I have a very important tip for you. You will thank me very much, I'm sure," Guerrero began. "There is an Israeli nuclear scientist here who worked at your nuclear plant. This is a top man. He helped design your atom bomb and now he's going to sell his story. And he wants to defect."

Guerrero babbled on for a few more minutes before Kliman cut him off. He had heard enough. It was a waste of time. An Israeli nuclear scientist defecting, talking about his work to newspapers, hooking up with a sleaze like Guerrero.

Kliman asked for the scientist's name, and Guerrero handed him a slip of paper with Vanunu's name and Israeli passport number printed on it. Kliman told Guerrero he would look into it, and the two men parted.

Guerrero had not mentioned the photographs. He was apparently intent on cutting two separate deals—one with Israeli intelligence for tipping them off to a traitor, and another with a newspaper or magazine for the photographs and a story by Guerrero about Vanunu, possibly including his arrest. The disappearance of Vanunu would enhance the credibility of the story and the photographs. Guerrero could have it both ways.

Despite his misgivings, Kliman contacted Tel Aviv when he returned to the consulate. On the face of it, the story was ludicrous. But if there were a kernel of truth to it, headquarters should know. Kliman cabled Vanunu's name and passport number and a terse account of Guerrero's tale. Was there anything to it, anything Sydney should worry about? he asked.

The query was similar to dozens that flood in every week to the Mossad, Israel's version of the American Central Intelligence Agency, and it was handled routinely by desk managers at headquarters, whose job it is to work with the field agents and provide them with any information they need. A check with the Interior Ministry confirmed that Mordechai Vanunu did exist, and that he had left Israel through Haifa on January 19. The Israeli Atomic Energy Commission, the agency nominally in charge of the Dimona plant, also confirmed that Mordechai Vanunu had worked there for a period of 8 1/2 years.

But far from being a scientist, he had been a control-room technician who, records showed, was laid off during budget cuts in 1985. His work mostly involved monitoring instrument panels in various sections of the reactor complex. It was a sensitive post, certainly, but Vanunu had only worked on a few aspects of a very complex project. The work at Dimona was highly compartmentalized, the AEC assured the Mossad. Vanunu could not know very much at all about Israel's nuclear program.

No one mentioned his long record of leftist political activity.

When Guerrero called the next afternoon, Kliman lit into him. "You wasted my time, made me look silly," he told Guerrero coldly. "Vanunu was just a lowly control-room worker. He does not know anything about the plant."

Guerrero, though, had one more surprise up his sleeve. "But, listen to me," he sputtered. "The guy's got pictures."

By the next afternoon, the evidence of Mordechai Vanunu's deceit was in the hands of the Mossad. Kliman had reacted with practiced skepticism to Guerrero's announcement, and demanded proof. True to form, Guerrero had given Kliman crudely printed copies of only four of the twelve photographs he had wheedled out of Vanunu's hands. He did not even mention the others; they could still be used to sell the story.

But the four snapshots were enough to sound alarms in Tel Aviv and spur the Mossad into action. While headquarters threw together a picture of Vanunu's life and work in Israel, a squad of seven agents was deployed to Sydney to monitor Vanunu's activities and attempt to determine if he had been in contact with foreign powers. Once that had been established, the Mossad could address the issue of how to solve the problem.

Vanunu, now working as a taxi driver, was shadowed wherever he went. Agents followed his cab as he made the rounds of the hotels, watched his apartment, even joined him at lectures and workshops at the church.

What they found was disquieting, but hardly uncontrollable. Vanunu had been discussing his work at Dimona with his friends at St. John's, "bored housewives and religious zealots who had absolutely no idea what he was talking about," one intelligence official called them. But there was no indication that Vanunu had contacted, or been contacted by, anyone else.

If there were a time to close the Vanunu case, this was it. In Australia, he could have been captured, even killed, and no one would have been the wiser. Guerrero and the parishioners at St. John's would assume he had drifted out of Sydney the same way he drifted in. And even if they suspected something, what could they prove?

The analysis was relayed to Tel Aviv, where a senior Mossad officer, Yeshayahu Levy, a forty-one-year-old agency veteran whose seventeen-year career had included tours of duty in Europe and Latin America, had been placed in charge of the operation.

Levy was an unfailingly efficient spy with a reputation for carrying out his orders without comment or complaint. But despite an unobtrusive, almost scholarly manner, Levy had a knack for keeping the men and women under his command focused on their objectives, no easy task in the often fractious world of Israeli intelligence.

"There are four things here," he told the team of agents assigned to the Vanunu operation. "What does he know? How do we get him back? And does he come back dead or alive?"

The operation was given the highest priority. Vanunu couldn't be allowed to roam the world with his photographs.

Israel had gone to great lengths to conceal the nature of its nuclear program from the world. For thirty years, successive governments had responded to reports and rumors about a bomb factory at Dimona by patiently repeating that Israel would never be the first to introduce nuclear weapons into the Middle East. It was a lie everyone could live with. It meant the Arabs did not have to save face by building their own bombs. It meant the United States would not have to debate the propriety of an Israeli nuclear force, and whether U.S. aid should finance the arsenal. And it meant Israel itself, born out of the genocide of the Holocaust, would not have to wrestle with the morality of weapons that could wipe out the world.

But Vanunu's photographs could shred the carefully constructed facade. The record of three decades of deceit would be absolutely devastating in the wrong hands.

Which, of course, was where they were.

Chapter 17

"It's bigger than Watergate," Oscar Guerrero said confidently, tapping the worn briefcase he clutched to his chest. "The story I've got in here, it's bigger than Watergate."

Wendy Robbins, a young summer intern at the *London Sunday Times*, eyed him quizzically across the table in the newspaper's cafeteria. What a very strange man, she thought to herself.

Guerrero couldn't sit still. His knees jiggled up and down and his fingers drummed the tabletop. He could feel it. He was this close to the big score. These guys were serious about his story, his pictures. They wanted to do business.

For a time, it had looked like a dry hole. After leaving Sydney, he flew to Madrid where he tried to interest several news organizations in his latest "exclusive." But Guerrero's reputation preceded him into many newsrooms; no one was biting. He was on the verge of desperation when he stopped by to see Tim Brown on August 26.

Brown, a stringer for a number of foreign newspapers and the *Sunday Times*, had some time on his hands. There wasn't much to do in the way of work in late August, and he was a little bored. If he hadn't been, he probably never would have allowed Guerrero through the door. But Brown invited Guerrero inside and listened to his story.

Since his near-miss with Kliman, the Colombian had refined the tale. Now, Vanunu was not only a top Israeli scientist, he was the father of his country's atomic-bomb program. Guerrero claimed to have been approached in Israel under the most mysterious circumstances by a group of leftists who asked him to meet with the scientist. A girl brought him to a secret rendezvous with Vanunu on the outskirts of Tel Aviv. Guerrero said he listened to the scientist's

81

story, then agreed to help spirit him out of Israel to Australia, where Vanunu planned to defect.

Brown did not believe the preposterous account. None of it made sense. But then Guerrero showed him several photographs that he claimed were shots of the top-secret Israeli nuclear plant at Dimona.

"Oh, that's worth a phone call," Brown thought after Guerrero had left. And he picked up the telephone and rang the *Sunday Times* foreign desk.

Stephen Milligan, the foreign editor, was intrigued. Of course, there was nothing certain about it. Guerrero's story could easily be a hoax. But Israel, nuclear weapons, smuggled scientists, defections—this was the kind of story the *Sunday Times* loved, a hard-news yarn that was fascinating enough to sell papers in the highly competitive British Sunday market.

Milligan walked across the cavernous newsroom jammed with cluttered desks and approached Robin Morgan, the newspaper's features editor and head of its Insight investigative unit.

"I've got this man in Madrid," Milligan began, and he told Morgan the story. "Tim Brown's talked to him. What do you think we should do?"

At thirty-two, Morgan had been a journalist for half his life. He broke into the business after leaving home and school at age sixteen, and had spent the last decade at the *Sunday Times*, working on some of the most important stories the paper had covered, including the investigation into the bombing of a Greenpeace (an environmental organization) boat in New Zealand by French intelligence agents. More recently, Morgan had served as news editor before shifting over to features and taking on Insight.

His quick rise and a condescending manner rubbed some people the wrong way. Morgan was too sure of himself, confident to the point of arrogance, and frequently unwilling to listen to advice. He had an irritating habit of sulking when he didn't get his way. More than a few reporters in the newsroom flatly refused to work with him.

Morgan also saw the potential of the Guerrero story, provided it wasn't a hoax. "Well, let's send a staff member, somebody we trust, over to Madrid to go through this guy's story with him," Morgan suggested to Milligan. The two men agreed that Jon Swain, a European correspondent based in Paris, was a good choice, and Swain flew to Madrid late that afternoon.

Swain wasted little time in offering his assessment. Within hours of his arrival, he was on the telephone to Milligan, urging him to pursue the story a little further. Guerrero was clearly an idiot and a liar, he told his editor, but he definitely knew someone in Australia. Brown had booked adjoining rooms for Swain and Guerrero at a Madrid hotel. The hotel had very thin walls and the Colombian was overheard placing a telephone call to Sydney.

And then there were the photographs. "You've got to see them and check them out," Swain counseled. "It's worth checking them out."

Milligan told Swain to bring Guerrero to London at the newspaper's expense. They arrived the morning of August 27 and went directly to the *Sunday Times'* office in Wapping, in London's Docklands section.

Guerrero couldn't have picked a better newspaper to approach, or a better time to approach it. It had been a tough, tumultuous five years for the *Sunday Times*, a rocky period that began in 1981 when Australian publishing magnate Rupert Murdoch bought the newspaper. The sale alarmed the British newspaper establishment, which worried Murdoch would turn the *Sunday Times* institution into the type of lurid, downmarket tabloid for which he had become notorious in Britain and other countries. His dismissal of the respected journalist Harold Evans as editor of the daily *London Times*, the *Sunday Times'* sister paper, barely one year later was taken as evidence that Murdoch meant to make drastic changes.

The *Sunday Times'* reputation suffered another blow in 1983 when it became entangled in the Hitler diaries scandal. Despite the misgivings of senior staffers, Murdoch agreed to pay $1.2 million to acquire the rights to publish excerpts from the purported diaries of the Nazi leader. The documents, which had been obtained by the West German magazine *Stern*, were quickly found to be forgeries.

Murdoch's legion of detractors thoroughly enjoyed the fiasco, and the publisher compounded the debacle with his nonchalance after the fraud was discovered. He dismissed the flap by saying, "Nothing ventured, nothing gained," and pointed out, "After all, we are in the entertainment business." Murdoch also noted with satisfaction that the *Sunday Times*, which was reimbursed for the $200,000 it had already paid *Stern*, gained more than 20,000 new readers as a result of its "scoop."

Checkbook journalism and sizzling, if dubious, exclusives have traditionally been mainstays of much of the British press, and other London dailies have fallen for hoaxes over the years. But despite the history, Murdoch's critics gleefully pounced on the Hitler diaries episode as evidence of the lack of standards at his British newspapers.

And much of Fleet Street would have relished another opportunity to embarrass him. In January 1986, Murdoch had decided to take on the powerful British labor unions, whose opposition to management modernization schemes had prevented most of the British media from moving into the 20th century. Without advance notice, he moved the offices of his company, News International Ltd., from antiquated, cramped quarters in central London to a brand-new, $180 million complex at Wapping on the Thames River. The modern plant boasted the latest in computerized production equipment and made it possible for Murdoch to publish without the intransigent labor unions with whom he had futilely attempted to negotiate new contracts. More than 6,000 production workers went on strike, but Murdoch managed to put out his newspapers with the help of the electricians union and his editorial employees.

The sometimes violent dispute was winding down in August 1986, but it had taken its toll, particularly at the *Sunday Times*. Dozens of senior staffers had either quit or been fired by Murdoch when they refused to move to Wapping in a show of solidarity with the striking production workers. While other British publishers secretly praised Murdoch in the belief his victory would benefit them economically, many British reporters and editors were outraged by his actions. Murdoch's papers became the objects of scorn.

The Wapping complex was a heavily guarded fortress surrounded by barbed wire. Editors and reporters frequently arrived at work in convoys that ran a gauntlet through mobs of jeering, brick-tossing strikers. The scene often turned bloody on Saturday nights when the striking workers tried to prevent delivery trucks from leaving with the week's press run. It was an ugly advertisement for a newspaper, and many staffers were depressed by their new status as pariahs. Reporters and editors spent hours on the telephones, hunting for new jobs.

There is nothing like an important international story to improve staff morale and a newspaper's standing among its peers. The photographs Guerrero was carrying in his briefcase certainly had the potential to do both. If true, the Dimona expose would send a signal that the *Sunday Times* was still in business as a major investigatory newspaper, that neither Murdoch nor Hitler nor Wapping had dimmed its glory.

Engrossed by the pictures, Milligan nevertheless decided this wasn't a story for the foreign desk. Too many checks would have to be made before the paper could even think about running with it, and then more work would be needed to whip it into shape. The foreign staff didn't have the time for such a consuming project.

So Guerrero was handed off to Morgan. This time, the Colombian added more bait to the hook. Israel was building a neutron bomb, he told Morgan. And the Mossad, Israel's CIA, was hunting for Vanunu right now. Sure, Morgan thought. The Mossad. Right.

Oscar Guerrero did little to boost the *Sunday Times'* confidence in the Dimona story. To the young editor, most of Guerrero's claims were rubbish, particularly the nonsense about how Guerrero smuggled Vanunu out of Israel with the help of left-wingers. But even if the fidgety man standing in his office was attempting a hoax, exposing him might still make a great story.

"I mean, the *Sunday Times* has always had this love of hoax stories as well," Morgan explained. "Everyone likes a good hoax. And when somebody comes in off the street with a story like this, you immediately know, your instinct tells you you're being hoaxed."

And again, there were the photographs. Morgan decided to make a quick attempt to confirm their authenticity. The shots of the out-side of Dimona appeared to match pictures in the newspaper's li-brary, blurry images taken from the highway that had surfaced in the past. But for all the *Sunday Times* knew, the other pictures could have been taken in any factory. Hebrew lettering on some of the instrument panels gave the photographs an Israeli flavor. But there was nothing to prove the equipment was part of a nuclear plant. A trained nuclear scientist was needed to pass judgment on the interior shots.

Morgan assigned the task to Peter Hounam, a tall bear of a man, with a slightly graying beard and long hair that fell almost to his shoulders. At forty-two, Hounam had moved somewhat late in his career into big-time British journalism. He had come to the *Sunday Times* in June, in the midst of the Wapping labor dispute, from the *Evening Standard*, where he had been chief investigative reporter. When Guerrero turned up in London, Hounam had been working with the Insight team only a few weeks. A gentle, polite man with a dry sense of humor, Hounam had a reputation as a dogged reporter whose main strength lay in his ability to follow leads to the bitter end.

Morgan sketched Guerrero's story. "I know this guy's completely crazy, but can you check out these photographs?" he asked.

Hounam and Guerrero drove to the home of a University of Lon-don nuclear physics professor recruited by Morgan to examine the photo array. The scientist was non-committal, but conceded the pic-tures could have been taken inside some sort of plant involving nuclear power.

That was confirmation enough to Guerrero, who wouldn't let the photographs out of his hands even while the professor was examin-ing them.

"I told you, I told you," he repeatedly squealed to Hounam on the ride back to Wapping. "This is the really big story, isn't it? This is the real thing. I told you it was the real thing."

Hounam had only known Guerrero for a few hours, but already he was tiring of him.

Chapter 18

Hounam's report convinced Morgan to move ahead, but he first needed the approval of the *Sunday Times* editor, Andrew Neil, an urbane thirty-seven-year-old veteran magazine journalist who had been hired by Murdoch in the wake of the Hitler diaries disaster. In tune with Murdoch's thirst for sensational headlines, Neil constantly pressured his correspondents to come up with blockbuster stories. But the 1983 humiliation was never far from Neil's mind, and Guerrero's wild tale had a hint of catastrophe about it.

Morgan had a solution. Instead of worrying about the Colombian's veracity, he suggested, the *Sunday Times* should simply pursue the story of how the pictures wound up in Guerrero's briefcase. Even if the newspaper ultimately discovered Guerrero was attempting a hoax, exposing him would still make an off-beat, exciting story. Neil agreed, and Morgan assigned Hounam to fly back to Australia with Guerrero that night to meet Vanunu. The Colombian was told to wait for Hounam at the nearby Tower Thistle Hotel, where the newspaper had booked a room for him.

Suddenly Guerrero became quite agitated. He didn't want to sit in a hotel room all day. He wanted to go out, do some shopping. He promised to return in time to make the plane.

Morgan and Hounam rejected the idea. Guerrero could not be left alone; for one thing, he might drop in on another newspaper and try to start a bidding war. But the *Sunday Times* couldn't keep him in the newsroom or at the hotel against his will. So Morgan asked researcher Wendy Robbins to babysit him.

It was the first out-of-office assignment for Robbins, an attractive, engaging brunette who had graduated from Leeds University a few months earlier and landed a temporary job at the newspaper while she awaited the start of graduate studies in the fall. But Morgan was not much concerned about Robbins' lack of experience. She was an aggressive and determined young woman who did her work well and with enthusiasm.

Over coffee in the cafeteria the previous day, Robbins had decided Guerrero was not a man to be trusted. Morgan had asked the young staffer, who had studied in Mexico and spoke fluent Spanish, to find out what she could about Guerrero's background. But from the start, he had thrown up smokescreens. At first, Guerrero told her that he was an Israeli, but when Robbins, who is Jewish, addressed him in Hebrew, Guerrero quickly shifted gears and claimed he was Mexican.

Robbins had not been told exactly what Guerrero was doing at the newspaper. But a man who lied about his nationality made her more than a little uneasy.

From the moment they left the office, there was trouble. Guerrero had not objected to Morgan's decision to send Robbins with him. Once outside, however, Guerrero demanded to be left alone. Robbins adamantly refused. She had her orders. "I'm to stay with you at all times," she insisted.

"No way," said Guerrero, shaking his head vigorously. "Look, it's very dangerous. I'm being followed. A lot of people want my ass. There could be trouble. You could be shot."

Robbins would not back down. Gurerro took one more stab at it. "You don't know how to duck bullets," he warned darkly, before giving up and getting into Robbins' car, muttering to himself.

They drove to Trafalgar Square, where Guerrero made two more attempts to escape from his minder. Finally, they reached a compromise. Guerrero said he had to meet a girl outside the National Gallery, on the north side of the square, and Robbins agreed to stand nearby during the rendezvous. She took up a position among the pigeons flocking around Nelson's Column and watched as Guerrero stopped on the sidewalk in front of the museum, pacing in small circles.

A few minutes ticked by, and Robbins, worried Guerrero might make another attempt to elude her, edged closer, taking cover behind the huge marble lions that flank the base of the column. Finally, a young girl threaded her way through the crowds of tourists swarming through the square, and approached Guerrero. There was a brief conversation. Then, suddenly, Guerrero and the girl hailed a taxi and jumped in.

Dejected, Robbins stood and watched in frustration as the cab pulled away from the curb and disappeared into heavy traffic. She headed for the hotel and sat down in the lobby to wait for Hounam, to tell him she had blown the assignment.

Ninety minutes later, Guerrero walked into the hotel. He was by himself. "See, I told you I'd show up," he said, grinning, as Robbins angrily harangued him for his disappearance.

Hounam arrived about 6 P.M. and Robbins was dismissed. She returned to the office and told Morgan about her experience, then went home, bewildered by the newspaper's involvement with a man like Oscar Guerrero.

The jumbo jet was in the air only a few hours before Hounam also started wondering about the entire venture. Traveling with Guerrero was torture. He spent most of his time crowing, "This is really the biggest story. We're gong to be rich, Peter. You're going to be famous and I'm going to be rich." He wandered through the passenger cabin trying unsuccessfully to strike up conversations with most of the women on the plane, returning to his seat only long enough to eat and drink everything that was placed before him.

A very strange character, Hounam thought as he settled in his first-class seat. But you meet strange characters all the time in the newspaper business. Best not to jump to judgments.

Still, by the time the plane landed in Sydney on the morning of August 30, Hounam was starting to wonder whether the trip had been a waste of time.

Hounam and Guerrero checked into adjoining rooms at the Sydney Hilton on Pitt Street. The reporter, exhausted after the twenty-one-hour flight, went to his room to take a nap, but Guerrero quickly left the hotel, saying he had to attend to some business. A few hours later, the telephone rang in Hounam's room. "Come over. I've got him here," Guerrero announced.

Hounam quickly dressed and went next door. He was anxious to meet Mordechai Vanunu.

"He was sort of standing rather stooped and nervous, shaking, almost. He was really petrified when I came in. We shook hands, and really I just sort of engaged him in small talk a bit, just to sort of try and get him to relax a bit."

Vanunu was initially suspicious. For all he knew, Hounam could have been a Mossad agent sent to bring him back to Israel. But he soon began to relax and the three men went back to Hounam's room to talk some more. With little prompting, Vanunu quietly began to tell his story. The session lasted most of the afternoon, but only a few minutes into the presentation, Hounam was able to confirm his suspicions: Guerrero's version of events was replete with lies. The Colombian was unfazed. He ignored Hounam's glares and whiled away the hours lying on a bed ordering beers from room service and smoking cigarettes.

Even stripped of Guerrero's embellishments, however, Vanunu's account was fascinating. Without bombast or fanfare, the Israeli showed the reporter the complete set of Dimona photographs, more than twenty of them now mounted on slides, which Hounam held up to the window to view. Hounam was impressed by the noticeable care Vanunu exercised in providing an accurate description of his duties at Dimona. He was quick to admit that he didn't know the answer to a particular question. And there was much he did not know.

"I don't know all the scientific background," he would tell Hounam in his accented English.

Politely but firmly, Hounam pushed Vanunu to explain why he had decided to talk publicly about his work. For an Israeli to be discussing such sensitive information with a British newspaper reporter was nothing short of extraordinary. Why, Hounam wondered, was he doing it?

The explanation didn't make much sense to the burly journalist. He listened skeptically as Vanunu argued that by baring Israel's nuclear secrets, he would help bring peace to the Middle East. Vanunu believed the world would pressure Israel to dismantle its arsenal. Without the bomb, Israel would be forced to make peace with the Arabs, and both sides could establish a nuclear-free zone in the Middle East, which would end forever the threat of a nuclear holocaust in the region.

As the conversation wore on, Hounam found himself in an uncomfortable position. Vanunu's arguments were incredibly naive and, even worse, illogical. Israel had never bowed to world opinion, regardless of the unpopularity of its actions. Moreover, Vanunu's story was likely to actually strengthen Israel's hand by showing the Arabs they could never defeat the Jewish state. Any settlement reached under those conditions would be highly advantageous to Israel, not the Arabs.

"But then I thought, as we talked like this, 'If I start arguing with him about it, he's not going to go through with it. He's not going to tell me anymore,' " Hounam recalled. "And it wasn't my job to sort of argue with him about it. I just listened and said, 'Yes, yes, yes.' "

The next day, Hounam had a slide projector brought to his room so he could better examine Vanunu's slides. He closed the curtains and Hounam and Vanunu spent several hours sitting in the darkened room going through the slides as Vanunu explained what they were seeing. The impressive presentation was interrupted only by an occasional "I *told* you, Peter," from an increasingly bored Guerrero, slouched on the bed.

The first burst of information went a long way towards quelling fears at the *Sunday Times* that the Dimona story was a hoax. Slowly, Hounam, Morgan and the Insight staff were coming to the realization that an important story had fallen in their hands. The world had long suspected Israel had nuclear weapons. But Vanunu's disclosures could allow the newspaper to paint a reasonably accurate and relatively detailed picture of Israel's nuclear weapons capability.

During his twelve days in Australia, Hounam developed a genuine affection for Vanunu. They frequently dined together and met for drinks, and Hounam found the intense Israeli to be courteous and reliable, punctual about appointments. He was fastidious about not profiting from his experience, even to the point of rejecting an occasional meal in an expensive restaurant. On days when interviews were scheduled, Hounam would pay Vanunu a small amount of money in compensation for keeping his taxicab off the road. But that, and a telephone call to Judy Zimmet in Boston, was all he got, or wanted.

Gerrero was a different story. Suspicious that he would be cut out of the deal he expected the *Sunday Times* to strike with Vanunu, the Colombian insisted on accompanying Vanunu whenever he met Hounam. One night the three men went to the Sydney Opera House to see Verdi's *MacBeth*. Guerrero snored through the performance.

Guerrero's ground rules were strict. All meetings between Hounam and Vanunu had to be arranged through him; Hounam was not allowed to know where Vanunu lived, or to call him on the telephone.

The reporter had grown to detest Guerrero. The querulous Colombian had stayed in the Hilton for several days, running up huge bills as he wolfed down steaks for breakfast and ordered the most expensive items on the menu at every other meal, before Vanunu quietly informed Hounam that Guerrero had an apartment in Sydney. Hounam had angrily evicted Guerrero, but he couldn't figure out a way to shake him for good. Guerrero was obviously not going anywhere until he was paid.

Vanunu was also not overly fond of Guerrero. The two men shared few interests, and Vanunu found Guerrero's lifestyle unappealing. The Colombian regularly spent time with prostitutes in Kings Cross, and urged Vanunu to join him. But the Israeli resolutely refused. "I do not want any woman who doesn't genuinely want to be with me," he would say. Still, he felt a sense of loyalty and gratitude to Guerrero, and had promised him $25,000 if the Dimona story fetched a fee.

Vanunu, of course, had no idea that Guerrero had been in touch with the Mossad. But Israeli intelligence was on his tail, watching him day and night, waiting for the order to move in.

Chapter 19

If the Vanunu story had arrived at a propitious moment for the *Sunday Times*, it couldn't have come at a worse time for Israel's spies. Rarely had the secret services been wracked by such controversy, rocked by such turmoil. For one of the few times in their history, they were playing defense. Blame and the best way to avoid it consumed the senior officials of the country's vaunted intelligence agencies.

The Shin Bet, Israel's internal security agency, had been under siege since 1984 when top officers, including director Avraham Shalom, ordered the beating deaths of two captured Palestinian bus hijackers, then lied to government investigators and tried to shift the blame to an innocent army colonel. Only the decision to issue presidential pardons to eleven agents averted the ugly specter of a trial, but the scandal was devastating for morale and set off a bitter fight for control of the agency.

Military Intelligence was suffering the fallout from the disclosure that Israel had been running a spy in the United States. A U.S. Navy intelligence analyst named Jonathan Jay Pollard had been recruited by a small Defense Ministry agency, and senior officials denied knowledge of the operation. But the cloud of suspicion had engulfed Military Intelligence as Jerusalem, anxious to appease its outraged ally, searched for scapegoats.

The Pollard affair had also stained the image of the Mossad, which was forced to admit it did not even know about the spy in Washington. The agency's reputation for infallibility had already been battered during a serious slump that began in 1982 when it led the campaign in favor of the Israeli invasion of Lebanon, an operation that quickly developed into a military quagmire and a political

93

disaster. The fiasco had substantially weakened the Mossad's influence, particularly after it was unable to locate Palestine Liberation Organization chief Yasser Arafat, a main target of the invasion forces.

Morale in the field suffered even more when Nahum Admoni, a cautious, politically minded bureaucrat whose career in the agency was marked by a singular lack of operational experience, was appointed as head of the agency.

The agency, officially known as the Institute for Intelligence and Special Services (Mossad is the Hebrew word for "institute"), had enjoyed vast powers since its creation in 1951 by David Ben-Gurion after a period of harsh infighting between existing intelligence services in the early days of the Jewish state. By 1986, the Mossad fielded about 500 officers and 1,000 to 1,500 other employees, and could call on the services of another 7,000 officers, soldiers and civilians working for Shin Bet and the foreign and defense ministries.

Specifically, the Mossad was responsible for all secret state activities outside Israel's borders. In Israel's situation, this covered a great deal of ground. The agency collected information on security issues, fought intelligence wars, handled research and evaluation in the political field, and conducted special operations, not always of an intelligence nature. It was also responsible for representing Israel in countries without formal ties to Jerusalem.

But in a country where information is the currency of survival, intelligence agencies dominate the governmental decision-making process, and the Mossad was perpetually locked in a struggle for supremacy with its sister services.

In 1986, Military Intelligence was threatening the Mossad's traditional role as the senior service. The defense agency, the preeminent intelligence unit in the years following Israel's birth, had gone into a tailspin after failing to predict the onset of the 1973 Yom Kippur War. But by 1979, the U.S. Central Intelligence Agency had concluded that Military Intelligence had again taken the lead role in "strategic and tactical intelligence," controlling preparation of national intelligence estimates and evaluation of all information dealing with Arab nations.

Burned once, Military Intelligence had also offered a far more cautious assessment of the Lebanon situation in 1982 and, in the wake of the disaster north of the border, it had once again supplanted the Mossad in the eyes of many political leaders as the premier intelligence agency. Enhancing its position was the new agency head, Major General Amnon Shahak, a much decorated army commander who had the added advantage of having played a key role in helping Prime Minister Shimon Peres develop his latest Middle East peace initiative. The proposal was at least tacitly opposed by Mossad chief Admoni, a long-time associate of Foreign Minister Yitzhak Shamir, a former senior Mossad operative and Peres' perennial political rival.

Admoni was suspicious of Shahak, who had made no secret of his interest in the Mossad post, and spent much of his time trying to undercut Military Intelligence. But the Mossad boss also had his hands full within his own agency, where he was not universally admired.

He had won the job almost by default in 1982. The scramble to succeed the retiring Major General Yitzhad Hofi, who had headed the Mossad since 1974, appeared to be over when then-Prime Minister Menachem Begin tapped a veteran army general, Yekutiel Adam, for the post. But Adam was killed in Lebanon in July, and the search was reopened. Admoni, the deputy director, was supported by Hofi largely because his two first choices had fallen by the wayside, one to terminal illness and the other because of his role in the Lebanon fiasco.

Admoni was more than acceptable to the political leadership, which had grown tired of dominating Mossad chiefs. The politicians wanted someone who would follow orders without delivering lectures, and the fifty-four-year-old Admoni fit the bill. He had begun his intelligence career during the War of Independence in 1948. After earning a master's degree in international relations at the University of California-Berkeley in 1954, he joined the Mossad, serving first as an instructor at the agency's training academy, then in a variety of posts overseas and in Israel before becoming deputy chief in 1976.

An unimaginative man whose major vice was a penchant for expensive clothes that earned him the nickname "Mr. Gucci," Admoni had made a virtue out of caution. He was the quintessential intelligence bureaucrat, a classic "little gray man." As he climbed the ranks, he had little to do with operations or running agents. Admoni spent most of his time dealing with other foreign intelligence agencies and handling relations with problem states.

His appointment to the top job was a triumph for passivity in an agency known for audacious acts. And by 1986 the Mossad had assumed his personality. The intelligence community believed the agency had become too reactive, too reliant on orders from the political sector. Admoni won't move without five okays, the standing complaint went, so that he can always blame failure on his political superiors.

Lebanon had taught him a valuable lesson. Admoni had assumed command of the agency on September 12, 1982, four days before Lebanese Christians massacred hundreds of Palestinians in the Sabra and Chatila refugee camps. The mass slayings touched off recriminations inside Israel, and heads rolled. Admoni, who had supported the drive into Lebanon, escaped the backlash, but came away with a keen understanding of the precarious nature of his post. He moved the Mossad into low gear. Scaling back operations to none but the most essential, he meekly bowed to the wishes of the political leadership.

The contrast to his predecessor, Yitzhak Hofi, could not have been more striking. In 1982, Hofi, convinced it was not in Israel's interest, actively campaigned to scuttle a proposal to stage a coup in Iran. Three years later, Admoni looked the other way when Shimon Peres involved Israel in the Iran-Contra affair, the American arms-for-hostages dealings with Iran.

And now, in mid-August 1986, Admoni was being asked for advice on how to handle the Vanunu situation. But he wasn't about to open his mouth until he figured out which way Peres wanted to go.

Israel's nuclear arsenal was built on a foundation of lies from the start, and no one knew more about that than Shimon Peres. He had been the architect of both the bomb factory at Dimona and the thirty-year effort to keep it a secret. As he huddled with his intelligence chiefs to assess the Vanunu situation, the prime minister was probably the only man in the room who understood the true dimensions of the dilemma.

David Ben-Gurion had concluded as early as 1948 that the horrifying threat of the power unleashed at Hiroshima could guarantee the survival of the newly created Jewish state. But only four countries—the United States, the Soviet Union, Britain and France—had the ultimate weapon in the years after World War II. To join the club would be an enormously expensive, technologically daunting undertaking, particularly for a country starting from scratch. But Peres, then the brilliant young director-general of the Defense Ministry, persuaded Ben-Gurion to pursue the nuclear option.

Peres first faced the task of finding someone to supply the necessary technology. A five-megawatt research reactor was built outside Tel Aviv in the early 1950s with American help under the "Atoms for Peace" program, but the facility was too small—and too closely monitored by U.S. officials—to build nuclear weapons.

France, which had launched its own nuclear program in 1954 over the strenuous objections of the United States, solved Israel's problem. Desperate for Israeli assistance in its ill-fated Suez adventure, France caved in to Peres' relentless campaign for a nuclear reactor. In October 1957, Prime Minister Maurice Bourges-Maunoury agreed to provide Israel with a twenty-four-megawatt reactor, large enough to produce one Hiroshima-sized bomb each year.

Hundreds of French technicians flooded the Negev to construct the facility, including a plutonium processing plant built underground to elude American and Soviet spy satellites. The complex was operating at full capacity in five years and by 1967 Israel had enough plutonium on hand to build its first bomb. Coupled with the acquisition and development of advanced missile and aircraft technology by the defense industry, another Peres achievement, Israel had gone nuclear.

Fueling the Dimona plant remained a serious problem. Small amounts of uranium and other materials needed to operate the reactor for peaceful purposes could be purchased through normal channels from countries like the United States and South Africa. But Israel could not openly obtain the relatively large quantities of uranium and other substances and equipment needed for weapons production without attracting suspicion.

To supply the scientists, Peres created a special intelligence agency, the Science Liason Bureau, known by its Hebrew acronym Lakam. The agency, so secret that only a few people inside the government knew of its existence, was immensely successful. Twenty-one tons of heavy water, used to cool the reactor, were purchased from Norway, which knew nothing about Israel's plans. About 220 tons of enriched uranium, enough to build as many as six weapons, were fleeced from a Pennsylvania company owned by an ardent supporter of Israel. Israeli agents were believed to have stolen 200 tons of natural uranium from a ship that sailed from Antwerp in 1968.

Ben-Gurion and Peres were convinced the bomb project had to be kept under wraps. They believed, correctly, that the knowledge that Israel had nuclear weapons would almost certainly prompt the Arabs to build or acquire some of their own and, more disastrously, pressure other countries to stop supplying Israel with the material it needed to fuel the desert reactor. At the very least, Israel, which enjoyed the sympathy and support of much of the world, would be excoriated by both its friends and foes for dramatically upping the stakes in the volatile Middle East. And the bomb was just as likely to be a problem at home. A bitter debate over the moral and political propriety of Israel's nuclear gambit could easily scuttle the project.

The solution was the strictest secrecy. Ben-Gurion never informed his Cabinet or the parliament and , at Peres' suggestion, not even the intelligence community was initially told of the plans. Seven of the eight members of the Israeli Atomic Energy Commission resigned in protest over the decision to build weapons, but their reasons were never made public. To explain the feverish construction activity in the Negev, Ben-Gurion announced Israel was building a textile plant.

After an American spy plane uncovered the existence of the nuclear complex in 1960, Ben-Gurion was forced to admit that Israel was erecting a second reactor. But he insisted the new facility would be used only for "peaceful" industrial, agricultural and health purposes. That party line was echoed throughout the decade; in 1963, Peres claimed the power produced at Dimona would be used to desalinate billions of gallons of sea water for the irrigation of the Negev. The announcement mystified the director of Israel's water company, who publicly insisted he was unaware of any such plan.

To placate the United States, Ben-Gurion agreed to permit regular inspections of the plant by American experts, but he secretly ordered severe restrictions on the inspectors' access, and the Nixon administration ended the program in 1969, As a result of the subterfuge, the tightly held secret of the real purpose of the desert facility never leaked, either inside or outside Israel. Successive Israeli leaders stood on a firm pledge, first uttered by Prime Minister Levi Eshkol in 1964: "Israel will never be the first to introduce nuclear weapons into the Middle East."

Throughout the 1960s, however, rumors abounded about Israel's nuclear capability. But to their delight, Israeli leaders discovered the rumors and their elaborately crafted denials created a surprisingly effective nuclear deterrent. No one could be sure if Israel had the bomb. But everyone, particularly the Arabs, had to worry about it.

Without a formal decision or even much discussion, Israel adopted this policy of deliberate ambiguity to deal with the nuclear question. Top officials began dropping hints about the country's nuclear capability on an almost regular basis. In the midst of negotiations over the purchase of F-4 fighter jets from the United States in 1969, Israeli officials asked that the aircraft be fitted with bomb racks to carry nuclear weapons. The officials knew the request would be denied. But they were equally sure the request would be leaked to the news media. In 1974, President Ephraim Katzir told a group of visiting American and European science correspondents that "Israel has nuclear potential." When one journalist wondered whether Israel was at all ambivalent about its capacity for destruction, Katzir replied, "Why should we be worried about that? Let the world do the worrying. . . . We should be concerned first and foremost about our survival."

Former Defense Minister Moshe Dayan, the legendary army commander, revealed to French television in 1976 that Israel has "the possibility of manufacturing the bomb now." Six months later, during a visit to Canada, Dayan commented, "Israel possesses the scientific and technological capability to produce an atomic bomb, should the Arab states threaten to use such a bomb, but Israel will never be the first to launch nuclear warfare in the Middle East."

The campaign continued into the mid-1980s. Professor Yuval Ne'eman, a former minister of science popularly known as Israel's "Dr. Strangelove," told an American reporter in 1984 that Israel could build an atomic bomb. But he stressed that "Israel has not yet crossed the threshold of manufacturing an atomic bomb." Pressed on whether Israel had nuclear weapons, Ne'eman replied, "Technically that is accurate, but it can also be misleading if one speaks in terms of the amount of time required for manufacturing a nuclear bomb."

The disclosure, denied by Israel, that Prime Minister Golda Meir had ordered missiles armed with nuclear warheads during the darkest hours of the 1973 war only served to heighten worldwide suspicion that Israel had nuclear weapons, and, more significantly, was willing to use them.

Deliberate ambiguity had been a success. Israel had managed a remarkable nuclear escalation without triggering the wrath of the world. But Vanunu was in a position to expose Israel's policy of deception.

Chapter 20

Ever cautious, Admoni waited more than a week before giving Peres the bad news. The Mossad chief wanted to know precisely how much damage Vanunu could cause before he informed the prime minister. Peres was a busy man in August 1986. He was deeply involved in negotiations to end a border dispute with Egypt, and visited the African nation of Cameroon to mark the restoration of diplomatic relations severed after the 1973 war. Thus, it was not until late August that Admoni had the opportunity to bring up the Vanunu matter.

Peres was staggered by the breakdown in security. Barely able to contain his anger, he slumped in his chair and shook his head in disbelief as the Mossad chief outlined the magnitude of the problem.

It had been a terrible year. Peres had spent the summer stamping out the fires of the Shin Bet bus-hijacking slayings, trying to head off a formal investigation that threatened to bring down the government. The fallout from the Pollard affair was still straining relations with the United States, and the arms-for-hostage deal with Iran was threatening to blow apart. His latest Middle East peace initiative was going nowhere.

The worst of it was the sixty-three-year-old leader of the centrist Labor party was only weeks away from swapping jobs with Foreign Minister Shamir, the right-wing Likud bloc chief and Peres' major rival, under an unusual rotation agreement forged after national elections in 1984 ended in a stalemate. Peres knew his chances of returning to the prime minister's office were not good. The politics of moderation that made him such a favorite in the United States and in Europe were rapidly becoming anathema to the Israeli electorate, which was moving sharply to the right.

Peres was far from washed up. He had earned kudos for shoring up the staggering Israeli economy, and would serve as foreign minister for the next two years. In addition, there was always the possibility that his Labor party could win outright in the 1988 elections. Still, the Vanunu affair had the depressing odor of political death about it. Peres' steady climb to the top of the Israeli government had been built on his success at the Defense Ministry, and the ostensibly peaceful nuclear project had been the cornerstone of that achievement, so much so that Peres trumpeted his role in the Dimona project in election advertisements in 1981. Now, all of that was threatened.

Admoni told Peres time was short, and the prime minister wasted little time in looking for a way out. A decision on Vanunu would be taken by the so-called "Prime Minister's Club"—Peres,Shamir and Defense Minister Yitzhak Rabin, who had each held the top spot—with the assistance of the intelligence chiefs and senior aides. The disaster would be another closely held secret, confined to the highest levels of the Israeli government. Informing the leak-prone, twenty-five-member Cabinet was out of the question; not even the ten-member inner Cabinet, which frequently decided government policy, would be consulted on this matter.

Peres called the first session of the Vanunu working team two days after talking with Admoni. The three ministers and a knot of intelligence officials and top-level aides gathered at the prime minister's office in Jerusalem. The curtains in the meeting room were drawn shut, blocking the spectacular view of the Judean Hills. Scattered around the long conference table were bottles of mineral water, pots of coffee and plates of fruit and olives. No one, however, had much of an appetite. The working group listened incredulously as a visibly shaken Peres briefed them on the photographs and Vanunu's discussions about his work. The former technician, who had worked in the most secret unit at Dimona, now planned to peddle his story to the news media, Peres explained, shifting nervously in his seat at the head of the table.

When he had finished, Shamir exploded in a storm of recrimination. He was incensed that security at Dimona was so lax that an employee could have waltzed inside with a camera and wandered around like a tourist, snapping pictures, without attracting any attention. Someone had better pay for this, Shamir snapped.

Peres assured the foreign minister that steps would be taken to punish those responsible. But the issue at hand, he stressed, was how to deal with Vanunu. "He is out and talking," the prime minister said somberly. "We have a major problem."

Rabin's first concern was the United States. Successive American administrations had largely ignored Israel's nuclear buildup, despite Washington's longstanding public opposition to nuclear proliferation. Even without knowledge of the underground facility at Dimona, the Central Intelligence Agency had provided regular updates on Israel's march into the ranks of the global nuclear club. By 1968 the CIA had concluded that Israel had the capacity to build a rudimentary bomb, and some intelligence officials believed Israel had as many as 200 warheads twelve years later. But U.S. presidents from Johnson to Reagan chose not to act on the information in the belief that a public confrontation with Israel, strategically vital to the United States in the Middle East, could serve no useful purpose.

No one in Washington, however, knew precisely how sophisticated and advanced Israel's arsenal had become. How the United States would react to disclosures about Machon 2 was anybody's guess. U.S. law required the president to cut off aid to any country in violation of the 1968 Non-proliferation Treaty, which Israel had refused to sign. The president could seek a waiver of the restriction, which had been done in the case of Pakistan, but the political fallout would be severe, and might even erode congressional support for Israel's $3 billion annual aid package. Without every penny, Israel would have to scramble to survive.

Rabin had served in Washington as Israel's ambassador and was sensitive to the delicate nature of Israeli-American relations. He wondered whether Israel should alert its closest ally to the possibility that Vanunu might talk. But Shamir, always disdainful of what he viewed as efforts to appease the United States, loudly rejected the suggestion.

"Never, never," thundered the foreign minister. "It is only our business."

Peres soon ended the meeting, telling his colleagues he would wait to see what the security services concluded about the Vanunu affair before making a decision on how to respond.

Admoni, who had contributed little to the discussion, was unhappy as he headed back to Tel Aviv. He could not act until he received some instructions from the politicians. And they seemed a long way from a decision.

But the prime minister was already toying with a radical idea, a proposal that he knew would be tough to sell to his colleagues. The genie was out of the bottle. Vanunu had already opened up to Guerrero and his church friends and possibly others beyond Israel's reach. The problem now seemed to be how to turn this calamity to Israel's advantage. Why not leave Vanunu alone, allow him to tell his story? It would essentially be another leak, this time designed to warn the Arab world how advanced and powerful the Israeli arsenal had become.

Peres knew support was growing within the defense establishment for a change in nuclear deterrent tactics. In a highly classified 1985 report, senior military analysts had recommended that Israel send a clear and precise signal to hostile states: the state of Israel has a sophisticated nuclear arsenal and is working on ways to make it feasible to use such weapons in the Middle East. The report urged that Israel abandon the policy of deliberate ambiguity and formally reveal the nature and extent of its nuclear capabilities as a means of placing the Arab world on notice. The political leadership had not acted on the proposal, but several ministers, including Peres and Rabin, were intrigued by the possibilities.

The concept was certainly not new. As early as the mid-1970s, influential defense experts had been debating the efficacy of going public as a means of reducing the tremendous expense of protecting Israel with conventional weapons. In 1978, Moshe Dayan had advocated a new policy based on naked nuclear deterrence. Defense spending was consuming roughly half of Israel's gross national product, and the costs showed no signs of easing. The top jet fighter in Israel's air force in 1967 was the French Mirage 3, which carried a pricetag of roughly $2.2 million. Twelve years later, the air force was flying U.S.-built F-15s, which cost about $28 million each. The story was the same throughout the military. The price of everything was going up. How long, Dayan wondered, could Israel, with its chronic economic problems, keep pace with the Arabs and their oil-financed armies?

"If the arms race in the Middle East continues—and it will become more intense—we will reach a situation in which there will be a tank in every Israeli backyard, an armored personnel carrier will be parked at the entrance to every house, and there will be a helicopter on the roof," Dayan cautioned. "The country will simply go bankrupt."

"We have to maintain a small, efficient, cheap, even professional army, for ongoing security and limited incidents, and nuclear arms for a general confrontation."

The argument took on added importance in light of the new challenges facing Israel. The assumption that the Arabs would only seek nuclear weapons if Israel forced their hand by publicly acknowledging its atomic arsenal was no longer valid. In 1981, Israeli jets had destroyed an Iraqi nuclear reactor under construction, ironically with the help of the French. But defense analysts glumly concluded that the nuclear threat from Iraq, one of Israel's bitterest enemies, would not disappear; Iraqi President Saddam Hussein was obsessed with the idea of developing an Islamic bomb that would help him lead the Arab world to victory over Israel.

Syria was an ever-present and growing threat. Israeli intelligence had uncovered evidence that President Hafez Assad was pushing forward with development of a powerful chemical-warfare capability. The use of poison gas in the Iran-Iraq war proved Arab leaders would have no qualms about using chemical weapons against Jews. Jerusalem also harbored suspicions that the Soviet Union, Syria's major ally and arms supplier, might provide Damascus with nuclear weapons, particularly if a Middle East peace agreement was reached without them. The Soviets had already supplied Syria with advanced SS-21 missiles that could be armed with either chemical or nuclear warheads.

Israel's fears about Syria had been exacerbated by the raw intelligence data it was receiving from Pollard, its American spy. At a minimum, Pollard had passed along more than 800 classified publications and more than 1,000 classified messages and cables, most of them dealing with two subjects: Soviet weapons systems and Arab military capabilities, including Syria's chemical and gas warfare factories.

"Literally everything I showed them set off alarm bells, particularly those things pertaining to nuclear and chemical warfare advances in the Arab world," Pollard told *Jerusalem Post* Washington correspondent Wolf Blitzer, author of *Territory of Lies*, an account of the Pollard case.

Peres knew the world had changed. Perhaps it was time for Israel's nuclear policy to catch up with the new realities.

Chapter 21

Peres advanced his proposal at the next meeting of the Vanunu group in early September. The headache was growing; the Mossad reported that a *Sunday Times* reporter had arrived in Australia to interview Vanunu. The secrets of Dimona were spreading even further.

Peres began with a detailed account of Vanunu's political activity during his last few years in Israel. Shamir was livid. "With that background, this man was allowed to work at Dimona?" he asked.

"Let's concentrate on what we do now," Peres urged.

Shamir, the former Mossad officer, looked around the table and shrugged.

"It's obvious, isn't it?" he said.

The room went silent. Peres fumbled distractedly with a sheaf of papers in front of him. Everybody at the table knew what Shamir was suggesting, but no one seemed to want to confront the issue.

Peres finally broke the impasse. "No, I don't think we kill Jews," he said firmly.

But Shamir was not dissuaded. The diminutive man with the hunched shoulders and bushy grey eyebrows may have looked like a kindly grandfather, but he had grown up as a ruthless street fighter, battling the British in the struggle for Palestine and then the Palestinians in Europe during ten years with the Mossad. To Shamir, the issue was clear. Vanunu was a traitor, he argued angrily. And there was only one way to deal with such a man.

But Rabin, a Labor party power broker whose relationship with Peres had always been strained and occasionally stormy, now joined the prime minister in opposing the Shamir solution. "It's too late for that anyway," he added. Vanunu had already talked.

The discussion turned to other choices, and Admoni ran through the options. Asking the Australians to formally arrest and extradite Vanunu was quickly ruled out. That could do Vanunu's work for him, dragging his story into the public spotlight. Sending a team of agents to kidnap him was risky. The operation could backfire if word leaked that Israel had broken Australian law. Vanunu might be bullied into silence, but that was a long shot.

From the list of choices, Admoni recommended a kidnapping. It was true that Vanunu had already talked to Guerrero and Hounam, but his disappearance would effectively kill the story. Without Vanunu, Guerrero was hardly credible, and Hounam would have little to write about if his source disappeared at this stage.

Peres sat quietly throughout most of the discussion. He knew how unpopular his proposal would be. But after the ministers and intelligence officials had run through the most obvious options, he decided to bring it up.

"I've been thinking about what might happen if we let him talk," he said.

Shamir, who had been foreign minister when Menachem Begin ordered the bombing of the Iraqi reactor, vigorously registered his disapproval. Vanunu knew Israel's deepest secrets. His revelations would be a major foreign policy debacle. And what about the Americans? They had not been told all the details of Israel's nuclear program. Vanunu's story would shatter the flimsy charade under which the two allies had operated all these years. If Israel's enemies in the United States got wind of what was going on in the Negev, Washington might be forced to take some action against Jerusalem.

Peres stood firm. Vanunu had already talked, he stressed again. Now the idea was damage control and, if possible, gleaning something positive from this disaster. Vanunu's information would quickly lead experts to conclude that Israel's nuclear arsenal was larger and much more sophisticated than anyone had believed. This would be a sobering signal to the Arabs, particularly Syria and Iraq, who had no idea just how powerful Israel had become. It would be a warning that they must stop their escalation of the Middle East conflict or face dreadful consequences.

The realization that Israel had such an advanced nuclear capability might even bring the Arabs to the peace table, Peres believed. It had worked with Egypt. One factor in Anwar Sadat's decision to seek peace was his conclusion that Egypt could never defeat Israel militarily because Israel had the bomb—a weapon Egypt could not afford to develop. A few Israelis had even suggested that a formal admission by Israel that it had nuclear weapons might permit the return of the occupied West Bank and Gaza Strip—major stumbling blocks in peace talks—by eliminating the military need for the defensive buffer zones. In a 1982 book, *Israeli Nuclear Deterrence*, Shai Feldman, a senior research associate at Tel Aviv University's Jaffee Center for Strategic Studies, argued that Israeli acknowledgment of a nuclear capability and a willingness to use it, coupled with a decision to relinquish the occupied territories, would make an Israeli bomb a more effective deterrent and perhaps end the Arab obsession with building their own.

And the beauty of this plan, the prime minister concluded, was that Israel could formally deny the report, just as it had in the past. *The Sunday Times*, after all, had published the Hitler diaries. Disclosures about Dimona in a newspaper with a tarnished reputation would never push the Americans into a situation where they might be forced to act.

For the first time, Admoni voiced some concerns. The Mossad urgently needed to interrogate Vanunu to find out if he had spoken with agents of enemy powers. And even if he hadn't, he must be arrested. He could not simply be allowed to float around the world with secrets still untold, an inviting target for the Soviets or the Arabs.

Peres waved off his intelligence chief's worries. Of course, Vanunu would be punished. The Mossad would stay on his tail and if it appeared he was preparing to speak with a foreign government, steps would be taken to prevent it. And in the end he would be brought back to Israel and placed on trial in secret. Something like this could not be permitted to happen again. Punishing Vanunu would send a signal to other potential whistleblowers that such actions would not be tolerated by Israel.

After forty minutes of debate, Shamir remained unmoved. But Rabin was reluctantly coming to realize that Peres might have a point.

In reality the solution to the Vanunu problem was strictly Peres' call. The prime minister had sole authority over the intelligence agencies. And he had made up his mind.

"Unless someone has a better suggestion, which I haven't heard, I'm going to do it this way," he said firmly.

Shamir still harbored serious reservations. But if Vanunu was eventually to be arrested and punished, and if Israel denied his story—well, it was Peres' idea. In a few weeks, Shamir would be prime minister.

It was done. A decision had been made at the highest level of the Israeli government. Mordechai Vanunu would be allowed to tell his story to the world.

Chapter 22

By the second week in September, the *Sunday Times* had heard enough. Reporter Max Prangnell had been sent to Israel to investigate Vanunu's background, and he was beginning to confirm much of what the Israeli had claimed. Hounam was sending back a steady stream of credible information. By all accounts, the world's knowledge about the operation at Dimona was very limited. And Vanunu appeared to be providing new information, including the fact that thermonuclear weapons were being manufactured at the plant.

But there were still a few more questions and one major test. Vanunu and his photographs would have to pass muster before an expert. Hounam was told to bring the Israeli to London for a final debriefing.

From the start, Vanunu had understood the *Sunday Times* was only interested in his story if he agreed to be named. The credibility of his entire account rested on the fact that the newspaper could identify its source as someone who had actually worked at Dimona. Unless the source could be produced, the story would be ignored. Hounam had explained all this to Vanunu at the outset, and Vanunu agreed. But as Hounam prepared to fly back to London with Vanunu, a snag developed.

The Israeli had become increasingly concerned about the ramifications of his decision. He was worried about his safety, the impact of the publicity on his family back in Israel, about whether he might wind up in prison. Vanunu had voiced some of his doubts to Stephen Grey, one of the St. John's clergymen.

"I gained the distinct impression that he was caught between what he felt he must do according to his conscience and what that meant in terms of his relationship, to a large degree, with his country," the minister said. "I suspect, to a greater degree with his family. I cannot put in words exactly why that should be, but I know Motti well and it came across quite strongly. There was a quietness about him, there was a loneliness about him. And I just feel that he was a really torn person."

A few days before they were due to leave, Vanunu called Hounam and asked if they could get together, alone, at a bar near the Hilton. Vanunu came straight to the point. "Look, I've been thinking about this," he told Hounam. "I want this story to appear. It's important that the world knows what is going on. Everything I've told you is true. But I've decided that you should only publish the story and the photographs if my name is kept out of it."

Vanunu's announcement rocked Hounam. He couldn't go back emptyhanded. After three weeks of legwork, the newspaper was extremely excited about the prospects for the story. It was going to be a blockbuster. The reporter had been involved in big stories before, but this one, with its international dimension, was easily the biggest of his career. Vanunu had to be persuaded to continue cooperating. Even with the scientific, political and military implications of his revelations, Hounam realized, "at least half of the story was, 'Here is the man who has worked in this place, the inside story of Dimona.' And if he's anonymous, then it's not such an interesting story." The use of Vanunu's name was vital to the *Sunday Times*. Without a warm body, Fleet Street would hoot down the "exclusive" as another Murdoch-inspired excess.

No way was the reporter going to permit Vanunu to back out now. "Not on your life. That's just not on," he told Vanunu firmly. "The fact is, we have to use your name. We have to describe who you are. Otherwise, the story doesn't stand up."

It was a difficult few hours. As they sat in the bar, Hounam battered Vanunu with one argument after another. In desperation, he brought up the question of how Guerrero would react if Vanunu scrapped the plan and cost him his payoff. "Oh, I will deal with him. He will have to do what I say," the Israeli said confidently, suddenly unusually assertive.

Switching gears, Hounam pointed out that the Mossad would almost certainly deduce that Vanunu had been the source for the story, even if his name was left out, and they would just as certainly come after him. Anonymity in this instance was absolutely no protection, Hounam stressed.

At length, the journalist managed to convince Vanunu he had already gone too far. There could be no turning back. Vanunu grimly conceded the point, and agreed to fly to London.

The night before their departure, Hounam and Vanunu met for a last time with Guerrero in Hounam's hotel room. Hounam was beginning to breathe a little easier. He had overcome Vanunu's last-second change of heart and even Guerrero seemed to have been moved to the sidelines.

The *Sunday Times* wanted Vanunu to return to London without his "agent," and Hounam was authorized to give Guerrero a letter promising he would be paid $25,000 out of any money that Vanunu might be paid in connection with his story—but only if Guerrero would stay behind in Sydney. Guerrero, who had believed the story would be worth millions, reluctantly agreed, but he was resentful. Vanunu had sold them short.

In fact, Vanunu was beginning to understand what his story might ultimately be worth. Days before he left for England he told Stephen Grey he expected to get about $450,000 for a book about his story, and would use the money "for God's work."

As the three men lounged around Hounam's room, everything appeared to be on track. But without warning, it fell apart again. As Hounam outlined the plan one last time, Guerrero stood up and angrily withdrew his approval. "I'm sorry. I don't agree with all this. You're trying to cheat me," he told Hounam.

"And in any case," Guerrero added, "the photographs have all been stolen."

Shortly after he had arrived, Hounam had insisted that Vanunu put the negatives and the prints and slides in a safe-deposit box at the Hilton, and keep the key. But without telling the reporter, Vanunu had given the key to Guerrero. Now Guerrero was saying he had taken the photographs and placed them in his briefcase, which was stolen on the subway.

The affable, mild-mannered Englishman was furious. "This is absolutely ridiculous," he said, glaring at Guerrero.

The Colombian smirked. "Oh, Peter, you know I'm sorry," he said with exaggerated innocence. "They've been stolen. Nothing I can do." Hounam grabbed Guerrero by the lapels of his jacket, dragged him across the hotel room, opened the door and flung him into the corridor. "If you don't come back with the photographs within one hour, that's the end of it. Sod off," Hounam roared.

Terrified, Guerrero picked himself up and scurried down the hall. Hounam went back into the room where Vanunu was sitting stiffly in his chair with a look of abject dismay on his face.

"Well, look, I'm sorry," Hounam said listlessly, falling heavily on the bed. "The whole thing is off now." The two men lapsed into silence.

About an hour later, there was a knock on the door. It was Guerrero, very apologetic and very frightened. "I didn't tell you the truth," he began sheepishly. "The photographs, I took them and left them at a bank."

"Well, get them out of the bank!" Hounam demanded.

"I can't. It's the middle of the night," Guerrero pleaded.

"Well, when can you get them?"

"Not till half past nine in the morning."

Hounam scowled. This could be another ploy. On the other hand, Guerrero did seem a bit shaken.

"Right, at ten o'clock, we meet," Hounam said finally. "Downstairs in the coffee bar. You hand me the photographs and we go off to the plane."

Guerrero was waiting with the photographs the next morning, September 12. Vanunu went home to pack and Hounam arranged to meet him at Sydney airport, and Guerrero slunk out of the Hilton.

"Thank God I'll never see him again," Hounam thought to himself as he watched the Colombian walk away.

Several parishioners gathered at St. John's for prayers, then drove Vanunu to Kingsford Smith International Airport for his flight to London. They had a blurry notion that Mordechai was going to England to participate in some sort of discussion about nuclear weapons and disarmament, and would return in three weeks. Only three ministers, McKnight, Grey and David Smith, knew what Vanunu was really planning, and how risky it was.

At the airport, Hounam stood to one side and watched Vanunu say goodbye to his friends. The reporter had not met McKnight or any of the church people during his stay. He had purposely maintained a low profile to make sure Australian newspapers or even the country's intelligence service were not alerted to his presence. But he knew how deeply Vanunu cared for these people, the respect he had for McKnight. The church on Darlinghurst Road had been his entire world for three months.

Now Vanunu was on his own again. Sitting in the airport waiting for the flight to be called, he scribbled off a note to Meir. He was involved in something he couldn't explain, he told his brother, and wasn't sure where it would end.

"I decided after a long debate with myself that there is no middle way," Vanunu wrote. "There is something I have to do, and I am going to do it."

Meir was alarmed when he received the letter. But by that time, it was to late for anyone to help Mordechai Vanunu.

PART III

Abduction: The Prime Minister Gets a Present

Chapter 23

The numbing flight through eleven time zones drained Hounam and Vanunu, but there was time for only a few hours' sleep at the Tower Thistle after they arrived in London early on the morning of Friday, September 12. Morgan, eager to push forward, had arranged a luncheon meeting at a wine bar in the hotel.

The Insight editor was delighted by the explosive story that had fallen in his lap. In Morgan's mind, it was potentially the biggest story in twenty years in the British press. Moreover, he believed it was easily the most significant piece of investigative journalism by the *Sunday Times* since a campaign in the 1970s to win compensation for babies born with deformities resulting from their mothers' use of the sedative Thalidomide. The international and historical dimensions of the Dimona story, Morgan believed, would be huge. "The scoop of a lifetime," he said later. The editor couldn't wait to meet the man who promised to deliver it.

Vanunu, barely awake after his trip halfway around the world, was not an especially effective salesman during lunch. He sat next to Hounam and said little, retreating into a protective shell of suspicion in the face of strangers, as Morgan and Insight reporters Max Prangnell and Roger Wilsher sketched the newspaper's plans. In Sydney, Vanunu had given Hounam his passport, his separation agreement from Dimona, and several other documents to help confirm his identity. But now he would undergo an intensive interrogation led by a nuclear-weapons expert before a final determination was made about his credibility. Only after the newspaper had nailed down every last detail would it be prepared to publish.

Morgan also stressed the *Sunday Times* would cover Vanunu's expenses in London, but would under no circumstances pay him for the story. Freelance journalists might be compensated, but the newspaper had a rule against paying sources for information. "What we can do as journalists is take the individual decision to write a book with you," Morgan added. "Ghostwrite it. Do it on your behalf. Sell it on your behalf. We'll take no fee. You take the money from the book. That's different. That's reasonable."

Vanunu drowsily nodded his agreement. He was exhausted, and wanted to go back to bed. But when the reporters asked him to explain why he was revealing his country's secrets, the Israeli sprang to life with a spirited defense of his decision.

"In Britain and in France and America, they're democracies. You know you have the atom bomb. You know you have the hydrogen bomb. You know where they're built. You know where they're tested. You know how they're carried, by submarine or airplane or whatever," he told the journalists.

"In Israel, we're a democracy, modeled on the British form of democracy. But we have none of this. We don't know any of this. We're not allowed to know any of this."

In a democracy, Vanunu continued, the people should decide the nuclear issue. He wanted to give Israelis the opportunity denied to them by their government.

The journalists were impressed by the arguments. The man must be telling the truth, Morgan thought. If he's a fake or an Israeli agent sent to plant a false story, he's damn good.

Morgan, however, wanted to make sure Vanunu understood the risk he was taking. He sensed Vanunu was frightened and, despite the passion of his explanation, still uncertain about his decision. And Morgan also had an entirely selfish reason for spelling out the dangers: if something happened to Vanunu, if he were arrested or even killed, the editor didn't want to feel responsible.

"You're dealing with a newspaper, and not some kind of Hollywood version, either," Morgan cautioned. "Journalists aren't policemen. We won't be able to give you a new identity, or protect you for the rest of your life. One thing you should understand is that no story in the world is worth your freedom or your life. Whatever happens, Israel is not going to be very happy. You've got to very,

very seriously think about your life and what's going to happen to you. We can look after you for a year, maybe. But what happens to you in five years? Ten years?"

"It's your decision. It's not my decision," Morgan said. "You have to decide now. Do you want to carry on with what we're doing?"

Thousands of miles from anyone who could even remotely be considered a friend, surrounded by strangers who believed he and his story were immensely important, Vanunu said yes.

About 4 P.M., Wilsher drove Vanunu to the Heath Lodge Hotel in Welwyn, about thirty miles north of London, where a room had been booked for the visitor under the name "George Forsty." From the newspaper's point of view, the Heath Lodge was a perfect location for the debriefing. Sparsely occupied, the hotel was close enough to the main roads into the city so that Vanunu was accessible to the staff, and far enough out of the way that anyone looking for Vanunu, particularly the *Sunday Times'* rivals, would not find him.

But Vanunu, eager to sample London, was displeased with his isolated lodgings. When he expressed his disappointment, Morgan instructed the Insight reporters Wilsher and Prangnell to entertain the newspaper's star source while he relaxed over the weekend.

On Saturday, Prangnell drove Vanunu into London for some sightseeing. They spent a few hours wandering through the trendy shops and restaurants of Covent Garden, stopping to watch the jugglers and mime artists working the streets, then strolled west to Picadilly. Both men were in high spirits. Vanunu was satisfied that the *Sunday Times* was beginning to believe him, and Prangnell was happy to be working on what promised to be a major story.

Their euphoria quickly evaporated. As they walked along Regent Street, Vanunu spotted a familiar face on the crowded sidewalk. It was an old acquaintance from Ben-Gurion University, Yoram Bazak, and he was gazing intently in Vanunu's direction.

"Quick, turn around," Vanunu whispered to Prangnell. "I know that man. He is from Beersheba."

But it was too late. In an instant, Bazak, accompanied by a

woman, was on him. "Motti, what a surprise!" he bellowed. "What are you doing in London?"

"Just visiting," Vanunu mumbled. Scrambling to explain his presence, he said he was winding up a European holiday with three days in London before returning to Tel Aviv. Bazak said he too was touring Europe, with his fiancee.

"We must have dinner. How about tomorrow night?" Bazak exclaimed.

Make it Wednesday, Vanunu said reluctantly, and he agreed to meet Bazak at his room at the Royal Scot Hotel.

Prangnell had slipped away during the chat, feigning interest in the goods displayed in a nearby shop window as the two Israelis exchanged small talk. The reporter didn't want Bazak to get a good look at him, and hoped to avoid any awkward introductions where the name of the newspaper might slip out.

Vanunu and Prangnell were shaken by the encounter. It was too much to believe it a coincidence. Out of nowhere, on the second day of Vanunu's secret journey to London, in the first hours he was actually on the streets, in public, he just happened to run into an old friend from college? Not very likely.

Surprisingly, neither man thought to notify Morgan. Even if the meeting with Bazak was merely a coincidence, Vanunu's cover was blown. Somebody—an Israeli, no less—was now aware that Vanunu was in London. It was a serious development that called for defensive measures, but none were taken. Prangnell and Vanunu went ahead with their plans Saturday night, attending a concert and having a late dinner before driving back to Heath Lodge, where they spent the night in adjoining rooms.

Morgan and Hounam did not find out about the meeting with Bazak until Monday morning, two days later, when Vanunu was brought to the *Sunday Times* newsroom for a first round of interviews. After relating the conversation, Vanunu said he had decided to keep the date with his old acquaintance. Hounam and Morgan were incredulous. Hounam immediately recognized the risks and warned Vanunu against going to dinner. Vanunu should be moved to a new location, and should call Bazak and tell him he was leaving London early.

But Vanunu rejected the advice. Although he offered no explanation, Vanunu apparently relished the idea of the confrontation. The meeting, in a way, would mark a milestone: for the first time since leaving Israel, Vanunu would challenge an Israeli with the complete break he had made with his country.

Anxious to keep Vanunu happy, the staff dropped its objections and even Hounam grudgingly gave in after Vanunu promised to say nothing about his plans. Hounam's concerns were also eased when Wendy Robbins accepted Vanunu's invitation to accompany him to the meeting. If Bazak had been sent by Israeli intelligence to forcibly retrieve Vanunu, Robbins would have been very little help. But it seemed unlikely that the Mossad would attempt an abduction in front of a British witness.

During his visit to the newsroom, Vanunu had noticed a necklace with a Hebrew inscription around Robbins' neck and began flirting with her. Delighted, the editors moved with alacrity to take advantage of the budding friendship. "I want you to get friendly with this fellow," Morgan told the young researcher. "You're both Jewish. You hit it off. Talk to him. Find out all you can about him."

Robbins was annoyed by Morgan's presumption that she and the dour stranger were somehow religious soulmates, but soon found she genuinely liked Vanunu. He seemed immature, a little silly, reaching over playfully to fiddle with the computer keyboard while she typed notes as he outlined his life story. But Robbins was happy to accept his dinner invitation. She had grown up in a traditional Jewish home where the existence of Israel was revered. Robbins had visited Israel as a teenager and planned to return. If nothing else, spending time with Vanunu would give her an opportunity to learn more about the country.

Chapter 24

Vanunu's debriefing began in earnest on Tuesday morning, September 16, 1986, four days after he arrived in London. The *Sunday Times* had asked Dr. Frank Barnaby, a nuclear physicist who had worked on Britain's nuclear weapons program and now headed the Stockholm International Peace Research Institute, to examine Vanunu's photographs and slides, and the scientist and a group of *Sunday Times* reporters and editors were waiting when Vanunu walked into a conference room at the Heath Lodge after breakfast.

As a slide projector was set up in the room and the curtains were closed, Morgan and associate editor Peter Wilsher pulled Barnaby aside.

"Look, do what you can to trip him up," Morgan told the scientist. "We really need to know right away if he's telling the truth."

The slide show and Vanunu's narration engrossed Barnaby. With his background, the scientist used the photographs of control-room instrument panels as maps to recreate the processes the Israelis employed in the plant. He was quickly able to assemble the various images into a fairly complete picture of how nuclear warheads were being produced at the Dimona plant. The photographs of the unit where lithium-6 was produced were especially exciting. One picture showed a white shell with a hollowed-out core. It would be meaningless to most people. But Barnaby realized it could easily be the casing for a thermonuclear bomb.

The photographs represented the first proof Barnaby had seen of Israel's expanded nuclear capabilities. Encasing an atomic bomb inside a lithium shell, as Israel seemed to be doing, was an expensive, relatively crude way of constructing thermonuclear weapons, a process long since abandoned by sophisticated nuclear powers like the United States and Britain. But there appeared to be an excellent reason for employing such cumbersome practices. The lithium method had been exhaustively tested by the superpowers, and had a good record of success. Israel therefore would not have to risk exposure of the Dimona secrets by conducting its own weapons tests, Barnaby explained to his audience.

Morgan struggled to keep his glee in check as he sat in the darkened room listening to Vanunu and seeing the photographs for the first time. The editor wasn't convinced yet, but his instincts told him the man was genuine. Vanunu didn't answer all of Barnaby's questions. Nor did he pretend to know everything. There were too many ragged edges. A hoaxer wouldn't have left so much to chance.

The slide show had been going on for about two hours when Barnaby suddenly called a halt to the proceedings, walked over to Morgan and Wilsher and whispered, "Let's go and talk."

In the corridor, Morgan asked Barnaby what he thought.

"I'm convinced he's an imposter," the physicist said forcefully.

Barnaby carefully explained that several key steps in the plutonium production process simply couldn't occur in the manner Vanunu described. "It just wouldn't happen. There are flaws. He hasn't got it right. It isn't scientific," Barnaby contended.

Pained expressions spread across the faces of the two journalists. Morgan was crushed, but he was also determined not to give up on the story without a fight. He urged Barnaby to take some time and analyze Vanunu's explanation to see if there was any way he could be right.

A few hours later, Barnaby returned, wearing a broad smile. "We've forgotten something," he said. "We've forgotten these are the Israelis."

The physicist had called several colleagues to discuss the apparent discrepancies in Vanunu's explanation. What had troubled Barnaby was Vanunu's assertion that the Israelis were recycling uranium during the production process, a practice never employed in British or American bomb production. It made no sense. But after further deliberation, Barnaby realized the Israelis had no choice but to improvise. Without a plentiful, easily available supply, they had to squeeze their uranium dry. That explained the odd process Vanunu had described, and some rough calculations proved the jerryrigged system could work.

"It is now clear to me that he is telling the truth," Barnaby told the relieved editors. "Vanunu is who he says he is."

Barnaby's change of heart elated the *Sunday Times* staffers. This single fact, this tiny deviation from the standard procedure, was the confirmation they needed. Vanunu could have known about such an arcane method only if he had actually worked at Dimona. And there was little chance he was an Israeli plant. An agent sent to feed the newspaper false information would never describe a process that wasn't generally accepted to the world scientific community. There would be too great a risk of having scientists brand him a liar.

No, Morgan told Peter Wilsher, this guy's for real.

Buoyed by the breakthrough, the reporters and editors attacked the rest of Vanunu's story with confidence it would not fall apart. They ran through his account of how he managed to snap the photographs, pressing him on the most minor details, searching for the slightest inconsistency. "My God, anybody would think you're the police," Vanunu complained as the journalists hunted for flaws.

But he was enjoying the grilling. Eager to demonstrate his scientific prowess, to prove conclusively he was not simply a "dumb Sephardi," Vanunu had badgered Hounam in Sydney to have him questioned by experts. Now, just days out of Australia, he had the rapt attention of a nuclear scientist. The experience was intellectually satisfying. There were elements of the production process that Vanunu hadn't understood and Barnaby was taking the time to explain them.

Later, as the fact-checking process stretched into weeks, Vanunu would grow restless, bored, even angry about the constant questioning. But that first day, tired and lonely and a little bit scared, he loved it. At the end of the first session, Vanunu turned to Hounam and asked, "What did you think?"

"I thought you did very well," the reporter said as Vanunu beamed. "People were impressed."

Chapter 25

The Dimona story held the promise of ending an agonizing drought that had shattered the Insight team's image as the premier investigative unit in British journalism. The crisis of confidence and morale that enmeshed much of the *Sunday Times* was perhaps most acute at Insight, which had seen its reputation savaged and mocked even inside the newspaper.

When Harold Evans assumed the editorship of the *Sunday Times* in 1967, the Insight team consisted of three reporters and a researcher assigned to churn out short features for a newspaper rich in foreign reportage, opinion and criticism. The unit had just begun to tinker with investigative reporting, and Evans accelerated the process. In its new incarnation, Insight became a close-knit band of talented eccentrics who threw their spotlight on a bogus auto insurance firm, then moved on to bigger game: an expose of the CIA's role in Guyana elections, and lengthy, in-depth coverage of spy scandals, violence in Northern Ireland and Lebanon, the 1973 Yom Kippur War and Portugal's return to democracy in 1975. Several of the projects later became books.

But Insight's status had taken a rough tumble in recent years. Aside from a thorough report on a police siege of the Iranian Embassy in London in 1980, the unit managed to scrape together little of consequence. Most *Sunday Times* reporters wanted nothing to do with it, and the team's dwindling ranks were filled with less experienced staffers.

"Part of the problem was you never got into the paper," a former Insight reporter recalled. "You worked on a team and the team got the credit. Egos couldn't handle it. And sometimes the team wouldn't have anything in print for weeks on end. It was terribly frustrating, just not very rewarding at all."

Andrew Neil, however, was unwilling to give up on Insight. The unit's distinctive black-and-white logo was important to the *Sunday Times*, he told his editors. It sold newspapers, and underscored a commitment to investigative journalism.

Just what Insight was supposed to be doing, however, was a matter of some uncertainty. The competition between reporters for space in a newspaper that only published once a week was bitter, and the pressure to come up with splashy "exclusives" was blinding. For decades, the *Sunday Times* and the rest of Britain's so-called "quality" newspapers had contemptuously dismissed their tabloid competitors, who feasted on a journalistic diet that often consisted of half-baked investigations, dubious revelations about the royal family, and bawdy, salacious accounts of the private lives of public people. But the race for a share of the market had tightened, and even the *Sunday Times* had jumped off its pedestal. For fifteen years, it had been the biggest, richest, hottest-selling Sunday newspaper in Britain, and it was desperate to stay that way. So when a blockbuster wasn't available for the front page, editors were frequently tempted to sensationalize an average story, even if that meant trivializing the important and headlining the trivial.

"The *Sunday Times* could treat an art fraud as if it were the Third World War," one of its reporters recalled.

The dismissals and resignations at the start of the 1986 labor dispute had cost the paper some cooler heads, senior editors and reporters who might have exerted a moderating influence on the newspaper's operations, and under editor Neil's prodding the Insight team embarked on an urgent drive for the big story, hoping to heal the wounds of Wapping. In his first weeks on the job, Peter Hounam had reeled in an article on financial mismanagement at the National Theater and the Royal Shakespeare Company. Neil was pleased, and pressed for more.

But reporters on the Foreign or Home staffs were zealously guarding their turf, taking pains to prevent Insight from snagging any story with even a remote chance of making it into print on

Sunday. Relegated to the sidelines, Insight was often reduced to shuffling through domestic stories of minor interest, to the amusement of the rest of the newsroom. "It wasn't a collegial atmosphere. There was too much pressure," one reporter recalled.

When the Vanunu story walked in the front door, and the foreign desk passed it off, the Insight team was ecstatic. It was true they were on their own, without the newspaper's science writers or foreign affairs experts to guide them through the intricacies of nuclear physics and the subtleties of Middle East politics. But that was fine with the Insight team. "It was handed to us by the foreign desk. We were asked to look into it. And there was no question of us handing it back," Hounam said.

The newspaper's more seasoned journalists didn't want to help. Few of them relished the thought of working with "Robin Morgan and his kids," as one staff member put it, particularly when the payoff was a shared byline. And after the Hitler diaries, many of the reporters were gunshy about involving themselves in a story that reeked of disaster. "Some people wouldn't have wanted to handle it because they just might have ended up with mud in their eye," Hounam acknowledged.

But in a sense, the lack of help from more experienced reporters didn't really matter. For the *Sunday Times* to make the most of the Vanunu story in the overheated British newspaper market, packaging and presentation would be the most important elements. The key to making sure readers picked up the paper and never stopped reading was personalizing the story. And the Insight team had Mordechai Vanunu. Peter Hounam had seen to that.

Vanunu's meeting with Bazak was a disaster from the start. When Vanunu and Robbins arrived at Bazak's room at the Royal Scot on Wednesday evening, he had just come out of the shower and his fiancee was speaking on the telephone in Hebrew to someone in Israel. She quickly hung up when Vanunu arrived.

"Oh, you're still dressing. We'll wait for you downstairs," Vanunu said.

"No," Bazak said quickly.

"Why?" Vanunu asked.

"You're going to run away."

Robbins was puzzled. Why would he run away? But Vanunu assured Bazak they weren't leaving, and he and Robbins went downstairs. Bazak, his hair still damp, and the woman joined them a few minutes later.

Bazak and his fiancee suggested seeing a film or a play, but Vanunu had developed an aversion—an "absolute phobia," Robbins called it—to anything even remotely frivolous. He insisted on seeing only something serious or tragic, preferably with a political or social message. After combing through the theater and film listings without agreement, the four decided to scrap the plan and instead have dinner.

They walked to an Italian restaurant in Leicester Square, where the already tense situation quickly deteriorated. Vanunu and Bazak began quarreling about politics, attracting stares as they shouted at each other in Hebrew. Robbins finally insisted they speak in English since her command of Hebrew was weak, but the change in languages had no effect on the tone of the debate. Vanunu was criticizing everything about Israel. He attacked Judaism and hinted that he had renounced his faith. At one point, he even ripped into the quality of Israeli meat, comparing it to the steak on his plate.

"It's disgusting," he said of the meat at home.

"It's the best you ever had," Bazak retorted.

As the two women tried in vain to end the argument, Vanunu lambasted Israel's military policies, further angering Bazak, who struck Robbins as extremely conservative and nationalistic.

Before dinner, Vanunu had told Robbins that he wasn't going to mention to Bazak that she worked for a newspaper. Instead, he was going to introduce her as a classmate from a school where he was taking an English-language course. But in the heat of battle, Vanunu blurted out his secret.

"What if I were to tell you that Wendy works for a newspaper and I'm about to tell them everything I know about you-know-what?" he asked.

Bazak evinced no sign of surprise at the astounding disclosure.

Staring impassively at Vanunu, he quickly and quietly replied, "I would take you back to Israel and I would put you in court."

Vanunu rose and headed for the bathroom. As he walked away, Bazak turned to Robbins and remarked, "The stupid ideas he had at university seem to have got worse."

The two couples parted after dinner, and Vanunu and Robbins ducked into a nearby pub. It was nearly closing time, so they each ordered three glasses of wine and sat down at a table. Vanunu, in a reflective, almost depressed mood after the stormy evening, talked at length about his decision. The encounter with Bazak had rekindled his concerns about his safety, draining him of the certainty with which he defended his position to Morgan at lunch only a few days before. Things were going wrong, Vanunu told Robbins as she tried to reassure him.

"All I want is to live on an island with a wife and some children I can kiss," he said glumly, his face only inches above the tabletop. "But before that happens, I'll end up in jail."

At the end of the evening, Vanunu made a pre-arranged rendezvous with Prangnell at a Covent Garden restaurant, and the young reporter drove him back to Heath Lodge. Remarkably, even after disclosing his intentions to a suspicious Israeli and despite Hounam's worries that the Mossad might have picked up his trail, Vanunu spent the night at the hotel by himself.

Chapter 26

Dismayed by Vanunu's threat, Bazak wasted little time in contacting his government. The next morning, he telephoned the Israeli Embassy in London and spoke with a security officer there, who listened to Bazak's report and thanked him without comment.

The message was relayed to the Mossad station at the embassy, but it came as no surprise. Israeli intelligence had been on Vanunu's tail since his jetliner left the airport in Sydney. The agents in Sydney, jolted by Hounam's arrival on August 30, were incredulous when Kliman relayed the orders from Tel Aviv to allow Vanunu to leave Australia. "The politicians," Kliman said darkly by way of explanation, "have made up their minds." There would be no move against Vanunu. Keep an eye on him, but let him go.

After learning through surveillance of Hounam's plans to return to Britain, two Mossad agents booked tickets on the same flight, sitting a few rows behind the reporter and Vanunu on the journey to London, and an agency team was posted outside the Wapping complex to monitor Vanunu's movements posing as a television news crew covering the ongoing labor dispute. To buttress the Mossad station working out of the Israeli Embassy near Kensington Gardens, the agency's special operations division dispatched a team of agents to maintain surveillance of Vanunu during his stay in Britain. The Vanunu squad reported directly to Tel Aviv; Israel's ambassador in London and his staff were not officially informed of their presence, a standard method of insulating them in case the operation went sour.

Admoni was increasingly leery of Israel's plan to take advantage of the security debacle. To his considerable consternation, the circle of people who knew about Vanunu's intentions was widening. Guerrero had boasted about his involvement in the Dimona story to a former agent of the Australian Secret Intelligence Organization, who immediately alerted the agency. Within hours, Telex messages were dispatched as a professional courtesy to both the Mossad and the British intelligence agency MI6, reporting that a British newspaper reporter was returning to London with an Israeli who claimed to possess knowledge about an Israeli nuclear weapons program. When Hounam and Vanunu landed at Heathrow airport, their trail was picked up by Special Branch, the British internal security and anti-terrorism agency.

Two more Israeli agents were also on hand to follow the two men into the city. But what should have been a routine assignment quickly took on a Keystone Cops air. During the drive into London, the Mossad operatives detected the presence of another tail. The agency immediately assumed the worst—Russians, maybe, or Arabs—and the Mossad station at the embassy scurried to identify the interlopers. After determining the strangers were British agents, Tel Aviv was informed that the operation in London had already been compromised to a certain degree.

The news could not have been much worse. Relations between the two secret services were never warm. The British frequently went out of their way to hinder Mossad operations in England, and the Israelis detected a distinct pro-Arab bias among London's agents. Now they knew about Vanunu.

The story was leaking in Israel as well. It is never easy to ask questions about sensitive security subjects in Israel without attracting suspicion, but the *Sunday Times'* fact-checking foray had been especially heavy-handed. One interview with a young woman whose name had been supplied to the newspaper by Vanunu was disastrous. After rebuffing reporter Max Prangnell's efforts, the woman notified her army reserve unit commander that a British journalist had attempted to interview her about a man she knew who worked at the Dimona plant, and the commander passed the information to the Shin Bet. Both the woman and the commander had been admonished to keep quiet, but there were no guarantees.

Now Bazak knew about the Vanunu case. Things, Admoni decided, were getting out of hand.

The Shin Bet did make a half-hearted effort to frighten Vanunu into silence. Five days before Vanunu left Australia, two agents paid a visit to Albert Vanunu at his carpentry shop in Beersheba, and asked whether he knew where his brother was currently living. Albert said he didn't know. His parents had received a few postcards, but no one was sure where he was right now.

"Well, he's in Australia," one of the agents said. "We know where he is, and what he's up to."

Albert had no idea what they were talking about, but the agents were only too willing to tell him. Mordechai had been talking to a British newspaper about his work at Dimona. "You should contact your brother and tell him this is not good. Not good," one agent said. "This can come to no good end."

Albert protested again that he didn't know where his brother was.

"Well, if he contacts you, you should tell him. He is in trouble," the agent warned.

Before leaving, Albert was forced to sign a secrecy agreement, and was cautioned that he faced fifteen years in jail if he discussed the conversation. A second Vanunu was now living under the sword of Israeli security.

Vanunu's presence in London posed additional problems. Peres had instructed the Mossad to seize Vanunu once his message had been delivered. Israel, like most nations, has never had many qualms about staging intelligence operations in friendly countries without the knowledge of its "hosts" when national interests dictate such actions. But given its paramount security concerns, Israel is perhaps less concerned than most with the potential political fallout. In the wake of the 1967 Arab-Israeli war, for example, the Mossad launched a bloody secret war against Palestinian terrorist groups that saw suspected terrorists shot to death and blown up in the streets of European capitals with little regard for world opinion. "We have no choice but to strike at the terrorist organizations wherever our long arm can reach," Prime Minister Golda Meir once explained.

But unlike the many countries where Israel felt free to operate with impunity, abducting Vanunu in Britain was fraught with pitfalls. If the operation went awry, if word leaked that Vanunu had been kidnapped on British soil in violation of British law, the fallout could be devastating.

The last thing Peres wanted in September 1986 was trouble with British Prime Minister Margaret Thatcher. Improved relations with London had been a major Peres goal, and he had made some progress. In Israel's estimation, Thatcher had pushed her government out of its long-standing and irksome pro-Arab posture toward a more even-handed approach to the Middle East. The British leader had made a rare visit to Israel. Even the relationship between Israeli and British intelligence, chilly since 1977 when the British began working closely with Arab security services, had thawed slightly.

Only a few months earlier, Britain had arrested a Palestinian terrorist for secretly placing a bomb in the luggage of his unwitting Irish girlfriend when she boarded an El Al jet bound for Tel Aviv. The act of terrorism was believed to have been sponsored by Syria in retaliation for a botched Israeli attempt to seize a jet thought to be carrying a group of radical Palestinian leaders home from a summit meeting in Damascus. An angry Thatcher had temporarily severed diplomatic relations with Syria and the terrorist was sentenced to forty-five years in prison, despite Arab threats of reprisals.

The Vanunu operation held the potential of undoing Peres' efforts. At best, exposure of Israeli violations of British law would deeply embarrass Thatcher. At worst, she might demand the extradition of the agents involved or the release of Vanunu, or even take action against Israel as she had against Damascus. In any event, Peres' painstaking diplomatic initiative would be doomed.

The abduction of Vanunu could go wrong, and now was not the time, Peres stressed to Admoni. Before he flew to Washington on September 14, 1986, for talks on the stalled Middle East peace process, the prime minister hammered home one point: the Vanunu kidnapping must not take place on British soil.

Chapter 27

Heartened by Barnaby's assessment, the Insight team burrowed into Vanunu's story to ferret out any inaccuracies in his account. As many as eight people were assigned to the task under Morgan's direction. Hounam went to work nailing down the scientific aspects of Vanunu's revelations. Prangnell and Robbins delved into Vanunu's personal life, trying to determine what had prompted the Israeli to betray his country and abandon his religion. Morgan, who had assigned himself the task of writing the final story, believed the answers to those questions were almost as important as what Vanunu had to tell the world about nuclear weapons. Vanunu was regularly brought into the *Sunday Times* newsroom to work with an artist on a detailed diagram of the plant, and he was questioned almost daily for about two weeks.

Bedeviled by the specter of the Hitler diaries, the staff moved slowly, anxious to prevent the kind of momentum that allowed the fraudulent German documents to snowball their way into print. The newspaper's painstaking approach was time-consuming, and Vanunu was exasperated with the delay. "Why is it taking so long to publish my story?" he heatedly asked.

Morgan and the others tried to calm his fears. "We said, 'Well, we're sorry, you know, do you want this story to appear in print this week and have everybody just knock it down and rubbish it when you know it's the truth?' " Morgan recalled. " 'Or do you want us to prove it beyond a doubt so that everybody has to accept it? If you want the latter, you have to wait. You have to accept the fact that we have to check it out all the way down the line.' "

In addition, editor Andrew Neil remained troubled by the Vanunu project. It rubbed him the wrong way, made him feel a bit dirty. A good story, perhaps, but still messy. "What if this were a British technician going to a German or an Italian newspaper with the secrets of Britain's atom bombs?" he asked Morgan one day. "How would we feel about the man?"

Neil's discomfort was manifested in his requests for corroboration of virtually every detail in Vanunu's account. If experts and government officials told his reporters the French had built Dimona, a fact not in much dispute by anyone, Neil wanted them to find someone in France who actually worked on the job. If five scientists approved the newspaper's description of how nuclear bombs are built, Neil asked for a sixth. No one could quarrel with the emphasis on sound journalistic standards, but it almost seemed the editor was stalling for time while he debated the propriety of publishing the story.

Not everyone agreed with the editors' approach. Hounam complained the story should have been run in the first week. He conceded there was still a great deal to check. Vanunu didn't understand all that he had seen or photographed, and there were inconsistencies in some of the stories he told. The *Sunday Times* had to eliminate them. But getting at least some of the story out, he felt, was a good way to protect Vanunu from Israeli retribution. With the world's attention focused on the Dimona revelations and the man who made them, Israel was less likely to move against Vanunu.

In reality, the *Sunday Times* was in no position to adequately assess the risk to Vanunu. Fearful of a hoax, the staff operated from the start under the assumption that the Israeli could be a fraud. If he was lying, the only danger he faced was exposure. If he was an Israeli agent, all he faced was failure. In that context, leaving Vanunu in the hands of Prangnell, Robbins and Roger Wilsher, three relatively inexperienced journalists who certainly had never before had to worry about protecting a source on this scale, was clearly an acceptable gamble. And if Vanunu was genuine—well, he had approached the *Sunday Times* with his story. He should have realized the dangers.

Despite the hard work, the Vanunu project was fun. The extraordinary demands did not dampen the enthusiasm of the Insight staff.

Reporters and editors were living a journalistic fantasy, pursuing a story of international proportions, traveling to the United States, France, Israel, spending some of Murdoch's millions. Morgan remembers the period with a broad smile.

"There was a lot I did which the team never knew about, just simply in terms of security. I had friends—nothing to do with the trade whatsoever—who had certain envelopes, which in the event of certain things happening, me disappearing or whatever, things would have been done with those envelopes. I mean, just to make sure that the story wouldn't die if Vanunu was knocked off or kidnapped."

"I mean, one does the most ridiculous things in a situation like this. Hiding stuff behind a bath panel in a hotel room that's been booked in somebody else's name, whatever. Crazy, crazy, crazy things. Just to insure that you watch your back. One borrows what one can from the movies, books."

"Fun is the right word, actually. I mean, I think a journalist would have to be a fool to say this story wasn't fun."

Vanunu was quickly tiring of life in the country. There was nothing to do at Heath Lodge, he whined to Morgan. It was like being back in Beersheba. Vanunu had tasted the loose, free nightlife in Soho and the West End, and he wanted more. He enjoyed the noise, the hustle, the bright lights, the restaurants, bars and movie theaters. He wanted to move into the city.

Vanunu's demand posed new headaches for the *Sunday Times*. He wasn't a prisoner and hadn't signed any agreement to cooperate. If he wanted, Vanunu could pick up and go at any time, leaving the newspaper without its star source on the eve of publication.

He was entirely dependent on the newspaper for his hotel and meals, as well as a daily allowance of about $60, and Morgan could have told Vanunu that if he didn't do as he was instructed, the money spigot would be turned off. In a strange country with little or no cash of his own, Vanunu would have reluctantly been forced to agree. But he also would have been unhappy, and the *Sunday Times* needed a cooperative Vanunu to handle the expected crush of post-publication publicity, when Vanunu would be trotted out for news conferences and interviews aimed at giving the exclusive even greater exposure. It was important to keep him happy.

On Friday, September, 19, 1986, Vanunu was moved into London, taking a room at the Tower Thistle under the name "John Smith." The change of scenery did not immediately lead to the freedom Vanunu had sought, however. Wilsher and Prangnell were still under orders to stay with their charge at all times, and they kept him on a tight leash. Vanunu didn't trust either man, and he regularly lashed out in anger against their restrictions. Most galling was their refusal to allow him to go out to meet women, which the newspaper considered an unacceptable risk that could tip off other newspapers as well as the Mossad to Vanunu's presence if he disclosed his activities in London. "You don't give me enough freedom," Vanunu would complain to the two reporters.

To solve the problem, Hounam once raised the question of whether the newspaper should hire a prostitute for Vanunu, but Morgan had rejected the idea, snorting he was not a pimp.

Weary of the battle and wondering why Morgan and Hounam didn't assume some of the babysitting burden, Wilsher and Prangnell began leaving Vanunu's entertainment in Wendy Robbins' hands. The researcher didn't object; she was dismayed at the lack of concern for Vanunu exhibited by most of the Insight team. Only Peter Hounam seemed to care about Vanunu as more than just a news source to be milked and discarded.

Vanunu obviously preferred spending time with a woman, and the staff viewed Robbin as a safe answer to Vanunu's constant nagging about the need for some female companionship. The arrangement settled into a routine. About six o'clock, the staff would leave for the night literally abandoning Vanunu in the emptying newsroom, and Robbins would take him out for the evening, making the cultural and culinary rounds of London.

The professional relationship between Vanunu and Robbins soon developed into a friendship. Vanunu occasionally tried to inject some romance, but Robbins politely rebuffed him. Constantly thinking about sex, he had become "subtly desperate" about the subject, in Robbins' view. On several occasions, Vanunu told her he hadn't slept with a woman in nine months. An affectionate, outgoing woman, Robbins was not offended when Vanunu put his arm around her or kissed her on the check. But she made it clear she was not interested in anything more.

Returning to the hotel one night after the opera, Vanunu asked Robbins up to his room. Searching for a way to spare his feelings, she lamely told Vanunu she couldn't go upstairs because she was afraid of heights. But Vanunu persisted, promising to behave, and Robbins reluctantly agreed. Once in the room, Vanunu made a spiritless attempt to hug her, but when she gently pushed him away, he accepted the rejection gracefully and immediately escorted her downstairs. He didn't want anyone, Vanunu said somberly, who didn't want him.

As Robbins and Vanunu grew closer, she began to challenge him about his decision to spill the Dimona secrets. The researcher realized that engaging Vanunu in a debate on the issue was rather unprofessional behavior for a journalist working, however peripherally, on a story. But she was also a Jew and a strong supporter of Israel. The conflict created a degree of ambivalence in her mind about Vanunu's efforts, and Robbins took Vanunu to task for acting in a "cowardly" way. If he felt so strongly about the nuclear issue, she insisted, he should be back in Israel organizing demonstrations and trying to initiate a public debate on the issue. What he was doing was simply going to hurt Israel—a horrifying thought to a woman who from childhood had listened to her parents stress the importance of a Jewish state. Israel was necessary because of the Holocaust, Robbins reasoned, because Jews had been persecuted for thousands of years, because they needed a safe haven in an all-too-often cruel world.

Vanunu derisively swept aside her arguments. Demonstrations wouldn't work, he sniffed. Israelis wouldn't listen. This was the only way to bring the nuclear issue—the issue of Israel's immoral use of its power—to the public consciousness. This way, Israelis would have to listen. And he wasn't particularly concerned about the impact of the disclosures on the state of Israel. Vanunu told

Robbins she had been brainwashed, like so many Jews living outside Israel, about the extent of the need for a Jewish state. Like many Sephardim—and, to a degree, like many young Israelis born after World War II—the Holocaust was an abstraction to Vanunu. Few Sephardim had suffered personally from the Nazi atrocities. They experienced none of the pain and loss so acutely felt by European Jews.

"He had no comprehension of the Holocaust," Robbins recalled. "He didn't believe even in the right of Israel to exist where it did. [He believed] the Jews should have established a post-war homeland in Uganda or somewhere else in Africa where their presence would not have dislocated the Palestinians."

"He hated Judaism, Israel with a vengeance."

When Robbins would gently taunt him about the money he might reap from the sale of his story, implying his motives were purely financial, Vanunu would irately maintain the purity of his beliefs. He had money, he contended, almost $40,000 in a Boston bank account. It was enough for the life he planned to lead, once Dimona was behind him.

Chapter 28

After two weeks of intensive research, the Insight team believed they had tied up most of the loose ends. The story was "copper-bottomed," as Morgan liked to call it, and publication was tentatively scheduled for Sunday, September 28.

All that remained was to obtain some reaction from the Israelis. The newspaper decided to approach the Israeli Embassy in London with an outline of the story, a few of Vanunu's pictures and some of his identification papers. On the afternoon of Tuesday, September 23, Hounam and Peter Wilsher drove to the embassy at No. 2 Palace Gardens, a modest two-story brick building hidden from the street by hedges, across from Hyde Park and Kensington Palace, and were ushered into the office of embassy press attache Aviat Manor. The two journalists showed him a selection of the photographs, gave him copies of Vanunu's passport and his Dimona severance agreement, and handed him a letter that described in detail the story they planned to run on Sunday.

"Please find enclosed some supporting documentation which refers to the subject we discussed at this afternoon's meeting," the letter read. "It includes a brief synopsis of what we propose to publish this coming Sunday, together with a selection of photographs showing the Dimona site, a floor plan of the plutonium separation plant, and a few of the units involved in producing the metal. There are also two photostats, one showing the opening page of our informant's Israeli passport, and a copy of the document he received when he left his employment at Dimona on October 27, 1985.

"Obviously we should be grateful for any comment or elaboration that the ambassador, or the Israeli government, care to make," the letter concluded.

Manor nodded slightly, then turned to the synopsis. Hounam and Wilsher watched the attache's face harden as he discovered what the *Sunday Times* planned to publish.

"We plan, on Sunday September 28, to run a major investigation piece, finally confirming the long-suspected existence of Israel's nuclear-arms capacity, and describing the highly advanced, sophisticated and rapidly developing facilities devoted to this purpose. This will state:

(a) That Israel, which despite regular denials is widely believed to be capable of producing, perhaps, one atom bomb per year, has in fact since 1970 been steadily accumulating the material for such weapons at an annual rate of between six to ten, and that there are now the makings of over 100 fission devices in her nuclear arsenal.

(b) That the plutonium separation plant needed for this programme, which has never been located or proved to exist, occupies six underground floors beneath an apparently innocuous two-story building on the site of the Dimona reactor, built by the French for 'scientific research' in the late 1950s.

(c) That the power of the reactor, never officially admitted to be more than 26 megawatts, is in fact at least four, and probably more like ten times that size, and that its output is almost entirely devoted to arms production.

(d) That the separation plant was supplied and installed by the French, despite the often-cited statement from President de Gaulle's memoirs that he had effectively blocked Israeli efforts to acquire the facilities 'from which one bright day atomic bombs might come.'

(e) That since 1980 Israel has built elaborate and power-hungry extensions to the Dimona site, which enable her to produce substantial quantities of both lithium-6 and tritium. These are the essential extra ingredients needed, first for massively boosting the yield of first generation fission bombs, and second for proceeding, if this is ever required, to the construction of a thermonuclear device—hydrogen bomb or neutron bomb. We do not know how far Israel has progressed down that road but there are now no further raw-material obstacles in her way.

(f) That in addition to the manufacture of all these materials there is an even more secret and secure section in which highly skilled technicians machine the materials into parts for bombs. In other words, the production does not end with the stockpiling of materials for nuclear weapons, but goes right through to the manufacture of at least screw-ready devices.

To this package we shall be adding detailed graphics of the Dimona site, floor-plans and cross-sections of the secret separation plant, many pictures taken inside the control room and the area for weapon development, and the personal testimony of the man who smuggled those pictures out after spending more than eight years at Dimona as a key technician on the plutonium, lithium, and tritium programmes."

It was a staggeringly powerful presentation. Spread out in front of Aviat Manor were secrets that had survived three decades. In a matter of days, they would be splashed across the front page of a British newspaper for all the world to see.

When he finished reading the document, Manor glanced worriedly at the journalists. "Are you sure it is safe for me to see this?" he asked solemnly.

No one was quite sure what he meant.

As they returned to the newsroom, Hounam spotted a two-man videotape crew outside the gates of Wapping. Plant security guards had been keeping an eye on the crew because of its odd behavior. Unlike most of the news photographers camped outside the newspaper offices during the protracted strike, the two men were photographing every person and vehicle that entered the complex. Questioned by guards, one of the cameramen claimed he was covering the dispute for a student group. The other said nothing.

Curious, Hounam thought as he and Wilsher drove past the two men and into the complex. Those blokes look very Middle Eastern.

The next afternoon, Manor telephoned Peter Wilsher and read him an official response to the *Sunday Times* blockbuster. Peres and Shamir were both out of the country, in New York for the annual meeting of the United Nations General Assembly, and the two-sentence statement had been drafted by mid-level Foreign Ministry officials unaware of the intrigue unfolding at the highest level of their government. It was another of the terse denials that Israel had routinely issued over the years in reaction to reports of its involvement in nuclear-weapons production.

"It is not the first time that stories of this kind have appeared in the press," the statement read. "They have no basis whatsoever in reality and hence any further comment on our part is superfluous."

Chapter 29

The telephone rang as Peter Hounam sat at his cluttered desk in the crowded newsroom on Thursday afternoon, September 25. It was Oscar Guerrero. He was back in town.

When Hounam and Vanunu flew off to London two weeks earlier, they left behind one unhappy and bitter man. Unnerved by the angry confrontation over the photographs, Guerrero was convinced he would be cut out of a share of the Dimona riches. Hounam had signed an agreement to honor Vanunu's promise of the first $25,000 from any payment, but the scrap of paper meant little. It was simple: if the *Sunday Times* had Vanunu, it didn't need Guerrero. The irritating Colombian was history.

But Guerrero was nothing if not resourceful. Without Vanunu's knowledge, he had kept thirty-seven prints of the Dimona photographs—the heart of the *Sunday Times* story. The newspaper's competitors, Guerrero was certain, would be delighted to beat it to the punch.

Flying to London only hours behind Hounam and Vanunu, he headed straight for the offices of the *Sunday Mirror*, a popular tabloid owned by Rupert Murdoch's major competitor, press baron Robert Maxwell. The two men were ferocious rivals who had squabbled publicly over the right to buy several London dailies for their ever-expanding empires. Guerrero figured no newspaper would be more interested in skewering a Murdoch exclusive than Maxwell's *Sunday Mirror*.

His calculations were on the money. Tony Frost, the *Sunday Mirror's* news editor, was tantalized by the Dimona tale, which Guerrero this time had spiced with the claim that Israel had actually built an arsenal of neutron bombs. After showing Frost the pictures of

Dimona and his suspect scrapbook of snapshots with world leaders, Guerrero made his offer. He told the editor he was seething about his treatment at the hands of the *Sunday Times*. The *Sunday Mirror* could have the story for about 200,000 pounds, about $320,000.

Frost's enthusiasm ebbed appreciably, and he firmly told Guerrero the newspaper would never pay that much money for the Vanunu story. But Guerrero was ready to negotiate.

"Over the course of three days with us, he came down drastically. From 200,000 pounds to saying he would accept 25,000 pounds ($40,000) for this world exclusive," Frost said. "Because he felt so greatly aggrieved by the *Sunday Times*. This was his motive: to get back at the *Sunday Times*."

As he dickered with Frost, Guerrero was also shopping the story in at least one other newsroom. He offered the photographs to the *London Observer* for $35,000, but the *Observer* rejected the proposal, saying it did not pay money for stories of that sort.

The *Sunday Mirror* finally talked Guerrero down to 2,000 pounds ($3,200), and went to work attempting to verify the Colombian's account. With Guerrero in tow, a reporter spent a week showing the photographs to several nuclear weapons experts around Britain in search of confirmation of their authenticity. No one could say for sure, and as usual, Guerrero's behavior struck virtually everyone as odd. He traveled everywhere with the Vanunu photographs tucked inside his black leather briefcase, and refused to open the bag in public. When the photographs were needed for inspection, Guerrero would duck into a bathroom and return with them in his hand.

But Guerrero already had the *Sunday Mirror* on the hook. The newspaper was paying most of his expenses in London. After returning from the cross-country confirmation trip, Guerrero spent two nights at the Southway Hotel on Gillingham Street in southwest London. On September 22, he asked to move to the Ecclestone Hotel, registering under the name "Jorge Bueno" and a false home address in Spain, and quickly made himself at home. A *Sunday Mirror* reporter who stopped to see Guerrero at the Ecclestone one morning found him having breakfast with a young, heavily made-up blonde woman who Guerrero claimed was a bus courier at nearby

Victoria Station. They had spent the night together, he bragged.

Suspicious of a hoax, *Sunday Mirror* reporters searched Guerrero's hotel room while he was being interviewed at the office, but found nothing incriminating. A background check, however, was more productive, turning up his criminal record, a reputation in Bogota as a swindler, and the sale of bogus news stories to newspapers and magazines by using phony press cards.

The editors confronted Guerrero in his hotel room on Thursday, September 25, demanding an explanation for his police record and global reputation for dishonesty. Unless he could refute the evidence, they warned, the newspaper was prepared to conclude that Guerrero was a fraud. The Colombian pleaded for time to buttress his story, and agreed to another meeting later in the day at the *Sunday Mirror* offices.

He never showed up. Instead, Guerrero telephoned Hounam. Crying, he confessed his dealings with the *Sunday Mirror*, omitting any mention of the latest setback. The reporter was hardly surprised. The *Sunday Times* had long ago formed the view that Guerrero would work for anybody. The trick now was to see whether there was any way to prevent the *Sunday Mirror* from walking off with the *Sunday Times* exclusive. Barely able to contain his anger and disgust, Hounam tried to calm Guerrero and persuaded him to meet with Robin Morgan at the Tower Thistle that night.

Guerrero didn't keep that appointment, either. Perhaps, Hounam thought bitterly, he's found another buyer.

Dissatisfied with the embassy's reaction to the story, *Sunday Times* editor Andrew Neil had ordered his staff to seek a reply directly from Jerusalem. To handle that task, the *Sunday Times* turned to Hirsh Goodman, the defense affairs correspondent for the *Jerusalem Post*. Many Israeli reporters have "stringer" relationships with foreign newspapers, alerting their clients to important stories and guiding foreign correspondents through the bureaucratic thicket that often makes reporting in Israel so difficult. Goodman had been the *Sunday Times* stringer for several years. In recent months, he had cut back his involvement, but remained available for major projects. The Vanunu revelations fit that bill.

A few hours after Manor telephoned with the embassy statement, Morgan called Goodman in Jerusalem, briefed him on the Dimona story, and asked him to request an official reply from Shimon Peres.

This must be bullshit, Goodman thought as he hung up the telephone. An Israeli disclosing his country's secrets? A Dimona worker sneaking a camera inside the plant and giving his pictures to a London newspaper? And Israeli intelligence didn't know about it? Goodman was far too familiar with the defense establishment to rule out a major foulup, but this was a bit much to believe.

Goodman's home was only a few minutes from the hilltop government complex, and he jumped in his car and raced up to see Uriel Savir, the prime minister's media advisor. Before Goodman explained the purpose of his visit, Nimrod Novick, a senior Peres aide, walked into the office and joined the meeting.

"Listen," Goodman began, "my employers have phoned me from London and they claim they have this story." He outlined the Dimona revelations, gave the two Israeli officials Vanunu's identification-card number and a few other pieces of information that appeared to confirm his identity, then asked for some official comment.

It was obviously the first Savir and Novick had heard of Vanunu. Savir looked shaken, and for a moment Goodman thought he was going to faint. There was an awkward hush while the two officials studied the notes Savir had made during Goodman's report. Finally, Novick told Goodman they would need some time to prepare a response, and the reporter left.

How much Peres told his aides about the Vanunu operation is not known. But when Savir telephoned Goodman later in the day, he relayed a "reply from the prime minister."

"We have no formal comment. Our ambassador has been approached in London, and a channel of communication will be through the embassy," Savir said.

"No denial?" Goodman asked in surprise when Savir paused.

"That is the formal reply," the press spokesman said, and he hurriedly hung up before Goodman could ask another question.

Convinced a more detailed response would not be forthcoming, the *Sunday Times* asked Goodman to fly to London to attend a meeting on Friday, September 26, at which time a final decision on whether to publish the story was to be made. A car was waiting when Goodman arrived at Heathrow and he was driven directly to Wapping, passing a crowd of angry strikers picketing across the road from the Pennington Street complex.

The meeting began around noon in the *Sunday Times* newsroom. Neil, Morgan, Hounam, Peter Wilsher and several other reporters and editors involved with the Vanunu story nibbled at a cold lunch as they walked through the story, analyzing every item in the proposed article. Peter Wilsher and Goodman were told to argue opposing sides on the major questions, and the rest of the staff members jumped in and out of the debate. Strangely, the discovery that Guerrero had been talking to the *Sunday Mirror* was not a factor; Neil was only interested in making sure his newspaper's story was airtight. Besides, the *Sunday Mirror* didn't have Vanunu, whose recollections seemed indispensable to the Dimona expose.

The session dragged on all afternoon. Eventually, about six o'clock, Neil announced he had decided to postpone publication. Hounam and several others vehemently protested the decision, but Neil was unmoved. The Israeli reaction had not erased the editor's doubts about whether the newspaper was being conned, and there was still no official confirmation that Vanunu had worked at Dimona. In addition, Neil was perplexed by Vanunu's increasingly erratic behavior. The Israeli's determined attempts to elude the reporters assigned to watch him and his strident demands to be left alone sharpened suspicion that he might be a hoaxer, or an Israeli agent. The staff's monthlong efforts had yielded a solid piece of work, Neil acknowledged, but he was still apprehensive.

Goodman agreed with the decision to hold the story for further checks. The *Sunday Times* story still had some holes that needed filling, he thought. The reporter had arrived in London with more than a few misgivings about the report. As a journalist, he agreed it was a hell of a story, but as a Jew and as an Israeli, he was dismayed by the damage the revelations might cause to his country's security.

Goodman felt better about it after the meeting. He still believed that allowing the world to peek inside Dimona could be hazardous. But what they saw just might convince Israel's enemies of the futility of their military efforts. Either way, Goodman decided as he shuffled out of the newsroom, it's good for the Jews.

Chapter 30

The imminent publication of the *Sunday Times* story posed two problems for Israel that required immediate attention. Obsessed with preventing any damage to Israeli-British relations, Peres intended to forewarn Margaret Thatcher about the revelations to ensure she was not caught by surprise. The prime minister also planned to minimize the exposure the story would receive at home by urging Israeli newspaper editors to play down the disclosures.

After learning from the London embassy about the *Sunday Times'* plans, Peres telephoned Admoni on Thursday, September 25, for a briefing on the Vanunu operation. The prime minister, not knowing Neil would decide the next day to postpone the story, assumed the Dimona revelations would be published on Sunday, and he wanted to make sure the Mossad was ready to move. Admoni assured Peres that agents were in position in London, prepared to pounce on Vanunu once the *Sunday Times* story appeared. Peres, haunted by his concerns about Thatcher's reaction, asked if the operation would violate any British laws. No, Admoni assured, Vanunu will leave England voluntarily before the Mossad seizes him. Satisfied, the prime minister indicated he didn't want to hear any more, and instructed Admoni to inform him when the agents completed their mission.

Admoni understood and even approved of Peres' disinterest in the details of the operation. It was important for government officials to be able to deny any knowledge of the dirty tactics employed by their spies. But Admoni was edgy. The scandal and turmoil that had shaken Israel's intelligence community had scrambled the rules. If the capture went amiss, Admoni would be very much on his own.

A few hours later, Peres contacted Margaret Thatcher to inform

her about the Dimona problem. The Israeli leader was breezily unconcerned about Thatcher's reaction, certain she wouldn't object.
After all, the British also hated traitors.

The conversation was exceedingly friendly. Thatcher commiser-
ated with Peres about Israel's dilemma as he explained that Vanunu,
a junior technician at an Israeli nuclear facility disgruntled about his
dismissal, had sold some photographs of the plant to the *Sunday
Times*, which would publish them that weekend. Israeli agents intended to seize Vanunu and bring him back to stand trial, and the
Mossad had devised a way to capture the traitor without violating
British law. No illegal acts will occur on British soil, Peres
stressed.

Thatcher promised British authorities would not intervene, provided Israel kept its pledge not to violate British law. Impressed by
Peres' assurances, she later ordered British intelligence to end its
surveillance of the Israeli team tracking Vanunu. On this occasion,
the Mossad was free to operate in London without fear of interfer-
ence from their wary British colleagues.

Peres' meeting with the Israeli editors also went well. Under a
long-standing quasi-official arrangement, a prime minister concerned about a story's impact on national security can request the
cooperation of a so-called "Editor's Committee" in squelching the
sensitive news report. Over the years, the committee has invariably
bowed to the government and agreed to self-censorship. Only the
newspaper *Hadashot*, a relative newcomer to the Israeli journalism
fraternity, routinely refused to abide by the committee's decision.

If they differed on the proper approach to the Vanunu problem,
Peres, Shamir and Rabin were unanimous in believing the Israeli
news media could not be permitted to report the Dimona revelations
in detail or, even worse, follow up on the story with new disclosures. Extensive coverage could provoke a debate on the nuclear
issue, and politically damaging criticism about the security lapse.
And, in a country where leaks are legion, reporters could conceivably stumble on the truth about the way the government handled the
Vanunu case.

In the modern communication age, it was impossible to prevent word of the *Sunday Times* report from reaching Israel. Israel's editors, however, could help ensure the story would fizzle once it crossed the border.

At 2 P.M. on Friday, September 26, while Neil and his staff were still debating the decision to publish, the editors gathered in Peres' office. The prime minister could not wait any longer; the Jewish Sabbath would begin at sundown and the editors would be out of contact until the traditional period of rest ended Saturday evening. By then, the *Sunday Times* would be on the streets in London.

The prime minister appeared nervous and somewhat agitated to several of the editors as he ran through the Vanunu problem, then asked the committee to play down the story out of London. "Please confine yourselves to reporting only what is in the *Sunday Times*," Peres told the editors. "Don't start digging into Vanunu's background, or try to uncover any more on this subject."

After an apathetic discussion, the editors agreed. None of them asked whether the *Sunday Times* story was true.

Vanunu had no idea Guerrero had returned to London, and it was just as well. His tensions were climbing as the days passed without publication of his story. On September 23, the day Hounam and Peter Wilsher visited the Israeli Embassy, Vanunu moved from the Tower Thistle to the Mountbatten Hotel, on a quiet street not far from the hustle of Soho, again under the name of "George Forsty." The hotel staff paid scant attention to the foreign-looking gentleman in Room 105 who kept to himself, rarely requesting any of the hotel's services. "Mr. Forsty" rose early, had breakfast and then left the hotel for much of the day and early evening. His debriefings virtually complete, Vanunu had little to do, and the Insight staff largely ignored him as they hurried to finish the story. Even Wendy Robbins, back in school and plunging into her studies, ducked many of Vanunu's invitations to join him for drinks or dinner. He had time on his hands.

Soho was much more to Vanunu's liking than the isolation of Heath Lodge. The area derived its name from the rallying cry shouted by hunters who roamed central London's parklands centuries ago, and it still teemed with thrill-seekers. Prostitutes, sleazy pubs and strip joints competed for customers with cut-rate shops, theaters, cheap restaurants and fast-food outlets, a few serving Middle Eastern fare. Just as he had in Sydney, Vanunu eagerly embraced the city's sin district. Even better, from Vanunu's vantage point, Soho attracted hordes of young people of all nationalities. There was a loose, continental feeling about the area that he enjoyed.

But the new surroundings didn't hold his attention for long. Vanunu was tired of waiting for the *Sunday Times*. He wanted to get on with his life. And no one at the newspaper was giving him straight answers about when he might be able to move. Vanunu suspected Neil and his superiors were under pressure from Israel to kill the story. Once convinced the editors shared his ideological motives for exposing the Dimona operations, he now realized in dismay that the *Sunday Times* was interested only in selling newspapers.

Morgan saw another reason for Vanunu's frustration. The editor had concluded that Vanunu believed the story was his one chance for fame, however fleeting. "My gut reaction was that here was a guy who was quite intelligent. Because of his background, his upbringing in Israel, he never found himself a role, but was intelligent enough to know that he could do something quite intelligent and constructive, useful," Morgan said. "And he wanted to play a role, wanted to be important, wanted to be maybe even famous. I'm sure he wanted to be successful with girls. He just wanted to be somebody. He was intelligent enough to be somebody, but he wasn't anybody."

"And he wanted to make a mark. [The story] became his torch."

More than anything, however, Vanunu was frightened. As the days dragged by, he became increasingly convinced the Israelis were on the verge of capturing him. He felt he was being followed.

Then, on Wednesday, September 24, Vanunu's spirits brightened. The Israeli spent most of his days in the area around Leicester Square, a small, leafy park flanked by movie theaters, hot dog stands, restaurants and cheap pubs. For Vanunu, the area was an engrossing street theater. In good weather, there was rarely an empty bench around the large statue of William Shakespeare in the middle of the park, and Vanunu found he could lose himself, and often his worries, in the milling throngs.

Wandering past the fashionable shops along Regent Street late in the afternoon, Vanunu stopped to examine the merchandise in one store window. He was quickly joined by a woman, young, in her mid-twenties, short and somewhat pudgy. Her blonde hair appeared bleached and she wore too much makeup. But to Vanunu she was attractive, and, best of all, she was alone.

He had been through this before. During his lonely tours of central London, Vanunu, still incurably shy, had occasionally sidled up to a woman standing by herself and tried to make eye contact in the vain hope she would make the first move. It never worked.

But as he stood next to this woman, staring at the window display, she turned her head slightly and smiled tentatively at him. Bored, tense and very much alone, Vanunu screwed up his courage and struck up a conversation.

She introduced herself as Cindy Hanin, an American from Florida, on holiday in Europe during a break from classes at a beauty school. After a few minutes of small talk, the woman agreed to have a coffee with him.

The first date lasted several hours and before they parted Vanunu arranged to meet Cindy again the next afternoon in front of the Tate Gallery, near Lambeth Palace, the London home of the Archbishop of Canterbury. If you can't make it, Vanunu told his new friend, call me at the Mountbatten Hotel.

Elated, Vanunu returned to his room and telephoned Robbins for directions to her parents' house, where he was to dine Thursday night. Robbins apologetically canceled the date; she had a meeting at the university. "But what about a week from Thursday?" she asked. Vanunu said he would look forward to it, then launched into his now-familiar litany of complaints about the way the *Sunday Times* was handling his story. After a few minutes, Robbins asked Vanunu where he was staying. He gave her the telephone number of the Mountbatten. "But don't tell Max I told you," he added. "They don't want anyone to know where I am."

Vanunu never mentioned his meeting with Cindy to Robbins, his closest acquaintance in London and the one person with whom he had shared his most intimate thoughts. Perhaps he feared the *Sunday Times* would learn of the encounter and prevent him from pursuing the relationship.

The next day, Prangnell picked Vanunu up at the hotel about 1 P.M.to take him to the newspaper for a previously scheduled appointment that Vanunu, in his excitement, had forgotten when he made plans with Cindy. "I'm supposed to meet someone at two o'clock. A girl," he told the reporter with a proud smile. Annoyed, Prangnell reluctantly agreed to swing by the Tate so Vanunu could explain the muddle to Cindy.

Prangnell sat in the car and watched as Vanunu talked to the woman, making arrangements to see a Woody Allen film, *Hannah and Her Sisters*, that night. The woman seemed reluctant to come near the car, but the reporter was still able to get a good look at her. She was wearing a plain brown coat over a brown tweed pantsuit and high heels. A brown trilby-style hat covered thick blonde hair, which was either a bad dye job or a wig, Prangnell thought. Vanunu's new friend also wore far too much makeup. Not much to look at, he sniffed. Still, maybe she would keep him happy.

Making Vanunu happy was precisely what Cindy had in mind. It was, in fact, her job. Cindy Hanin was a Mossad agent, sent to London to help capture Mordechai Vanunu.

Chapter 31

Seizing Mordechai Vanunu should have been a simple task for Israeli intelligence. He was a confused, restless and frightened man, stranded in a strange country. He harbored doubts about his actions and was anxious to elude the people who had helped put him in his current situation. Above all, he was alone—cooped up in a hotel room with no friends or family to offer advice, no one to sound alarms or provide protection. He was, by any measure, a supremely easy target.

But Peres' order to avoid any acts of illegality in Britain meant the Mossad needed to figure out a way to persuade Vanunu to voluntarily leave London. Some weakness would have to be exploited to convince him to drop his guard. A woman seemed the best bet.

The Mossad knew Vanunu was desperate for a romantic relationship. The subject of his sexual frustrations had surfaced in interviews with people who knew Vanunu in Israel, and the surveillance of Vanunu in London had been so tight that agents actually overheard the target himself complain to Max Prangnell one day that he wanted to meet some women.

Like most spy agencies, the Mossad had enjoyed great success with the use of "honeytraps." The lure of sex had led to one of Israel's greatest intelligence coups. In 1966, an America-born agent traveling on a U.S. passport had gone to Baghdad and lured an Iraqi fighter pilot to Paris with promises of a sexual tryst. There, she talked him into flying to Israel, where he was persuaded to defect with one of Iraq's brand-new Soviet-supplied MiG-21 jets, the first to fall into Western hands.

The Vanunu case was a bit more mundane, but to the Mossad

planners a honeytrap was the right approach. Now all they needed was the bait.

In 1978, Cheryl Hanin was living in Florida in the shadow of a fantasy. Walt Disney had come to Orlando and built his Magic Kingdom, a splashy theme park that sprawled across more than 27,000 acres of prime central Florida real estate, twice the size of the borough of Manhattan in New York City. Disney's extraordinary creation transformed the torpid Southern community, which for years had lived off the orange groves and herds of cattle that surrounded it, supplemented by a short burst of tourist activity in the late winter when major league baseball teams turned up for spring training. The Magic Kingdom made Orlando one of the country's most popular tourist destinations. Suddenly, the city was awash in cash.

Cheryl's father, Stanley, rode the crest of Disney's wave to financial success. Fueled by his gift for promotion—friends say it was Stanley Hanin who came up with the concept of the screaming television salesman to flog his wares—Hanin's auto supply business mushroomed into a chain of stores, making him the tire king of central Florida.

The Hanins lived in Longwood, a small community of about 10,000 people just outside Orlando, and Cheryl and her brother, Randy, and sister, Penny, dwelled in sun-drenched suburban comfort. The parents were fairly active members of Orlando's small but expanding Jewish community. It was not an especially religious family, but Stanley was a generous contributor to Jewish philanthropies and his wife was active at Temple Israel.

Cheryl was an average American teenager, a bright, bubbly, pleasant-looking girl with a little weight problem and a touch of insecurity. She earned As and Bs at Edgewater High School, but didn't really stand out, "kind of faded into the background," assistant principal Lowell Boggs put it. "She was one of those that nobody ever really noticed too much, if you know what I mean," he added. Still, she was a fighter when she had to be. If a teacher scheduled a test on a Jewish holiday, Cheryl was the one who insisted on special arrangements for Jewish students.

It was a comfortable life. But there was something missing, and Cheryl felt it. Like Mordechai Vanunu, she was dissatisfied with her surroundings. Like Vanunu, she was searching for something more, a chance to make a difference. Unlike Vanunu, however, she found her opportunity in Israel.

In 1978, in the winter of her senior year, Cheryl, then seventeen, went to Israel to study for a few months. Her parents had imparted a reverence for the state of Israel, and the importance of its existence as a safe haven for the Jewish people. But nothing they told her prepared Cheryl for what she found in Israel. The experience exhilarated her. Israel, Cheryl thought, was so different from the affluent but morally dissolute society she had left behind. It was a country on the make, carving a place in a hostile world. There were problems, certainly. But in her dazzled eyes, the people—the Jewish people—seemed to be struggling together with a determined optimism and glowing idealism to create a real miracle and build a true magic kingdom.

What happened to Cheryl Hanin was not unusual for a young American Jew. Dissatisfied with life at home and enthralled with the notion of a country where being Jewish is the norm, many move to Israel, study, join the army, and go to work. One day they look up and the years have gone by and they are Israelis.

It is a process that Israel assiduously exploits. The government spends millions of dollars to woo young foreign Jews, and to the annoyance of many American Jews, who believe they can aid Israel just as easily from abroad, Americans are a favorite target. They bring with them good educations, high standards and a bristling sense of purpose that eagerly lends itself to the concept of a Jewish state. The point is made over and over: the Jewish state needs you. Here you can make a difference. Here you can help ensure the survival of a homeland for your people.

Young American Jews emigrate to Israel for a variety of reasons. Some are motivated by devoutly religious beliefs. Others are fleeing personal problems at home. And then there are a few who see in Israel the opportunity to make a difference in life.

Cheryl was turned on by the idea of building a nation. In Israel she could have an immediate impact on the world around her and she was anxious to get started. The sense of commitment and purpose that Cheryl did not find in the United States was waiting in Israel. Life would be a little harder, but the sacrifice was worthwhile. A girl who would never have considered military service in the United States avidly anticipated a stint in the Israeli army. It was part of the fabric of the society, part of building the country.

Cheryl Hanin was exactly the kind of pioneer that David Ben-Gurion had sought.

After returning to Orlando for her high school graduation, Cheryl moved to Israel for good. She had grown up in a fantasy, and when the wonder wore off, she went in search of another one. In Israel, she had found what she was seeking.

And in 1986 she was offered the chance to make a major contribution to her new homeland. Cheryl Hanin became the key to capturing Mordechai Vanunu.

Finding a woman for the Vanunu kidnapping was not easy. Women rarely receive much operational experience in the Mossad; most are assigned to administrative tasks. Part of the problem is their inability to operate in the male-dominated Arab world, but there is also an element of benign discrimination, perhaps a legacy from the days of legendary Mossad chief Isser Harel, who was reluctant to send women overseas because of the danger. Harel was also zealously puritanical. He would sternly chastise male staff members who even touched female workers at headquarters. And he insisted on using women in vital operational roles only as a last resort, after all other alternatives were dismissed.

A woman, however, was essential to the Vanunu mission, and optimally a woman with an American background. Vanunu's involvement with Judy Zimmet and his plan to travel to the United States had not escaped the attention of Mossad planners.

The agency's decision to go outside to find their agent was not unusual. Because of chronic manpower shortages, Israeli intelligence frequently calls on the services of "part-timers"—particularly foreign-born Israelis with knowledge of other countries and languages and possession of foreign passports—to handle some operations.

Cheryl was an excellent candidate for the Vanunu job. She was twenty-five years old, originally an American, reasonably attractive, and a veteran of an elite army unit where she had received some intelligence training. She was married to an Israeli, Ofer Bentov, a major in Military Intelligence. Best of all, Cheryl Hanin Bentov was an ardent Zionist who would do whatever was necessary to serve Israel.

When the Mossad came knocking on her door, Cheryl readily agreed to help. She was shocked to learn of Vanunu's deceit, and expressed the hope the Mossad could capture him before he talked about Dimona. No one knew enough about the government's plans to tell her that wasn't the idea.

Chapter 32

She looked good on paper, but the use of Bentov was risky. If the plan went wrong, an unmitigated disaster would result. And fresh in the minds of Mossad planners were two blown intelligence operations, both involving the use of "part-timers:" the Pollard affair, which had seriously strained relations with the United States and the all-important American Jewish community, and the nightmare in Lillehammer, Norway. There, in 1973, a Mossad assassination team gunned down a Moroccan waiter in front of his pregnant wife in the mistaken belief that he was a leader of the Palestinian terrorists involved in the 1972 Munich Olympics massacre of eleven members of the Israeli Olympic team. Several Israeli agents were arrested and served time in prison for the slaying. Two of them had also been "part-timers," a Danish-born Israeli businessman and a Swedish-born woman recruited because they spoke the language and knew the social and geographical landscape. Neither had any idea of the nature of their work. They had simply been asked to "perform a service for the state of Israel." Arrested by Norwegian police, the woman panicked and gave authorities the address of a Mossad safe house where police arrested the two case officers who led the operation. The businessman was afflicted with claustrophobia, a fact either not known or ignored by the Mossad, and he quickly cracked after spending some time in a small, dark room awaiting interrogation. Terrified, he confessed not only to taking part in the waiter's murder but to at least one other Mossad operation—the hijacking of the uranium ship in 1968.

In the Vanunu case, everything again depended on a "part-timer," and the consequences of a failure were staggering. If Vanunu somehow made it to the United States, for instance, the retrieval operation would be greatly complicated. Israel was reluctant to run the risk of staging another intelligence operation in the United States so soon after the Pollard debacle.

Unknown to Peres, a worst-case solution was also on the boards at Mossad headquarters. If Bentov failed, Vanunu would be killed. The death would appear to be the result of a drug overdose or a simple street mugging.

There was another potential problem with the Mossad plan: it called for Guerrero to introduce Bentov to Vanunu. No one was enthusiastic about the Colombian's involvement. The Mossad had been on his trail since he arrived in London, and was aware of his dealings with the *Sunday Mirror*. But it was of minimal concern to the agency. Guerrero did not have any knowledge of the operations at Dimona and only a general idea of Vanunu's duties. The *Sunday Mirror*, moreover, was certain to discover Guerrero's shady background, casting more doubt on his credibility. Finally, a story based on Guerrero's information would actually aid the plan by creating an aura of confusion about Vanunu's allegations.

The agents in London were told not to worry about Guerrero's involvement with the *Sunday Mirror*. It was all part of the plan.

With Bentov on board, the operation came together quickly. The woman and about ten other agents would be sent to London. Posing as an American journalist who had been tipped to the Dimona story and Guerrero's whereabouts by a friend at the *Sunday Mirror*, Bentov would contact the Colombian and offer to outbid the British newspaper. She would tell Guerrero that she knew where Vanunu was staying and ask his help in obtaining Vanunu's cooperation. Just as they determined a woman would be Vanunu's weakness, the Mossad knew greed was the way to reach Guerrero. Bentov's proposal would be exactly the kind of doublecross that a man like Guerrero would understand and appreciate.

After gaining Vanunu's confidence, Bentov would lure him out of England to his arrest. Once in custody, Vanunu would be whisked back to Israel.

The London team arrived on September 20, traveling separately or in pairs on false passports from several European countries, and checked into four different hotels in central London. There was no record of any of them leaving Israel. Bentov's 1986 Interior Ministry travel card—a record kept on all Israelis leaving and entering the country—shows she left Israel only twice, once between July 1 and July 11 and again between October 24 and November 7, when she went to Florida for her brother's wedding. Both times she traveled on her Israeli passport, No. 1338394.

This time, she was traveling on her U.S. passport, No. 040936379, issued at Miami, Florida. Bentov took a room, No. 209, at the Ecclestone Hotel, registering under her maiden name and giving her father's home address in Florida.

Shortly after arriving, she called Guerrero at the Southway Hotel. As the Mossad had predicted, Guerrero jumped at the chance to make some more money, and instantly agreed to meet her at the Ecclestone the next morning.

The encounter went poorly. Bentov was immediately distrustful of the erratic Colombian. He rambled on about his desire to punish both Vanunu and the *Sunday Times* for pushing him out of the deal, and then made several clumsy passes at Bentov before she sharply told him to stop. Finally, Bentov called an abrupt end to the meeting.

Listening to Bentov's report, the Mossad team concluded Guerrero was a liability who couldn't be involved any further in such a sensitive operation, and Tel Aviv readily agreed. Bentov checked out of the Ecclestone and moved into a Mossad-leased apartment in central London.

Eager to nail down his latest score, Guerrero moved to the Ecclestone the next day, only to find "Miss Hanin" had left. The Mossad placed him under twenty-four hour surveillance as a precaution, but the agents were not worried. Guerrero, fearful of jeopardizing his already tenuous relationship with the *Sunday Mirror*, would never mention his contact with another journalist. And even if he did, the newspaper would probably think he was lying in a last-ditch attempt to drive up his price.

Without Guerrero to make the introduction, however, Bentov's task was greatly complicated. She would have to meet Vanunu on her own. She would have to pick him up.

Vanunu was not an easy catch. For three days, Bentov, shadowed by as many as five other agents, made herself available. She hung around the lobbies of Vanunu's hotels and strayed across his path as he aimlessly wandered the streets of London, drinking coffee and staring at shop windows. Nothing worked. It wasn't that Vanunu had lost interest in female companionship. The team reported back to Tel Aviv that he appeared to have a consuming interest in many of the women he passed, and even struck up brief conversations with a few. But he never bit on Bentov. Part of the problem was that she couldn't be too forward. When Vanunu boasted about his "conquest" to the *Sunday Times*, as the Mossad assumed he would, it had to appear that Vanunu made the first move.

Bentov was becoming frustrated. Even with her coat unbuttoned in the September chill, exposing an attractive blouse and tight-fitting pants, Vanunu never seemed to notice the girl who had blended into the background back at Edgewater High School. "What do I have to do? Strip?" she asked the team after the second night.

No one laughed. It was agonizing to the other agents. At times, when Vanunu turned unexpectedly or when the shadow teams inadvertently crossed paths, the agents were close enough to Vanunu to reach out and touch him. Nothing would be simpler than to shove him in a car and shoot off for the airport. Why couldn't the job be done that way?

But Vanunu must not be taken in Britain. That was the order. Bentov would have to handle it.

In Tel Aviv, planners nervously drew up a backup plan. The Mossad enlisted the help of a Ben-Gurion University engineering student named Ofer Keren, who had been friendly with Vanunu. Keren was told only that his government required his services. If Bentov failed, Keren would be flown to London where he would introduce the agent to the target or induce Vanunu to leave Britain himself.

But Keren wasn't needed. On September 24, the operation finally clicked.

Bentov had followed Vanunu out of the Mountbatten and down

Earlham Street, where he turned left and began walking slowly along Charing Cross Road. At New Coventry Street, he turned right and headed into Leicester Square, with Bentov several paces behind him and three other agents close on her heels. The odd parade continued for about twenty minutes before Vanunu stopped in front of a store just off the square and began peering into the window.

Bentov drew up alongside Vanunu, feigning interest in the window display. Vanunu suddenly noticed her reflection in the glass. The woman seemed to be smiling at him. He turned toward her and, summoning up every ounce of his courage, said hello.

"Hi," Bentov replied brightly. "How are you?"

It was over quickly. After several minutes of small talk, Bentov, using the name and profession of her twenty-two year-old sister-in-law, introduced herself as Cindy Hanin. Emboldened by his initial success, Vanunu suggested they go for coffee. As they walked into a nearby restaurant, one of the trailing agents slipped into a telephone booth and dialed the Mossad safe house where a command post had been set up.

"She's with him," he said, and hung up.

Chapter 33

The *Sunday Times* had resisted the temptation to rush into print to avoid a Guerrero-supplied article by the *Sunday Mirror*, but the Insight staff was nevertheless concerned about the impact of a Dimona story in the rival newspaper. Three things could happen as a result—none of them good for the *Sunday Times*. Other newspapers could try to locate Vanunu. The Israeli, alarmed by the unexpected publicity, might flee. Or the Mossad could grab him before the *Sunday Times* published its account.

Losing Vanunu at that point would have dealt a serious blow to the *Sunday Times'* plans. In addition to a book, from which only Vanunu would have benefited financially, the newspaper was contemplating an extensive publicity campaign designed to advertise its achievement. News conferences would be held with Vanunu as the star attraction. The serial rights to his story would be sold to American newsmagazines. Vanunu could conceivably be asked to testify before the U.S. Congress if the revelations, as expected, provoked angry protests in Washington. But without Vanunu, none of this would be possible. The *Sunday Times* would again face charges of sensationalizing a story and hostile questions about the credibility of its expose. The tremendous boost that the newspaper hoped to receive from the Dimona story would never materialize if Vanunu was not available to defend it.

Neil's decision to postpone publication only enhanced the possibility of disaster. Worried the *Sunday Mirror* would run a Dimona story that weekend, Morgan sent Prangnell and Roger Wilsher to the Mountbatten Friday night, September 26, to urge Vanunu to be more careful. The reporters were instructed not to inform Vanunu about Guerrero and the *Sunday Mirror*. Just urge him to be even more conscientious about security as we near publication, Morgan said.

Vanunu was not at all receptive to the new warnings. Tired of waiting after almost a month of interviews, he frostily demanded to know when his story would be completed, and when Prangnell explained that a few more checks were being made, Vanunu erupted in fury. "Every day that goes by without the story being published puts me in more trouble," he raged. The journalists offered to provide full-time protection, but he angrily turned them down. The pressure had finally become too much to bear. Gesturing wildly and pacing the room, Vanunu abruptly announced he was leaving London, perhaps even England, and might go ahead to join his brother in the United States. Alarmed, Roger Wilsher tried to calm Vanunu by promising to discuss a trip with Morgan, but he hesitantly cautioned against it because of the security concerns. Vanunu spurned the advice.

About 8 P.M., Prangnell gave Vanunu some more money and drove him to the Tower Thistle to pick up some laundry he had left behind when he changed hotels. Returning to the Mountbatten, the reporter stopped by Wapping to make a telephone call at the office. Not wanting to bother with obtaining the required visitor's entry pass for his charge, Prangnell left Vanunu in the car by himself.

Still in a state of agitation, Vanunu met Cindy Hanin later that evening. Over a drink, he poured out the story of his work at Dimona and his subsequent involvement with the *Sunday Times*. The young American expressed shock. "Mordy," she said, "this could be very dangerous. Why are you taking such a big chance?" Cindy implored him to reconsider his arrangement, warning the *Sunday Times* couldn't be trusted, and urged Vanunu to retain an attorney. She knew a good one in New York.

As the date ended, Vanunu invited Cindy to his hotel room, but she politely turned aside the pass, saying the discussion had left her too tense for romance. Still, she hinted flirtatiously as they left the pub, there would other opportunities.

On Saturday, Vanunu kept a date to attend the opera with Trina Talbot, Robin Morgan's secretary. Prangnell had failed to obtain the tickets, so Talbot and Vanunu went out to dinner instead. Vanunu was restless, distractedly picking at his food and unreceptive to Talbot's attempts at conversation. The strain of waiting was showing.

As Trina climbed into a taxi in front of the hotel at the end of the evening, Vanunu suddenly grabbed her and tried to kiss her cheek. Talbot pulled her face away, and the two parted awkwardly. Upset by her reaction, Talbot went home and telephoned Wendy Robbins. "I feel so guilty," she told Robbins. "He was obviously so lonely."

It could have been worse, the *Sunday Times* editors agreed after seeing the *Sunday Mirror's* story on September 28. Instead of the front page, the Vanunu story was buried deep inside the newspaper. And far from stealing a beat on the *Sunday Times*, the article ridiculed Guerrero and his claims about Dimona.

"The Strange Case of Israel and the Nuclear Conman," blared the headlines on page 24. "Exclusive Report: Hoax fear after neutron bomb revelation."

Most of the accompanying story detailed Guerrero's attempts to sell the *Sunday Mirror* the Dimona photographs and an account of Vanunu's work at the plant, and the newspaper's intrepid efforts to debunk his claims. Typically, Guerrero had come up with yet another version of how the story fell into his hands. "I was in Australia writing a book," he told the newspaper. "Vanunu approached me out of the blue. Friends in Israel had given him my name and address. He told me he was a scientist who had played an important part in Israel's nuclear program. Vanunu told me, 'I love Israel. I am a man of peace, not violence. Israel should use its powers to make peace. Something has to be done to stop this madness.' "

The story was accompanied by two of Vanunu's photographs, and selections from Guerrero's "world leaders" collection. A caption under Guerrero's photos stated experts believed the pictures were doctored.

The *Sunday Mirror* did not pass up the opportunity to tweak its competitor. It merrily report the *Sunday Times* had believed Guerrero's story, even to the point of promising to pay him, and broadly implied that Murdoch's flagship newspaper had fallen for a hoax. Two scientists who had examined the Dimona photographs had pronounced them frauds, the *Sunday Mirror* announced, and the Israeli Embassy said Vanunu had been only a junior technician at Dimona.

"So what really is the truth of the matter?" the report concluded.

"It could be that the garrulous Guerrero was merely after a good pay day."

"In a story that has more twists and turns than a Le Carre novel, it would make as much sense if he was an agent in disinformation with any money he extorted counting as his bonus," the newspaper concluded, protecting itself against every eventuality.

The story prompted only a mild response from Jerusalem. In a news release issued by the Government Press Office, the Israel Atomic Energy Commission stated, "The article published by the *Sunday Mirror* on September 28, 1986, ranges itself alongside a long list of publications on Israel's nuclear activities. The Israel Atomic Energy Commission has not reacted in the past and does not intend to react at present to publications dealing with this subject."

The reaction in the *Sunday Times* newsroom was one of relief. The Insight team was confident of the authenticity of both the photographs and Vanunu's claims, and no one was perturbed to see Guerrero exposed as a conniving hoaxster. The staff had already drawn that conclusion.

"Whatever they are, they are not idiots," Hounam later said of his colleagues at the *Sunday Mirror*. "They did a professional job on Guerrero, exposing him for the crook he is."

The only worrying note was the *Sunday Mirror's* publication of a photograph of Guerrero with Vanunu, taken in Australia. If Vanunu saw the picture, he might bolt. Still, the photograph was not on the front page of the tabloid. Prangnell was dispatched to the Mountbatten on Sunday morning to prevent Vanunu from reading a copy of the newspaper.

Vanunu had not seen the *Sunday Mirror*. He appeared relaxed, almost pleased to see Prangnell, and turned surly only once, when the reporter told him the newspaper might move him to another hotel.

"Fuck off!" Vanunu retorted, and Prangnell quickly changed the subject. The two men had lunch at Tuttons, a restaurant in Covent Garden, and Prangnell bought Vanunu several English grammar texts at the Claude Gill bookshop in Piccadilly Circus before leaving him at the Mountbatten about 5 P.M., confident that Vanunu was not interested in reading the Sunday papers.

But Cindy had seen them, and when she showed up at the hotel that evening with a copy of the *Sunday Mirror*, the woman was near tears. Insisting the picture placed Vanunu in tremendous jeopardy, she beseeched him to leave London for a few days, until the buzz created by the *Sunday Mirror* story died down. And she offered an enticement. Cindy frankly acknowledged she was attracted to Vanunu, but the idea of an affair in a hotel room left her cold. The tensions created by the Dimona story also made her too uncomfortable to act on her impulses. In another setting, she suggested, she might feel less inhibited.

Leaving the question unresolved, Vanunu and Hanin decided to see a movie, and headed for a theater near Leicester Square. On the way, the couple was spotted by David Connett, another Insight reporter. Surprised to find Vanunu with a woman, he followed them for a few minutes, then broke off the surveillance when they neared the theater. Better let Robin Morgan know first thing tomorrow, Connett told himself as he walked away.

Vanunu turned up in Morgan's office late Monday morning and announced he was thinking of leaving town, going to Europe for a few days. He was concerned about his safety, and had decided he was better off protecting himself. If the *Sunday Times* couldn't keep the story from the *Sunday Mirror*, how could it possibly make sure the Mossad didn't find him?

Morgan had his own plans for Vanunu in the wake of the *Sunday Mirror* disclosures. He wanted to send Vanunu and one of his reporters on a bus trip through Scotland or Wales, a kind of "magical mystery tour" that would keep the Israeli out of sight until the *Sunday Times* story was on the stands. The itinerary would be known only to Morgan and the reporter on the bus with Vanunu, and when the story broke, the newspaper would send a helicopter to meet

Vanunu at a previously arranged rendezvous, bring him to town for press conferences and television appearances, then fly him back to the hinterlands.

Morgan urged Vanunu to consider the proposal. Leaving the country entailed using his passport, creating a paper trail that would make him easy to trace. If he wanted to get out of London, taking the bus trip, staying in rooming houses in out-of-the-way towns, paying cash, would be the way to go.

But Vanunu wasn't interested in spending a few weeks on the road. He was leaving.

"Is this woman going with you?" Morgan asked casually.

If Vanunu was startled to learn that Morgan knew about Cindy he showed no sign of it.

"Maybe," Vanunu answered curtly.

"I don't think that's such a good idea," the editor said tentatively. Vanunu didn't respond.

Morgan gave up. There was little else he could do.

"We couldn't nail his feet to the floor, you know. He was an individual. We could advise, we could impress, we could hold the door shut and say, 'No, you cannot go out.' But the alternative was to create such a ruckus that hotel security would be down on us. In the end, you just have to open that door and say, 'Okay, go. But on your head be it.'

"I would have liked to have nailed his feet to the floor, but I'm not a policeman. I'm not a security guard. We couldn't do that. We had plans to look after him. But we weren't a professional police force. We're not the FBI, we're not Mossad.

"And if Mossad wanted him, they were going to pick him up, sooner or later."

There was one last possibility. Hounam might be able to pound some sense into Vanunu, Morgan thought. The man who brought him out of Australia was the only member of the Insight team who Vanunu trusted. But Hounam, busy with the story, had seen very little of the Israeli outside of hurried chats in the newsroom.

Hounam was not pleased to find Vanunu at Wapping on Monday morning. If the Mossad was searching for him after the *Sunday*

Mirror story, one of the first places they'd look would be the *Sunday Times* offices. The reporter's mood darkened when he discovered that the staff, with Morgan's acquiesence, had not followed through on the plan to keep a constant eye on the Israeli.

Hounam and Vanunu sat down to talk in the *Sunday Times* newsroom, nearly deserted on a Monday morning. For the first time, the reporter learned about Cindy, and he was immediately suspicious. "You know," he quietly pointed out, "you shouldn't be doing this. It's quite possible she's a plant. She could be a Mossad agent."

Vanunu blew up. This was crazy, he shouted. The first person to pay attention to him in days, to care about what happened to him, about how he was feeling, and the *Sunday Times* thinks she's a spy.

"You don't know what you're talking about, Peter," he said with disgust. "She's an American tourist, a student, that's all. Don't involve her in this."

Surprised by the virulent reaction, Hounam tried to persuade Vanunu that the *Sunday Mirror* article necessitated even tighter security, an around-the-clock guard, maybe even a change of hotels. But in Vanunu's mind, that was completely out of the question. How could he hope to pursue his relationship with Cindy with some reporter hovering over them? Moreover, he was disdainful of the expressions of concern prompted by the *Sunday Mirror* story. Where was the *Sunday Times* during the last couple of weeks? Wasn't his security at risk then?

"I don't know what you've heard," Vanunu added, jerking his head in the direction of Morgan. "But I just want to get out of London for a few days. I need a break."

"You must not do this," Hounam pleaded. "You've just got to be patient."

The admonition rankled Vanunu. "Well, when are you going to publish the thing? I've been here now three weeks," he demanded.

"It should be this week."

"Well, you said that last week," Vanunu replied, but with a bit less conviction.

The conversation returned to Cindy.

"Look, we haven't been out together for a long time," Hounam said. "Why don't me and my wife and this girl and you go out for dinner tonight?" The Hounams had other plans for the evening, but the reporter was prepared to cancel them to babysit Vanunu.

Vanunu said he couldn't make it. He wouldn't say why, but made it clear that he and Cindy were busy.

"How about tomorrow night, then?" Hounam asked.

"Fine," Vanunu said. "That's great. We can do that. We'll go out tomorrow night."

But Cindy wasn't interested in having dinner with Peter Hounam. As she sipped a glass of wine with Vanunu Monday night, the woman slipped an airline ticket from her shoulder bag and laid it on the table. The next afternoon, she was flying to Rome, where her sister had an apartment.

Vanunu panicked. He had been making some progress with Cindy. It couldn't end now. "What," he asked hesitantly, "if I go with you?"

Cindy smiled. Rome, she told him, could be a lot of fun.

There was still the problem of the dinner date with Hounam. Vanunu called the newsroom, but the reporter had already gone home. "Well, tell him I've changed my mind about tomorrow night. I'm going to leave the country for a few days," Vanunu told the staffer who answered the telephone.

The message was relayed to Morgan, who called Hounam at home and gave him Vanunu's room number at the Mountbatten, urging him to make one more attempt to talk Vanunu into remaining in London. Hounam rang Vanunu's room repeatedly, finally reaching him about 11:30 P.M.

"And he said, yes, he was leaving. He was very sorry that he couldn't come to dinner the following night. He would be back by the end of the week. Not to worry, he knew what he was doing. He was just leaving the city. Didn't say he was going abroad. And I tried to dissuade him, but in the end I couldn't.

"So I said, 'Well, look, whatever you do, wherever you are, ring me twice a day, or, failing that, ring the office. Just to let me know you're all right. Reverse the charges.' At least we would know where he was because usually when they reverse the charges they tell you there's a call coming in from so-and-so."

Vanunu agreed to stay in touch, and the two men hung up. Minutes later, Vanunu picked up the receiver and called Wendy Robbin's house to say goodbye, but he transposed the last two digits of the telephone number and reached an old man who lived around the corner from Robbin.

"There's no Wendy here, mate," he said. Confused, Vanunu hung up.

As midnight slid into early morning, Vanunu sat in his room, unable to sleep. The situation was unraveling. Guerrero's dealings with the *Sunday Mirror*, the *Sunday Times* dragging its feet on the story—events had closed in on him over the last month. The sense of doom that had dogged him since he arrived in London shrouded him. He was alone and in trouble.

Several times during his stay in England, Vanunu had called John McKnight in Sydney to bring him up to date on developments. It was somehow reassuring to talk to McKnight and the others at St. John's, the one place where Vanunu had been comfortable. He could speak freely with his friends at the church, secure in the knowledge they understood and loved him. Now, as the clock moved toward 1 A.M., Vanunu picked up the telephone again and dialed Sydney. McKnight was not in, but Stephen Grey took the call.

"He seemed alone, worried, disturbed, disillusioned," Grey later remembered. "And he spoke about the damage that Oscar had done—not in detail, but just that Oscar had done them a great deal of damage and that he didn't feel safe anymore, that he was feeling very alone and that he wanted to be back here at St. John's with us."

After joining the minister in a brief prayer, Vanunu thanked Grey for his concern and said he hoped to see him soon.

"Be careful, Mordy," the minister replied.

At mid-morning, Vanunu called the newspaper office, looking for Andrew Neil or Robin Morgan. Neither could come to the telephone, and after a brief chat with Morgan's secretary, Vanunu asked to speak with Hounam. The reporter was pleased; Vanunu had promised to stay in regular contact and here was the first call.

Vanunu sounded calm and relaxed. He told Hounam he was leaving in a few hours, but wouldn't disclose his travel plans other than to say he expected to return by Thursday, October 2, when he was due to sign a contract to write a book about his experiences. He promised to called Hounam at home every morning and every night, and after apologizing for canceling the dinner plans, he said goodbye.

Shortly after 11 A.M., Vanunu checked out of the Mountbatten. Cindy was waiting outside the hotel. That morning, she had purchased a round-trip business class ticket for him from a Thomas Cook travel agency on Berkeley Street. "It's okay," she told him. "You can repay me when we get back."

Chapter 34

To the Mossad, Rome was a perfect location for the kidnapping. The operation had to be staged quickly, out of sight, and moved off foreign soil at the earliest possible moment. And it had to occur relatively close to Israel, a place where Vanunu could be quickly and unobtrusively whisked away. Those conditions ruled out several potential sites. The initial suggestion had been to talk Vanunu onto a ship off the British coast. But Admoni thought even that might be too close to London for Peres and the politicians, and Vanunu in any case was likely to be suspicious of an effort to isolate him. Other European capitals were also rejected because of possible political repercussions if the plan failed.

Rome, on the other hand, seemed ideal. Airport security was ridiculously lax, and the city was near a port. Italy was close enough to Israel to ease the return trip and far enough away to minimize Vanunu's fears. The political landscape was also favorable. Israeli intelligence had an excellent relationship with its Italian counterpart that dated back to their cooperation during the 1970s in the war against Italian terrorists. In addition, the domestic political picture was, as usual, fragmented. The current government, like most of Italy's postwar administrations, was in a fragile position. Even if something went wrong, Israel could weather an Italian storm. Within hours of Bentov's initial contact with Vanunu, six Mossad agents were dispatched from Tel Aviv to Rome, where they waited for Bentov to complete her part of the mission.

On Tuesday, September 30, Bentov and Vanunu hailed a taxi on Shaftesbury Road and headed for Heathrow airport. The driver was a Mossad operative, and two carloads of other agents followed close behind in case Vanunu had a change of heart. Arriving early,

Bentov and Vanunu checked in and ate lunch. About 3 P.M., they boarded British Airways Flight 504 to Rome, sitting next to each other in the sixth row of the business-class section of the jetliner.

As the plane droned on to Rome, Vanunu began to wonder about his decision. Peter Hounam's warnings echoed in his mind. But when he voiced his concerns, Vanunu noticed a change in Bentov's attitude. The soothing, compassionate woman with whom he had spent the last week was developing a hard edge. She impatiently dismissed his apprehensions, and testily demanded that he concentrate on enjoying his trip.

Flight 504 landed at Fiumicino airport at 6:38 P.M., 18 minutes behind schedule. With her arm around Vanunu, Bentov walked briskly out of the terminal and waved at a man slouched against a small red taxi. She gave the driver an address, and they headed onto the autostrada and into the city. The taxi careened along the highway at a high rate of speed, blending into the breakneck traffic flow. Bentov was tense and unresponsive when Vanunu tried to start a conversation. Vanunu began to panic. Something was terribly wrong, he thought as the taxi zipped past the houses and industrial complexes along the route to the city.

Dusk was falling as they entered Rome about thirty minutes later. The taxi passed the city gas works on Via Ostiense, then turned right and a few minutes later pulled up in front of a small apartment building in a working class neighborhood. Bentov paid the driver and waited while he slowly pulled away from the curb and drove off down the block. Without a word, she motioned at the building. Vanunu walked inside, with Bentov right behind him. They climbed the stairs to a second-floor apartment. Bentov drew a key from her shoulder bag and opened the door, standing aside to let Vanunu enter first.

The door slammed shut behind him. In an instant, he was attacked by two Mossad agents. Vanunu put up a brief struggle, but he was knocked to the floor on his stomach. As the agents knelt on either side of him, pinning his arms, Bentov took a syringe filled with a fast-acting sedative from a bag lying on a table. One of the agents pulled up Vanunu's right shirt sleeve and Bentov plunged the needle into his arm. In a matter of seconds, Vanunu was unconscious.

Bentov fell into a chair. For her, the operation was over. She had done her job.

The other agents draped Vanunu's arms around their necks and carried him downstairs to a sedan parked outside the front door. They shoved him into the back seat, got in the car, and raced off down the street.

Vanunu awoke a short while later and groggily looked around him. The auto was speeding down a highway, and through his drugged haze he could see two men sitting up front. When he made a sound, the man in the passenger seat turned and smiled at him.

"You are the Mossad," Vanunu said matter-of-factly.

"Yes, we are," the agent replied in English, with a smile. "You are going back to Israel."

For the rest of the drive, Vanunu lapsed in and out of consciousness When he was alert, the two agents engaged him in friendly conversation about subjects which Vanunu would not remember months later, and after about forty minutes, they reached the port of Fiumicino. About 8:45 P.M., just over two hours after his plane had landed, Vanunu was bundled aboard a small launch that cruised through the harbor to a larger ship lying offshore, an electronic-surveillance intelligence vessel. Vanunu was carried aboard and placed in a small windowless cabin, where he was manacled to a bed and fell into a deep sleep.

There was no celebration in the command center in Tel Aviv when the word of the successful conclusion to the operation was relayed from Rome. This was, after all, how it was supposed to work. A professional job by a professional intelligence agency. Still, Admoni was relieved as he accepted the quiet congratulations of several aides. He reached for a telephone to call Peres and give him the good news. It would be a nice present for the prime minister in his final weeks in office.

Chapter 35

Vanunu's story was now set to run Sunday, October 5, and the Insight reporters scurried to complete their final checks. Hounam flew to the United States to discuss the photographs and Vanunu's technical comments with Dr. Theodore Taylor, a scientist who played a key role in the development of U.S. nuclear weapons and once headed the Pentagon's atomic weapons test program. Max Prangnell returned to Israel to tie up a few loose strands, and Robin Morgan began piecing together the final story.

But now there were new questions about Vanunu. Despite his pledge to stay in touch, he had not been heard from since Tuesday morning. The Insight team began to wonder if Vanunu had actually been a Mossad operative after all, sent to plant the story about Israel's nuclear program. He's probably in hiding now, Morgan joked bitterly, living the good life courtesy of Israeli intelligence.

Hounam rejected the idea. Returning to London to find Vanunu still missing, Hounam was convinced the Israeli was in trouble. The only other possibility was that Vanunu simply tired of waiting and went to see his brother. Sitting in the newsroom on Thursday afternoon, October 2, the reporter tracked down Meir at his girlfriend's apartment in Boston, where it was about 7 A.M. After apologizing for the hour, he explained there was a problem regarding Mordechai. He had been helping the newspaper with a story, and had dropped out of sight.

"We can't seem to locate him. We don't know where he's gone off to," said Hounam, with forced nonchalance. "Have you by any chance heard from him?"

Mordechai wasn't expected until the end of the year, Meir said. The last he had heard, from Judy Zimmet, was that his brother was

in Australia. But Meir took Hounam's telephone number and promised to call if Mordechai turned up.

This is very strange, Meir told his girlfriend as he dressed. The
brothers were very close. If Motti was involved with a newspaper,
surely he would have contacted Meir to discuss what he was doing.

Meir had recently moved, and later that day he and his roommate
drove to his old apartment to see if any mail had arrived after he
left. Waiting for him was the letter Mordechai had written in the
Sydney airport. On the drive home, Meir read the letter several
times. "There is something I have to do, and I am going to do it."
Meir was worried. What in the world was Motti up to?

In the strangest of coincidences, Meir got an inkling that afternoon. A Jewish weekly newspaper had picked up the *Sunday Mirror*
story, and printed a short item about a "Professor Vanunu" who
claimed to have knowledge of Israel's nuclear program, but was
uncovered as an impostor by a London newspaper. "Well, here it
goes," Meir thought. "There's going to be a little bit of rough going
here."

But he was relieved. If this was what Motti had done, it would
certainly blow over. His "revelations" apparently amounted to
nothing. Motti must have felt he knew more than he really did, and
he was probably on his way to Boston right now.

For the next three days, Meir waited for a call from his brother.
At the Italian restaurant where he worked as a waiter, he spent his
idle moments staring out the front window, hoping to spot Motti
ambling down the street. Once or twice, he was certain he saw him
and started to call out, catching himself only after "Motti" turned
out to be a stranger.

Still, Meir wasn't overly concerned. Motti would turn up, soon,
chagrined but safe.

Vanunu's disappearance weighed heavily on the minds of the reporters and editors who crowded into Neil's office on Friday afternoon, October 3, for one last debate about whether to publish. It
was an acrimonious meeting, with several staff members urging
another postponement because of the renewed doubts about

Vanunu's true identity. The disappearance of their source threw into question everything he had told the newspaper, they contended. To publish now, without knowing where Vanunu was, would be an extraordinary gamble.

Hounam was incensed by the last-minute objections. Convinced the delay in publication had played a part in Vanunu's disappearance, Hounam forcefully argued that there was absolutely no reason why the paper should wait any longer. All the checks had been made, and everything in the story had been verified. The newspaper had the photographs, the experts' reaction, the response from Israel—everything they needed. The notable exception was Vanunu himself, Hounam admitted. But the reporter speculated that Vanunu had purposely gone into hiding "to provoke us into action in some sort of twisted way." Perhaps he planned to surface only after his story had been published.

Neil was now confident the story was true, but the editor still had qualms. Should the newspaper wait to publish until Vanunu was in hand so it could protect him when the story broke? "If he's just disappeared with a girl for a few days and he's going to resurface, and we go with the story, are we going to put him at risk?" Neil asked. "Should we go while we don't know where he is?"

As the meeting stretched into a second hour, two factors tipped the scales. In its zeal to help the *Sunday Mirror* knock down Guerrero's claim that he had been working with the father of Israel's bomb program, the government of Israel had pointed out that Vanunu was only a control-room technician at Dimona. To the *Sunday Mirror*, that made Vanunu a fraud. But the *Sunday Times* had believed all along that Vanunu was only a technician. The embassy's "no comment" to the question of whether Vanunu worked at Dimona bothered the Insight team, but by helping the *Sunday Mirror*, Israel had indirectly confirmed Vanunu's identity.

The editors' meeting with Peres—particularly the absence of any denial by the prime minister of the truth of the impending disclosures—also seemed to authenticate Vanunu's account. After the session, a reporter for the Israeli newspaper Hadashot called the *Sunday Times* and passed along the information, hoping for some advance word on the newspaper's exclusive. To the *Sunday Times*, Peres' attempts to limit news coverage in Israel appeared to be a tacit admission that the story outlined to the embassy and to Peres' top aides was accurate.

After ninety minutes, Neil signaled an end to the conference. He wanted one more chance to read over the stories. The Dimona articles would be readied for publication on Sunday, but replacement pages would also be prepared in case a postponement was ordered. "Let's all think about it overnight, and reconvene tomorrow morning," he told his staff.

A smaller group of reporters and editors met in Neil's office the next day. The editor had a few final questions, and after walking through the story one more time, he fell silent for a moment.

"Right," Neil said at last. "Let's go with it."

PART IV

Playing the
Diplomatic Game

Chapter 36

Quite a story, a once-in-a-career shot, Peter Hounam thought when he saw the October 5, 1986, edition of his newspaper, and it would be difficult to disagree with him.

"Revealed: the secrets of Israel's nuclear arsenal," screamed the stark headline that spanned all eight columns of a front page dominated by two large black-and-white photographs—one a closeup shot of the dome of the Dimona reactor, the other a picture of the Machon 2 underground control room identified by a caption as "the nerve centre of the bomb factory."

"The secrets of a subterranean factory engaged in the manufacture of Israeli nuclear weapons have been uncovered by the *Sunday Times* Insight team," the story began.

"Hidden beneath the Negev desert, the factory has been producing atomic warheads for the last twenty years. Now it has almost certainly begun manufacturing thermonuclear weapons, with yields big enough to destroy entire cities."

Most of Page One was given over to a story identifying Vanunu as the source for the revelations, which the *Sunday Times* said proved Israel now possessed the world's sixth most powerful nuclear arsenal, built in secret over more than two decades. The story cited scientists Taylor and Barnaby as having confirmed the evidence provided by Vanunu. Rather than the small, antiquated atomic arsenal it had long been rumored to possess, the *Sunday Times* reported, Israel had stockpiled as many as 200 sophisticated nuclear weapons, and had the technology required to build neutron bombs, which emit radiation that kills people but leaves buildings standing. Israel also held the means of landing the knockout punch—a fleet of U.S.-built F-16 warplanes and a homegrown missile, the Jericho, which

187

could deliver warheads within a range of 400 miles to targets in Syria, Iraq, Egypt, Saudi Arabia, Iran and the Soviet Union.

"There should no longer be any doubt that Israel is, and for at least a decade has been, a fully-fledged nuclear weapons state," Taylor told the newspaper. "The Israeli nuclear weapons program is considerably more advanced than indicated by any previous report or conjectures of which I am aware."

Spilling inside onto the second and third pages under the headline, "Inside Dimona, Israel's nuclear bomb factory," the story detailed the operations at Dimona, Vanunu's background, and the history of Israel's nuclear involvement. Accompanying the report were three more photographs—showing a control panel, part of a nuclear bomb apparently under construction, and the outside of the Dimona complex—as well as a diagram, which explained the functions of the six underground levels of Machon 2. Below the fold, under a smaller headline reading, "How the experts were convinced," the *Sunday Times* recounted the background of Vanunu's involvement with the newspaper, and how the Insight team had grappled with Guerrero before finally confirming Vanunu's tale.

Only near the end of the twenty-nine paragraph main story did the newspaper mention Vanunu might not be available for interviews. Concerned about his safety, the story said, Vanunu "went to ground" after the *Sunday Mirror* published its expose of Guerrero.

But to the Insight team, that was almost beside the point. Morgan was strutting proud. The *Sunday Times* had a reputation for investigative journalism, but Vanunu—this was the topper. Hugely significant, he told his colleagues, matched in impact only by the John Profumo scandal in the 1960s, a sex-and-spies uproar that rattled the British government.

Morgan's judgment, however, was not shared by the rest of the world. The *Sunday Times* expose was greeted with a collective yawn at home. The British government ducked comment on the issue, and Fleet Street was singularly unenthusiastic. Anti-Murdoch sentiment, the lingering specter of the Hitler diaries, and Vanunu's absence (the *Sunday Mirror* had reported Vanunu was "in fear of his life" and being hunted in Britain by the Mossad) led virtually all of Britain's national dailies and the Press Association news agency to ignore the scoop. Peter Hounam, who spent Sunday and Monday passing out copies of the Dimona photographs and sitting for a few interviews in an effort to draw attention to the story, was dumbstruck by the lack of interest.

Even among the *Sunday Times* staff there was grumbling that too much space had been devoted to the story. "The feeling was, where was the news?" one former reporter recalled. "Everybody went out for a drink and lamented how far the quality of the Insight team had fallen."

Instead of kudos, Neil was informed that Murdoch was not happy that the newspaper's only source was missing.

The picture was much the same in the United States, where the *Sunday Times* had expected enormous interest. The *New York Times* and the *Washington Post* printed short accounts, but only a few other papers around the country picked up cursory news agency reports out of London. And as the Israelis had hoped, the Reagan administration's reaction was measured. Asked about the report at his Monday briefing, State Department spokesman Charles Redman preferred to gently chide Israel for not permitting inspections of Dimona and the country's smaller reactor near Tel Aviv. The United States "is concerned about the existence of unsafeguarded nuclear facilities in Israel," Redman said. "We believe regional security would be enhanced if all states in the region would adhere to the Nuclear Non-Proliferation Treaty ... We urge Israel to accept comprehensive safeguards."

In Israel, the *Sunday Times* stories predictably provoked a much sharper response. As Peres had requested, Israeli newspapers summarized the exclusive without comment. Still, the news topped radio and television broadcasts all day Sunday, and made the Monday front pages of the Jerusalem Post and the seven Hebrew-language dailies, marking the first time stories about Israel's nuclear capability had appeared in the Hebrew-language press.

Censorship prevented anything more, however. The military excised references in the leftist newspaper *Al Hamishmar* to reports in past years about Israel's nuclear program, and an editorial set to run in another newspaper was banned—a measure that had been rarely imposed against Israeli newspapers since the early 1950s.

The government quickly closed ranks. Only one parliament member bothered to address the issue—and then only in the context of how much information the media should be permitted to publish or broadcast. No one else in the Knesset, Israel's parliament, expressed any interest in a debate on the matter, and Peres waved off expressions of concern from Cabinet ministers at their weekly Sunday meeting, saying the newspaper stories were of no import.

"We are used to these sensational publications," Peres told reporters with a bored air at a public appearance later in the day. "We never comment on it. One thing I can say and that is that the policies of Israel have not changed. Israel will never be the first to introduce nuclear weapons to the Middle East."

Communications Minister Amnon Rubenstein charged Vanunu had invented the story in revenge for his dismissal. "Yes, I'm sure that there's no truth to it," Rubenstein assured the country.

The public mostly shrugged. Most Israelis had long assumed their country had nuclear weapons; the *Sunday Times* had simply provided more details. No one, though, really wanted to know that much about it. Some Israelis even thought Vanunu had done Israel a favor—but certainly not the one he had planned. "The point of nuclear deterrents is that the other side should know that you have nuclear bombs in order not to have to use them," one Hebrew University analyst noted. "Let the Arabs know, and even better that it is not us who tells, but it comes in a roundabout way. Like through a report in the *Sunday Times*."

Arab leaders, predictably embarrassed by the obvious inference that its nuclear capability made Israel virtually unbeatable on the battlefield, were mostly mum. But an authoritative daily newspaper in Saudi Arabia did take notice of the new reality, pointing out that "any Arab army thinking of going to war with Israel in the future will have to take into account the fact that its enemy is able to use nuclear weapons against it." And a leading Arab analyst predicted the revelations would be a "major factor" in a decision about future conflicts. "Before the *Sunday Times* article, there had been speculation about Israel's nuclear capability, but no documentation," he said. "The material about Machon 2 and the separation plant is all new."

The Arab world had evidently received the message.

Judy Zimmet was on her way to Northeastern University in Boston for her first day of computer classes when a girlfriend asked if she had heard about the Israeli who had given his country's nuclear secrets to a newspaper in London. Images flashed through Zimmet's horrified mind—Motti at leftist rallies, Motti railing against the Israeli government, Motti disgustedly pointing out the road to Dimona and wondering why the Israeli people weren't told about the plant. The girlfriend couldn't remember the man's name, so at her first break, Zimmet raced to the library to look at the newspapers. She found nothing, but decided to call Meir. Vanunu's brother had heard about the *Sunday Times* account. Yes, he said gruffly, Motti gave a story to the newspaper and no one knows where he is. Meir resisted her efforts to pump him for more details.

Away from the romantic allure of Israel and after their lengthy separation, Zimmet was no longer sure what more she wanted out of the relationship. But she had been looking forward to seeing Motti again. Now she wondered if she ever would.

When Meir Vanunu actually read the story a few days later, it didn't take him long to decide his brother had done something extremely important. "Motti has touched history today," he told his roommate. "I'm not sure people are going to understand this right now. It might take a few years before they realize how important this was. But he's really carved himself a niche. He's affected history."

In Israel, however, the rest of the family had little time to ponder Vanunu's impact on history. Far from engaging in the debate Vanunu had wanted, Israelis instead turned on the man who made the revelations, quickly concluding that he was simply a traitor. At least 111 other families in the Negev region shared the Vanunu name, under three different spellings, and some petitioned the courts for permission to change their names to avoid any association with the Dimona turncoat.

Mordechai's family paid a heavy price. After enduring a day of taunts like, "Your son is an Arab," Solomon Vanunu shuttered his stall in the Beersheba market and kept it closed for most of the next month. He and his wife closeted themselves in their apartment almost as if they were in mourning. Solomon was shunned at the synagogue, ignored by his neighbors. One day, he left the house to buy some vegetables, and was recognized as he gave a bag filled with tomatoes to the sales clerk to be weighed.

"Ah, you're the father of that traitor, Vanunu," the clerk snarled. With that, he dumped the tomatoes out of the bag, filled it with garbage and handed it to the devastated old man.

The city government installed a security door in the Vanunus' apartment building in an attempt to ward off jeering neighbors, and a social worker was sent to help the family handle their unwanted moment in the harsh glare of the spotlight.

Their world had fallen apart. And worst of all, they could not ask their son to explain why he did it. No one seemed to know where he was.

The voyage home took a week. The two agents stayed with Vanunu throughout the trip, keeping him in a semi-conscious state by drugging his food and water. Once, Vanunu awoke to hear them talking in accented English about whether he would be killed.

On the morning of October 7, the ship docked at Haifa. Vanunu, in leg and wrist irons, was helped down the gangplank by his two guards, placed in a waiting car and driven to Gadera prison near Tel Aviv, where he was thrown in a cell with no light and only a mattress on the floor.

The Mossad, whose secret emigration network had helped the Vanunus flee Morocco two decades earlier, had brought Mordechai Vanunu home again.

Two days later, the door to Vanunu's cell opened and a uniformed police lieutenant colonel walked in. Speaking in a terse monotone, he officially informed Vanunu that he was under arrest and would be held for trial. The officer asked if Vanunu had anything to say. Vanunu shook his head silently. As the policeman left, a man in civilian clothes entered the cell, carrying a copy of the October 5 edition of the *Sunday Times*. He held it in front of Vanunu's face long enough for the prisoner to see the large black headline: "Revealed: the secrets of Israel's nuclear arsenal." After a few seconds, the man pulled the newspaper away and tucked it under his arm. "There," he said, staring angrily at Vanunu, "see what you've done."

Chapter 37

Hounam had hoped Vanunu would contact the *Sunday Times* once the newspaper published his story. When no message was forthcoming, the reporter was convinced something terribly wrong had befallen the young Israeli.

The Insight team gathered in Morgan's office to discuss its next step. There was still a considerable difference of opinion about Vanunu's whereabouts. A few people were sure he was a Mossad agent who had now gone underground after completing his mission, while others thought he was in Amsterdam or somewhere else on the Continent with a girl, and would return in due course.

Hounam contended Vanunu had run afoul of somebody, most likely the Israelis. As he reviewed the past few weeks, the reporter realized there had been hints the Mossad was on Vanunu's tail, like the suspicious television camera crew outside the gates of the Wapping complex. And shortly after he returned from Australia, Hounam had spotted a car crawling past his house early one morning. The driver was peering up at the building through a window that was rolled down, despite the chilly temperature. The incident had spooked Hounam so much that he refused to discuss the Vanunu story on his home telephone for fear it was bugged. There was no proof the Mossad had been lurking in the wings, but Vanunu's disappearance certainly suggested it.

The reporter wanted to contact British authorities with an eye toward launching an investigation. Morgan agreed, and Hounam telephoned Scotland Yard and reported Vanunu as a missing person.

Detective Inspector David Wood was assigned to the case and immediately began making inquiries. There wasn't much to go on. The staff of the Mountbatten Hotel identified a photograph of

Vanunu as the "Mr. Forsty" who had checked out on the morning of September 30, but there was no trace of him beyond that. There was also no record of Vanunu entering or leaving England; since authorities kept only random entry and exit records, however, that proved nothing.

British intelligence also wasn't any help, claiming it had never heard of the missing man. And officials at the Israeli Embassy politely but firmly declined to respond to any inquiries about Mordechai Vanunu.

The Israeli connection provided one possible lead. In July 1984 customs officers at Stansted airport outside London had become suspicious about two large wooden shipping crates being sent home by Nigerian Embassy officials. Ignoring Nigerian claims of diplomatic immunity, the customs officers opened the crates for inspection. In one they discovered Umaru Dikko, a former senior Nigerian government minister wanted for trial in Lagos following a coup. Dikko had been drugged into unconsciousness by a white man who was also inside the crate, holding an intravenous drip. Two other white men were discovered in the second crate, and all three whites were found to be Israelis, who claimed they had been acting on the orders of the Mossad. The Israeli government denied the charges, and the three were jailed, but the Dikko case enraged British officials who suspected the operation was part of Israel's determined campaign to strengthen ties with black African nations. The Thatcher government suspended diplomatic relations with Nigeria for violating British law.

The detectives investigating the Vanunu case remembered Dikko when a check of airport freight offices turned up records indicating a Tel Aviv-bound coffin had been placed aboard a jetliner at Heathrow airport by someone with ties to the London embassy. Embassy officials assured police the body in the coffin was not Vanunu's, but rebuffed further efforts by authorities to confirm the claim. After a few days, the police inquiry sputtered out.

The day after Hounam filed his missing-person report, a distraught Judy Zimmet turned up in the *Sunday Times* offices desperate for information about Vanunu's disappearance. She was joined a day later by John McKnight, who had persuaded his congregation to send him on a search for their missing parishioner. McKnight and Zimmet were the last people the Insight team wanted to see. The journalists had nothing to tell them. Zimmet was put up in Max Prangnell's apartment for a few days while the staff tried to convince her to return home. After a week of fruitless visits to the police and under pressure from the newspaper, she flew back to Boston. McKnight decided to remain in London a while longer.

The *Sunday Times* ran three more Vanunu stories the following week. On Page One was an account of an interview with the former head of France's nuclear weapons program who acknowledged his country had secretly supplied Israel with bomb-making technology thirty years earlier. Inside, on the third page, there was a photograph of Vanunu with the word, "Missing," stripped diagonally across the lower right-hand corner, and a story headlined, "Disappeared: the man who revealed Israel's nuclear-bomb secrets." The story included a photograph of McKnight, who told the newspaper, "If he wants to contact me, I'm here."

On page 12, the *Sunday Times* ran a lengthy account of worldwide reaction to their week-old exclusive, including an unsuccessful call by several Arab delegations to the United Nations for a General Assembly debate on the issue of Israel's nuclear program. The story also reflected some of the bitterness at the *Sunday Times* over the way the expose had been treated at home. "Fleet Street largely ignored it," the newspaper charged, "since the only way the story could be followed up (given that the Israeli government did not attempt to discredit it) was to give the *Sunday Times* full credit for a major international scoop."

With anti-Murdoch sentiment still running at a fever pitch, the staff hadn't been surprised, Morgan recalled later. Instead, the newspaper was mostly ashamed of its competitors.

"Ashamed of the British press. Ashamed of the British press for allowing commercial considerations to get in the way of their duty to the reader," Morgan said.

The trio of stories on October 12 largely emptied the *Sunday Ti-*

mes's files, and the staff slowly moved on to other matters. Hounam took a short vacation in the United States, then spent a week in Washington, D.C., working on another story. Morgan turned his attention to several long-delayed features, and the rest of the Insight team slipped back into the lethargy that had prevailed in the days before Mordechai Vanunu walked into the newsroom.

The police investigation had stalled, Vanunu was still missing, and Israel was not deigning to comment on the revelations. There wasn't much more the newspaper could do. At least not until the rumors started flying.

Chapter 38

The *Sunday Times* exclusive might have been largely ignored by much of the world media, but the disappearance of the newspaper's prime source was another matter altogether. This had a whiff of intrigue about it. Nuclear secrets and a missing person could only add up to one thing: a spy story. And reporters, like their readers, can't get enough of spy stories, especially when they involve Israel.

The rumor mill quickly cranked up into overdrive. Everyone had a theory. Vanunu was dead, killed by Israeli intelligence in a faked auto accident. Vanunu was in hiding, eluding the Mossad while he waited for the story to die down. Vanunu was a Mossad agent who planted the story and was now undergoing plastic surgery to alter his appearance.

Contributing to the confusion was the Mossad. With Vanunu safely behind bars, the agency had scurried to cover its tracks. All operations in Britain were temporarily shut down to make sure British investigators looking into the *Sunday Times'* missing-persons report did not accidentally stumble on an Israeli link to Vanunu's capture. The agents involved in the kidnapping rushed back to Israel, and Bentov flew to the United States to attend her brother's wedding. And when word of Vanunu's return began to leak, the Mossad mounted a disinformation campaign, floating bogus stories about the operation in the news media to make sure Britain was not implicated. In one instance, the agency put out the word that Vanunu had been lured aboard a yacht off the French coast, then captured by Israeli agents. The tale made its way into *Newsweek* in late October, a short item in the magazine's Periscope section under the headline "A Mossad Caper":

It could be the plot for Le Carre's next novel. According to officials close to the Israeli intelligence community, agents of its Mossad secret service ran a sophisticated land-sea operation to capture Mordechai Vanunu, a former nuclear technician who was the source for recent stories that Israel has stockpiled atomic weapons. The case had been called Israel's worst security lapse: though he made no secret of his Palestinian sympathies, Vanunu, 31, was allowed to leave the country after being laid off from his job at Israel's Dimona atomic facility last November. From a hiding place in Australia, he provided data about Dimona to the *Sunday Times* of London. Flow to London for further debriefing, he vanished.

As Israeli sources tell it, when Mossad got wind of Vanunu's whereabouts, they arranged for a woman friend to lure him on a trip through Europe. On the Mediterranean, he was persuaded to board a yacht and—once in international waters—was arrested by the crew of Mossad agents and returned to Israel.

Vanunu now faces a closed-door trial on charges of espionage and perhaps treason—and possibly a life sentence—according to Israeli sources. But skeptics in Europe and the Mideast suspect the leak was actually orchestrated by the Mossad as a warning to hostile Islamic nations, particularly Syria and Iran, that Israel's long-suspected nuclear capabilities are real. In that case Vanunu's case could quietly be dropped.

The Israeli government was, as always, officially mum. A prisons spokesman said Vanunu was not being held "in a prisons service jail." The Mossad and Shin Bet, which operates its own jail and commands wings in at least two others, maintained their usual silence. "We do not know anything about this matter," said a government spokesman.

But despite the denials, the *Sunday Times* rapidly came to the conclusion that Vanunu had somehow wound up back home, and dispatched reporter Rowena Webster to Tel Aviv to search for him. It would be embarrassing to discover that Vanunu was an Israeli agent, but learning about it from another newspaper or magazine would be humiliating. If the hunt was on, the *Sunday Times* had to be in the pack.

Webster, stripsearched by airport guards on her arrival and then stonewalled by government officials, came up with nothing. The newspaper told her to hire a lawyer, hoping an attorney with connections inside the Israeli legal system could pry loose some answers. Get the best, Webster was told, and she went out and asked around and came up with Amnon Zichroni.

At fifty-one, Zichroni was a lawyer between reputations. Once, he had been Israel's best-known civil rights attorney, with a client list made up primarily of Palestinians and left-wing Israelis. But to be a civil rights lawyer in Israel is to be on intimate terms with defeat. Long ago, the country decided its security was more important than individual liberties, and the mavericks who challenged that concept almost always lost. For Zichroni, the mission became madness.

In a way, he reflected his country. Once upon a time, when Israel was young and believed in magic, Amnon Zichroni lived for lost causes. But Israel was turning forty now, growing old and cynical, more interested in money than miracles, and Zichroni wanted his share. There were still a few civil rights cases, mostly for old clients. But more and more, Zichroni was squeezing his ballooning body into expensive suits, planting a Cuban cigar between his lips, and hopping a plane to some foreign capital to negotiate a deal for his flourishing roster of corporate clients. He threw himself into the new work with the zeal of a convert—marathon days, late nights, early mornings, Saturdays, Sundays and holidays, so many hours that his wife finally moved her office nearer to his so they could see more of each other.

The transformation was so complete that a magazine profile in March 1985 that touched on Zichroni's old reputation as "the Maginot Line of democracy in Israel" also ran a full-page, closeup photograph of the lawyer's cigar-adorned face with a caption identifying him as Israel's answer to Mario Puzo, the author of *The Godfather*.

Zichroni could chuckle over his new image. But he ruefully admitted that he missed the flush of publicity his civil rights work generated. If there was something Zichroni loved more than his fine cognac and his refrigerator full of Havanas, it was his picture in the newspaper.

Zichroni had his first taste of publicity at age nineteen when he spent seven months in an army prison for refusing to carry a gun. It ws not an attempt to evade military service; Zichroni would eventually rise to the rank of lieutenant in the army reserves, serving in the "Job unit," assigned to the grim task of reporting soldiers' deaths to their relatives. But his unwillingness to accept a combat assignment was an almost inconceivable act of conscience in a country where men and women accept without question the need for compulsory military service and a lifetime of annual reserve duty. It was even more courageous—and newsworthy—in the mid-1950s when the military, having saved the fledgling nation from annihilation and pledging to do it again, was in the process of becoming the most revered institution in the Jewish state.

The lawyer turned to leftist politics as a young man, becoming a leader of a small party headed by his good friend Uri Avneri, and once almost won election to the Knesset. Even without a parliament seat, he was highly visible, calling for talks with the Palestine Liberation Organization, defending friends and colleagues who defied government bans and met with PLO representatives, and warding off right-wing attacks on a newspaper run by Avneri.

The corporate world, though, was different. Most of his clients preferred to operate in the dark. Firms like the company forging business ties to South African-backed Botswana didn't want the media taking notes as they made their moves.

Now, Rowena Webster walked into Zichroni's cluttered, book-lined office on a quiet, shaded side street in central Tel Aviv and offered him an opportunity to make more headlines. The *Sunday Times* wanted him to find out if Vanunu was back in Israel and, if need be, go to court to force the government to disclose his whereabouts. "Would you be interested in handling this?" Webster asked.

Would I? thought Zichroni. Of course I would.

There was just one problem, something he couldn't share with the reporter. Amnon Zichroni was already representing someone in the case. His client's name was Mordechai Vanunu.

Chapter 39

In mid-October, Zichroni had received a telephone call from the attorney general's office. We have something important to discuss with you, the voice on the line said. Can you come around to the office?

Few attorneys in Israel are permitted to represent defendants charged with security offenses. The security services, which would prefer to avoid the trial process altogether, hold veto power over lawyers who handle cases involving state secrets and classified material. When the authorities decide to let a prisoner consult an attorney, sometimes weeks after his arrest, the suspect is given a list of acceptable lawyers from which to choose.

Zichroni's meeting with the attorney general was short. Mordechai Vanunu is in jail, he was informed. He needs a lawyer and he's asked for you. Zichroni quickly agreed to take the case.

A day later, he drove down to Gadera prison, a Shin Bet facility about twenty miles south of Tel Aviv, to meet his new client, who explained he had selected Zichroni because of the lawyer's reputation for taking political cases.

Conversant with the outline of the case, Zichroni didn't press Vanunu for details, and instead used the two-hour meeting to size up the prisoner. Vanunu expressed himself well, seemed extremely intelligent and was aware of the gravity of his situation. Despite his confinement, he appeared to be bearing up emotionally.

But there was little the attorney could immediately do to help Vanunu. Under his secrecy agreement with the government, Zichroni was prohibited from talking about the case with even the associates in his law office, and sitting on the country's biggest secret gnawed at him. One afternoon his friend Avneri had brought up the subject of Vanunu and, as he ran through the rumors and the speculation absorbing the public, Zichroni could only sit quietly and listen. He had the answers, but he couldn't tell anyone. It was a killer. Unless the government decided to disclose that Vanunu had been arrested, Zichroni knew his hands were tied.

And now, sitting in his office in Tel Aviv just a few weeks later, Rowena Webster was asking for his help. The prospect of adding a well-heeled client like the *Sunday Times* pleased Zichroni. The fee in the Vanunu case would be high, perhaps as much as $40,000, and the Vanunu family didn't have that kind of money. What was so wrong about the *Sunday Times* helping out a little?

It would be a strange situation, Zichroni realized, representing one client who wanted to know where another client was, and not being able to say. But, after all, he was not a volunteer.

Gazing dolefully at her through heavy, hooded eyes, Zichroni assured the reporter that he would do what he could to find Vanunu.

Vanunu's father also knew of his son's arrest. The Shin Bet had informed Solomon and Albert, the oldest son, but ordered them not to reveal the information to anyone else, even other family members, under threat of prison. The enforced blackout led to several days of grief for Meir Vanunu. In the days following publication of the *Sunday Times* story, Meir was on the telephone to Israel several times a day, running up bills totaling hundreds of dollars, trying to find out what his family might have heard about Motti. He received some strange signals from his father. Solomon, knowing his telephone was likely tapped but desperate to let Meir know that Motti was in prison, fell back on obscure Biblical references to send his message.

The effort backfired horribly. After several references that only mystified his relentlessly secular son, Solomon paraphrased one Biblical passage to tell Meir, "Mordechai is not in this world anymore." Albert then took the telephone to say, "Whatever I tell you about this, there is nothing to do anymore."

Meir was devastated. His father and brother were telling him Motti was dead. For two days, he lived in grief, trying to come to terms with the loss of his brother, his closest friend. During his next conversation with the family, Meir abruptly cut off a discussion of Vanunu's case. "Whatever happens now, what's the difference? Our brother is gone. He is dead."

"What are you talking about?" Albert asked apprehensively, worried that Meir had received some new information.

"What do you mean? Motti is dead," Meir replied.

"Dead?" Albert shouted in alarm. "Who said he's dead?"

The confusion was quickly cleared up when Albert blurted out that their brother was in prison in Israel. It was a huge relief, but Meir was also angry that Israeli laws had prevented his family from even telling him that Motti was alive.

Chapter 40

The rumors also convinced McKnight, who had been cooling his heels in London, to fly to Israel in late October. The story had shifted, and the minister was determined to stay near the center of the action. He arrived in Jerusalem on October 23, telling reporters, "Sometimes a shepherd has to leave his flock and look for one sheep that got lost."

For the media, starved for anyone to comment publicly on the case, the minister's visit was a godsend, and he was rewarded with packed houses at news conferences. It was a star turn for the cleric from Sydney. Everywhere he went, reporters followed. Everything he said was written down and recorded. He was clearly enjoying himself.

McKnight's first move, following an interview on state-run Israel Radio, was to contact the prime minister's office. But Shamir, who had replaced Peres a few days earlier under the government rotation agreement, instructed his aides not to meet with McKnight. An appointment, the reverend was told, would be useless because Israel "knows nothing about the matter."

Shut out of official circles, McKnight fell back on the media. He was staying at a YMCA on Nablus Road in Arab east Jerusalem when he was introduced to Israel Shahak, an Israeli human-rights activist. Shahak was taken aback by the Australian cleric's approach.

"He wasn't interested in me as a human rights expert, but as an expert in the Hebrew press," Shahak said. "I told him what was reported in the papers. On the basis of what was published, I told him that I was convinced Vanunu was in Israel."

McKnight pressed for more information. What would be Israel's legal justification for handling the case in this manner? Do priests have special status in Israel? What could Shahak tell him about Israel's nuclear program?

Neither a lawyer nor a nuclear scientist, Shahak told McKnight what he had read in the papers and passed along the latest rumors. Several Israeli journalists claimed to have seen court documents indicating Vanunu had appeared before a judge in secret. They had been prevented from reporting the news by censorship regulations, but that had not stopped them from freely discussing the forbidden story, and the news had filtered out.

Shahak stressed the shaky nature of much of what he had related, and urged McKnight to see the Israeli attorney general and pay a visit to Gershon Shocken, the well-connected editor of the respected daily newspaper *Ha'aretz*, if he really wanted to learn the truth of the matter. The minister did neither. But the next day, armed with Shahak's reprise of various rumors and newspaper accounts, McKnight held court at a crowded news conference at the American Colony Hotel in east Jerusalem.

Vanunu, he announced, had been brought back to Israel against his will and was now in jail. McKnight said he had learned that Vanunu had appeared before a judge in a secret hearing a few days earlier and had been remanded in custody for fifteen more days.

"We have solid information that he is here in Israel," McKnight said. "I do not believe he would have left England on his own free will."

Cross-examined by skeptical reporters, McKnight would say only that the information had come from a "number of sources" whom he refused to identify, explaining, "I have made certain commitments to sources to protect their identities.

Basking in the attention, McKnight talked at length about his friendship with Vanunu, the Israeli's conversion to Christianity, and his decision to make public the secrets of Dimona—an action that he contended was motivated by "very good and moral reasons."

The minister's news conference triggered a most extraordinary reaction from the government. The military censor had been working overtime to keep a lid on reports about the Vanunu case. Under

Israeli law, Israeli journalists and foreign correspondents alike are required to submit stories dealing with security matters to the office of the chief censor. The subjects on the censor's list are supposed to be limited to matters of military significance, but in a country that remains in a technical state of war with all but one Arab country, even seemingly routine issues such as road construction face the censor's scissors. In all, sixty-nine subjects are deemed censorable.

Everything about the Vanunu affair obviously fell under the censor's sweeping purview, and nothing more so than McKnight's remarks about Vanunu's activities and his current whereabouts.

But surprisingly, the government permitted accounts of the news conference to appear in newspapers and on television in Israel and abroad. Authorities realized how Israelis would react to the idea of being lectured by a Christian minister defending an Israeli he had wooed from Judaism and talked into spilling his country's secrets—and all from a podium at the American Colony Hotel, which over the years had acquired a reputation among many Israelis as a sort of unofficial Palestinian headquarters.

"We should have paid for his trip," one senior official joked.

The government calculated correctly. Israelis were considerably less than pleased with McKnight's campaign. If anything, the minister's presence deepened the antipathy toward Vanunu. Even without his white collar and black cleric's suit, abandoned in favor of a "civilian" jacket and tie, McKnight was a constant, painful reminder of Vanunu's decision to renounce Judaism and convert to Christianity. At every opportunity, he portrayed his "friend" as a good and decent man whose action—betrayal, most Israelis preferred to call it—was motivated by Christian ideals.

The reaction was scathing. A columnist for *Ha'aretz* ridiculed McKnight's attempts to justify Vanunu's decision as an act of faith. "Reverend McKnight has already piously announced that in his prima facie treason and in his handing over atomic secrets, Vanunu acted as a good Christian," the columnist wrote. "Did Vanunu have an earlier revelation, star-over-Bethlehem-like, which heralded his future conversion to Christianity and therefore led him to secretly photograph the nuclear reactor at Dimona, as claimed by the *Sunday Times*?

"This apparently is an innovation in Christian dogma, which over the past 2,000 years has yet to find anything good to say about Judas Iscariot."

By the time McKnight wound up his weeklong visit and returned to Sydney, amid rumors his trip had been financed by anti-Israeli political groups or by the *Sunday Times* to keep the story alive, the government had planted an important seed: Vanunu is no longer one of us.

As so often seems to happen in the Middle East, the campaign against Vanunu was also framed by tragedy. In the Old City of Jerusalem on October 15, several hand grenades were tossed into a crowd of army recruits and their families at an induction ceremony at the Western Wall, the holiest site in Judaism. The father of a soldier died and seventy other people were wounded in the attack, which authorities blamed on Palestinian terrorists. As they mourned the dead and raged against the Arabs who threatened their survival, few Israelis could forget Vanunu, the Israeli who had told the world about his country's most important weapons.

In a column entitled "Vanunu and the Judas Syndrome," which neatly summed up the two complementary strands of anti-Vanunu sentiment, *Ha'aretz* journalist Dan Margalit said Israel had to find Vanunu and punish him.

"In many democracies, Vanunu would have ended up as a corpse dumped on his father's doorstep. It can be supposed that in Israel, if Vanunu is captured, the affair will end in the courtroom, and if he is convicted—in prison. Another aspect which is perfectly clear is that whoever crosses the line in this way, whether he speaks lies or tells the truth, must not be allowed to get off without heavy punishment."

"If Israel has not yet suctioned Vanunu back to this country, the government should be asked why he is still free, and if Vanunu is already in hand the government should in no way be hampered," Margalit contended.

Chapter 41

The editors' committee decision to abide by Peres' request had effectively limited coverage of the Vanunu case in the Israeli press, but foreign correspondents ignored the restraints. The telephone in the office of Avi Pazner, Yitzhak Shamir's media advisor, never seemed to stop ringing. One particularly persistent British reporter called Pazner at home one night in mid-November and demanded information about Vanunu's capture.

"I cannot discuss this matter," Pazner pleaded.

"I need information," the reporter insisted. "If you are afraid to talk, I'm ready to use your remarks as background, not for attribution. If you can't talk from the house, I'll come to your office."

Pazner was unswayed. "I don't want you to come to my office," he said firmly. "I have nothing to tell you."

The reporter threatened to approach Pazner every morning when he arrived at work.

"You won't get me. I go in by car," the aide warned.

"I'll scream when I see you," the reporter retorted, and for the next four days she stood outside the office, shouting, "Mr. Pazner, I have a question—where is Mordechai? Will he be brought to trial?" before finally abandoning the effort.

Prime Minister Shamir was not about to be bullied into releasing any information about Vanunu. He complained to aides that the unchecked flood of foreign news reports regarding Vanunu had placed Israel in an untenable position. The prime minister was particularly incensed by what he considered blatant violations of Israeli censorship laws by foreign correspondents, frequently in collusion with Israeli journalists. Much of the information about the Vanunu case followed a route traced long ago as a means of circumventing the country's press restrictions. Israeli officials, including senior ministers or their top aides, leaked sensitive information to Israeli reporters, who tipped off foreign correspondents. Once the information appeared in print or on the air abroad, the Israelis reported it, citing the foreign news accounts as their sources.

Unswayed by the constant drip of the leaks, Shamir staunchly advocated stonewalling the entire matter. "He will be tried in secret and sentenced in secret. No one will know for sure where he is," Shamir told one aide. "The press will eventually get tired and forget about it."

There was certainly no legal reason why Israel had to say anything. Under Israel's strict security and espionage laws, a defendant can be held indefinitely and tried and sentenced in secrecy if the defense minister determines that state security is at stake. Israel's brief history is rich with such proceedings. In 1957, Mossad agent Mordecai Kedar was ordered home from Paris for questioning by his superiors about the murder and robbery of a Jewish businessman in Argentina. The victim had been Kedar's contact on an assignment there. Within hours of his return, Kedar vanished. He spent the next eighteen months in solitary confinement at Ramle prison, where even the guards did not know his name. There were rumors about a "Prisoner X," but the government never acknowledged his existence. Finally placed on trial in 1959, Kedar was sentenced to seventeen years in prison, and served the full term before his release in 1974. The government eventually admitted that a man, who was not identified, had been arrested for unspecified offenses. But to date Israel has not officially disclosed the nature of Kedar's crime.

Another former intelligence officer, Avri El-Ad, was arrested in 1958 on suspicion of spying for Egypt and was interrogated for nine months by the Shin Bet before standing trial in July 1959. Again, the proceedings were cloaked in secrecy. References to the case in the news media were censored, and El-Ad was known at Ramle prison only as "X4." Only after his release in 1967 did the public learn what had happened to him.

The years had not softened Israel's approach. In 1983, prominent Israeli scientist Marcus Klingberg, the deputy director of the government Biological Institute, where top-secret work on biological warfare is carried out, suddenly dropped from sight. His office was cleaned out and his files removed. Rumors spread that he had defected to the Soviet Union; his wife announced he was undergoing medical treatment in Europe. In time, it was learned that Klingberg had been tried in secret on charges of passing secrets to the Soviets, convicted and sentenced to life in prison. No official announcement was ever made.

And just months before Vanunu was captured, reports began circulating that an Israeli had been sentenced to twelve years in prison after a secret trial on charges of spying for Syria.

A secret trial for Mordechai Vanunu was hardly out of the question. And to make sure no one would care, the government orchestrated the simmering anti-Vanunu sentiment into a full-fledged smear campaign in early November.

The ban on Vanunu stories in the Israeli media had not prevented reporters from gathering information about the man, and authorities knew precisely what was sitting in the newspapers' files. In some cases, Shin Bet agents and other government officials had supplied editors and reporters with photographs or transcripts of interviews about Vanunu that painted him in the worst possible light. The effect had been to create a backlog of stories guaranteed to finish the job of besmirching his character, creating such a hostile atmosphere that Vanunu and his handful of supporters in Israel would have little opportunity to argue their side of the case. All that remained was to ignite the firestorm by lifting the censorship orders.

On Sunday, November 3, the restrictions were removed and the onslaught began. "Vanunumania," the Government Press Office mirthfully called the ugly orgy of halftruths and slanders, much of it provided by official sources, that engulfed Israel's news media.

Perhaps no newspaper more eagerly embraced the spirit of the occasion than the mass-circulation *Yediot Ahronot*. The paper had a field day on November 3, giving over whole pages to the Vanunu story. The front of the afternoon tabloid was dominated by a blowup of a photograph showing Vanunu at a pro-Palestinian demonstration holding a placard with the Hebrew slogan, "Israel-Palestine: Two

Countries for Two Nations." Inside, there was a report about *Newsweek's* kidnapping story, an interview with Vanunu's father ("Mordechai is not my son anymore"), and a full-page profile of Vanunu. *Yediot* carried an interview with Judy Zimmet, and a story that depicted Vanunu as an attention-seeking extrovert and discussed his nude modeling for Beersheba art classes. Accompanying the article was a sketch purporting to show Vanunu in the nude.

The thrust of the coverage was to portray Vanunu as a psychologically unstable, pro-Palestinian, Jew-hating communist willing to sell out the state of Israel for money. Virtually all the newspapers used the same photograph of their subject: a head shot showing a swarthy man with close-cropped hair and a shifty, suspicious look in his eyes. It would be difficult to imagine a picture that could make Vanunu look less trustworthy.

The vicious character assassination, which continued for days, perhaps reached its nadir when government-controlled television obtained a few pages of Vanunu's diaries and read them on the air. The television network then hired a graphologist, who analyzed Vanunu's handwriting and claimed it showed he was emotionally unstable and suffered from sexual disorders.

Vanunu's sex life was of great interest to Israeli journalists. Hadashot ran a story quoting an unnamed psychologist as saying Vanunu had problems with women, implicitly suggesting he was a homosexual. It seemed inconceivable that a psychologist in Israel, where the same standards of patient confidentiality apply as in the United States, would divulge this information to a newspaper, and Hadashot's editors privately had serious misgivings about the story. But the newspaper did not acknowledge its error until after the allegations were published. And the implications lingered on, despite a lack of evidence. Three years later, people familiar with the case referred to Vanunu's alleged homosexuality as if it were a well-known fact.

The record was replete with errors, but the government campaign backfired in only one regard. The picture drawn of Vanunu was so ugly that many Israelis, including some members of parliament, began to wonder how a man with such an unstable history could have remained on the Dimona payroll. One leftist newspaper called the disclosures about Vanunu "the last drop in the clouded-over, obscured sea which has surrounded 'the Vanunu affair' from the outset."

The feeling is that of an almost Orwellian world in which all information is perhaps a deception, with a substantial number of the deceptions likely to be [correct] information. We are hard-pressed to accept at face value the account according to which a relatively high-ranking technician in the Atomic Energy Commission could openly evince a total turnabout in personality and identity—including religious and political views—without such a change being noted by those parties responsible for security classification and categorization of 'reactor employees' (as stated by the foreign press).

The editorial concluded:

If Mordechai Vanunu in fact wanted to signal the Shin Bet that he was no longer fit to be employed in a sensitive position, he chose every conceivable means of doing so, in the most public way possible. Did those responsible indeed not see these blatant signals, which were the topic of the day in Vanunu's own surroundings? If so, this would appear to be an instance of a severe security breach which needs to be thrashed out and cleared up in the entire security system. If that's not the answer, then what in fact is actually happening here?

One security expert told the *Jerusalem Post*, "If an overt security risk like Vanunu could get away with it, imagine what someone subtle could have achieved."

The evidence of an egregious security lapse prompted calls from right-wing politicians for a purge of all "left-wingers" in the Shin Bet. With all that was known about him publicly, the critics charged, the only way Vanunu could have continued working at

Dimona was if officials sympathetic to his political beliefs looked the other way.

Perhaps most alarming was the realization that if Vanunu had secretly given his story and photographs to the intelligence service of a hostile country, instead of a newspaper that intended to publish them, the breach of security would never have been discovered.

Even the normally implacable Admoni was unhappy. The Vanunu affair had badly strained relations between the Mossad and Shin Bet, and during one of his weekly meetings with Shimon Peres in September, the Mossad chief vented his anger about the Shin Bet's errors. Admoni did not believe Shin Bet had been infiltrated, but he shared the fears of the right wing that something was seriously amiss at Shin Bet, and he believed the prime minister should do something about it.

Peres told his intelligence chief that he couldn't agree more that mistakes had been made. However, the prime minister, only a few weeks from stepping down, was not interested in stirring up more trouble. He rejected Admoni's demand for an investigation into the foulup. The Shin Bet, he told the Mossad boss, has suffered enough.

Aside from the criticism of Shin Bet, however, the anti-Vanunu media campaign was a brilliant success. It was clear that if Vanunu should suddenly be discovered in an Israeli prison and brought to trial on treason charges, there would be little public support for him. At the urging of reporters, legal scholars eagerly brainstormed ways in which Vanunu could be jailed without trial. Dr. Mordechai Kremnitzer, a Hebrew University law professor, said the government could hold Vanunu under an emergency powers act that allows the defense minister to order the jailing of any person for six months "for reasons of state security and public security."

The order, which can be extended indefinitely with a judge's approval, has been widely used against Palestinians in the occupied West Bank and Gaza Strip, but only rarely against Israeli citizens. Still, Kremnitzer saw a possible application in this case. "If the authorities say that there is no possibility of conducting a trial against Vanunu, because it would damage state security, but that he continues to constitute a danger, they could use this law," he said.

How long, the professor was asked, could Vanunu be held that way?

"Ad infinitum," he responded. "Ad infinitum."

In editorials that accompanied the frenzied coverage, several papers backed whatever action the government would have to take to place Vanunu on trial, regardless of the laws it might have violated. "If that did happen, we say 'Well done,' and we don't give a hoot whether he was brought legally or by subterfuge, by sea or by air, alive or dead," Ma'ariv commented.

Chapter 42

The media campaign further blackened the Vanunu family's anguished existence. The mood inside the parents' tiny apartment in Beersheba was somber. No one wanted to leave the house, and Mazal Vanunu could not stop crying. "People point at us in the street and we haven't done anything wrong to anyone," she wailed.

Solomon Vanunu, still in a state of shock, opened his stall in the central market only rarely, and he soon stopped going to the synagogue, an excruciating sacrifice for such a pious man. Two days after the avalanche of attacks on his son began, the seventy-five year-old father was assaulted in the street by two men who beat him with their fists, kicked him and hurled stones at him while groups of passersby gathered in the street to watch. As his wife begged for help, the old man fell in the street, sobbing loudly. "It's not my son. He's not my son anymore," he screamed at his attackers.

All they had accomplished, all their hopes, were being destroyed, and they were powerless to stop it. Albert watched in frustration as business at his carpentry shop dwindled. Another son, Asher, traveling in Europe after his military service, was in West Berlin when he saw Motti's picture on the front page of Yediot Ahronot. Asher felt sick, and thought seriously about not returning to Israel.

Some of their neighbors were sympathetic. "Poor people," one sighed. "They are mourning Motti as if he was dead. They, of all people, don't deserve this. They're the most religious people in the neighborhood."

Another neighbor concluded, "Now Motti to them is like Syria is to Israel."

Death threats turned up in the daily mail, and reporters and photographers buzzed around the Vanunu home; an intercom system had to be installed on the front door of their building to ward off the endless requests for interviews. And there was no place to hide. Israelis sporting T-shirts bearing the slogan, "I'm Vanunu," drew gales of laughter on the streets, and even the television offered no escape. One Friday night, Shlomo Nitsan, Israel's most popular comedian, delivered a monologue on his weekly variety program that focused on which country Vanunu might have been spying for.

"We are ashamed," Vanunu's mother told a reporter. "We had a good reputation in the neighborhood, people thought of us as a quiet family, whose children were successful, were in school, served in the army. We have had bad luck and it's not our fault."

"A month and a half ago we heard for the first time about this story and we were shocked. It fell on us like a bomb. Until this day, I still don't believe it's true. I can't accept what they're saying. I'm not willing to believe. I don't know what to think from then on. Our lives have been a nightmare. People are saying terrible things about us and are breaking our hearts. We haven't hurt anyone."

But, criminal or not, Motti was still her son.

"I just want to know where my child is, what's happening to him, so we'll at least know he's all right," she said, her voice quavering. "Motti was always a good boy. Please just tell us where he is, what's going on."

Despite the lynch-mob atmosphere, Shamir was still not inclined to reveal Vanunu's whereabouts. The day after the ban on Vanunu stories was lifted, the prime minister told reporters Israel "has its reasons" for keeping mum. "The Israeli government will say what she thinks is correct and will fulfill all obligations toward her citizens," Shamir added, in his government's first public comment on the case.

Inside the government, however, pressure was mounting for some sort of announcement about Vanunu's return to Israel. During three meetings in late October and early November, Foreign Minister Peres, with support from Defense Minister Rabin and Attorney-General Yosef Harish, told Shamir that Israel had little choice but to disclose Vanunu's capture.

Peres was pleased with the way in which the story had developed. Potential whistleblowers had been warned, and the message about Israel's nuclear capability had been delivered to the Arabs. But the fact that Vanunu was last seen in London and hints that he had been kidnapped on British soil still posed a threat to Israeli-British relations, and left London in a difficult position with the Arab world. Arab-British ties had been strained since Thatcher ordered a suspension of diplomatic relations with Syria over the Hindawi affair. Now, even relatively moderate Arab states like Jordan were charging that Britain had conspired with Israel on the Vanunu case—further proof, as they saw it, of a pro-Israeli tilt in London.

The speculation had also prompted calls in Britain for an official investigation into Vanunu's disappearance and the Thatcher government's role in it.

"Does the silence of the British Government over the affair imply complicity in his removal by Mossad?" the pro-Thatcher *Daily Telegraph* asked in a November 4 editorial.

"It would be scandalous if it had turned a blind eye to Mr. Vanunu's disappearance."

One member of Parliament from Thatcher's Conservative Party said he had been told by an Israeli "prominent in public life" that Vanunu was packed in a crate and smuggled out of Britain as diplomatic baggage. "The fact that there is a friendly relationship between Britain and Israel does not make the rules any different," the lawmaker contended. "When a country decides that there are some laws it obeys and some it doesn't, that there are some civilized attitudes it accepts and some it doesn't, that country is on a very slippery slope." His demand for an explanation from Jerusalem elicited a loud chorus of "Hear, Hear" from other MPs during a debate in the House of Commons on the matter.

Thatcher was managing to stave off an investigation, but the controversy, fueled in no small measure by pro-Arab members of Parliament, continued to hammer away at her government.

Curiosity was also growing in other countries, including the United States. U.S. Ambassador Thomas Pickering assured Shamir in early November that Washington would not take a position on either the question of Israel's nuclear arsenal nor its alleged involvement in the Vanunu case. Only days before, however, Pickering had received a "confidential" message from Secretary of State George Shultz requesting any information the embassy might develop concerning a news report about the alleged kidnapping of Vanunu.

The mystery of Vanunu's disappearance received prominent play in the *New York Times* and the *Washington Post* in the last few days of October. And from Boston, Meir was giving interviews to anyone who called, hoping to pressure Israel into an announcement.

In Australia, protesters in Sydney, some of them PLO supporters, dogged Israeli President Chaim Herzog as he arrived for a state visit, picketing his meeting sites with placards saying "Let Vanunu go" and chanting, "PLO, PLO."

Even Israelis who thought Vanunu should be brought to justice were beginning to believe the government should disclose what it knew about Vanunu's fate. "Old precedents for the secret jailing, interrogation and trial of persons who committed grave security offenses, followed by their secret incarceration, are not only extremely few, they are wholly inapplicable," the *Jerusalem Post* editorialized.

There were suggestions that the secrecy surrounding the case was solely designed to cover up the security lapses that allowed Vanunu to succeed. "Mordechai Vanunu is a traitor," said Yossi Sarid, a left-wing Knesset member. "As a traitor, he must be brought to trial. I am not that concerned how he is brought. The trial must be held behind closed doors. But one thing must not happen. A man cannot just disappear. Apparently there was a serious failure here. A failure can't be dealt with by silence or covering up."

The question came to a head on November 9 during a meeting between Peres, Shamir and Rabin in the prime minister's office. Peres had insisted on resolving the issue of a formal announcement before he flew to the United States the following day, and two new troubling developments had provided the foreign minister with additional ammunition.

The previous day, the *Financial Times* of London had reported that Thatcher had given Peres her approval for Israel's plans to capture Vanunu. The British leader denied the report, saying she had never talked with Peres or any other Israeli official about Vanunu, but as the Israeli leaders assessed the consequences of the story, even Shamir grudgingly conceded that Thatcher was increasingly exposed.

Indeed, the United States had worriedly concluded that the uproar in Britain could intensify if Israel did not move to quell the rumors. In a confidential cable to Washington, the U.S. Embassy in London noted in early November that the Thatcher government "is sticking to the line that there is no evidence that any crime has been committed, and therefore no investigation has been ordered, and there are no plans to approach the Israelis. Vanunu remains on the missing persons list."

"While [Britain's] response to parliamentary questions has thus far proved sufficient, the situation could rapidly escalate should Vanunu surface in an Israeli prison claiming he was forced to leave Britain against his will," warned the embassy assessment, which was passed on to Shamir.

More vexing were Zichroni's efforts on behalf of his client. The lawyer, acting at the insistence of Vanunu's family and the *Sunday Times*, had informed the attorney general that he planned to petition the High Court of Justice on Monday to force the government to reveal any knowledge about Vanunu's disappearance. A court hearing threatened to lay bare the government's role in the entire affair.

Buffeted by the Shin Bet scandal, the Pollard case, the government rotation, and a host of nagging domestic crises, the year had already been a trying one for Israel's leaders. On the horizon, storm clouds were forming over the Iran-Contra affair. Our plate is full, Rabin told Shamir. Let's not add to it.

The three leaders approved a draft statement drawn up by Peres' aides, and after the regular weekly Cabinet meeting, Cabinet Secretary Eliyakim Rubenstein walked over to reporters waiting outside the prime minister's office. In a high-pitched drone, Rubenstein read the short, three-paragraph declaration:

"Mordechai Vanunu is under lawful detention in Israel, in the wake of a court order which was issued following a hearing at which the lawyer he chose was present.

"Due to sub judice regulations [rules restricting comment on pending prosecutions], no further details will be published.

"All the rumors to the effect that Vanunu was 'kidnapped' on British soil are totally without foundation, and it follows that there is likewise no basis to the report that Mr. Peres contacted Mrs. Thatcher in order to inform her about something that never took place."

Shamir had not mentioned the statement during the closed-door Cabinet meeting—a session that delt at length on a routine Defense Ministry briefing, a discussion of a labor dispute involving teachers, and a report on immigration policy—and many of the ministers were not pleased to learn of the decision from the radio. Even President Chaim Herzog, himself a former chief of military intelligence, was kept in the dark as he traveled in Australia. The next day, Rubenstein was forced to apologize to a furious Herzog for the oversight.

But it had been a deliberate omission. The "prime minister's club" was not interested in other voices, other opinions. Like so many other important issues facing the country, they preferred to handle Vanunu themselves.

Even after the announcement, serious questions remained. Most importantly, how had Vanunu been brought back? Were international laws violated? Why didn't Israel seek his extradition in a legal venue? And how had all this happened in the first place?

The government wasn't saying. Vanunu would be tried in secret and very little would be released to the public. And neither the Cabinet nor the Knesset nor the Israeli public were much interested in filling the gaps.

"I think the right of the public to know what's going on is not in effect here," remarked one member of the Knesset Foreign Affairs and Defense Committee. "The public will hear whatever the government and the committee decide to give them, and I'm sure that's what the public wants."

The media, certainly, would get nothing more. "I understand that everybody is for freedom of the press, but I'm also in favor of freedom of existence, freedom of life," said Knesset member Eliyahv Ben-Elissar of Shumir's Likud party. "And I don't think we should write about everything just because we want to sell papers. We should put some stories aside, even if they would sell good."

"You know how you start in these kind of things, but you never know how you end."

Chapter 43

If the government thought the announcement would put an end to the matter, they were badly mistaken. The news of Vanunu's whereabouts only whetted the appetites of reporters in Israel and abroad.

The Vanunu affair dogged Israeli officials wherever they traveled, and they hewed closely to the party line. Herzog, on a three-day state visit to New Zealand, was pressed at every stop about the Dimona revelations. At one news conference, he was asked why Israel manufactured nuclear weapons.

"Who said we make them?" the president responded. "We've made it very clear that we will not be the first to introduce nuclear weapons in the Middle East."

Asked whether Israel had any nuclear weapons, Herzog was adamant. "The answer is no—an unequivocal no," he replied.

In Chicago, Peres called Vanunu a liar, but said he would be prosecuted for violating the law by disclosing state secrets, "or pretending to."

"This is pretended information," the foreign minister stressed.

"Israel stated very clearly that we shall not become the first country to introduce nuclear weapons into the Middle East. This is our stated position and we didn't depart from it," he said.

And far from satisfying officials in London, the Cabinet announcement triggered new calls for inquiries into the British government's role in the capture. To the Israelis, this was particularly galling. The last sentence of the Cabinet statement, denying rumors that Vanunu was "kidnapped" on British soil or that Peres and Thatcher had discussed such an operation, was included for the express purpose of calming the waters in Britain. But Jerusalem's refusal to officially disclose how Vanunu had been brought back precipitated a new wave of demands for more information.

The *Guardian* summed up the controversy in an editorial under the headline "Mr. Vanunu vanishes":

As soon as Parliament reassembles the searching questions need to be renewed about how Mr. Mordechai Vanunu came to disappear from London on September 30 and reappear in an Israeli prison. Downing Street has flatly denied that it was informed of any intention to seek his return. The Foreign Office's man in Tel Aviv is asking questions. But return he did, obviously against his will. The affair bears a striking, if so far superficial, resemblance to that in which the Nigerian Dr. Umaru Dikko was found on July 5, 1984, drugged in a crate at Stansted Airport (with an Israeli anaesthetist at his side) awaiting shipment to Lagos. The Nigerians' big mistake was not to ensure that the crate was part of their diplomatic baggage, for if it had been it could not have been opened.

Mr. Vanunu disappeared a week before his disclosures about the Israeli nuclear weapons programme at Dimona, in the Negev Desert, appeared in the *Sunday Times*. That newspaper took a little time to check his detailed and circumstantial account, which makes Israel an even more substantial nuclear power than had previously been suspected. Word obviously reached the Israeli authorities before the story appeared and someone on their behalf, who must surely be part of the Mossad Intelligence service, secured his abduction to Israel.

If the Prime Minister and Foreign Secretary were not themselves told by Israeli sources of the intended abduction, was there some connivance by the British security services? In that case were British ministers aware beforehand from non-Israeli sources, which is a question not covered in the denials? Or was the whole episode conducted under the seal of diplomatic immunity without any British cooperation? Unless Mr. Vanunu was first induced to leave the country voluntarily and then picked up abroad, the answer to at least one of those questions must be yes. Whichever question it is, it raises some pointed supplementaries. For if there was British connivance, what is the ethical distinction between Dr. Dikko's case, in which he was wanted on corruption charges, and Mr. Vanunu's, where he was wanted for betraying State secrets? If there was no British connivance, and Mr. Vanunu left with a diplomatic seal on his crate, is this not the type of abuse against which the Government has been vocal in its condemnation (rightly) of other diplomatic missions?

It was a highly uncharacteristic lapse by Shin Bet, the Mossad's domestic intelligence counterpart, which allowed Mr. Vanunu, with his known Arab sympathies, to roam at will through the Dimona plant so that he was able to sketch it and even produce photographs. Members of the Israeli security services would want to pick up some of the pieces after he had spilled them to a foreign newspaper. But an intelligence coup is useless if it aggravates relations between supposedly friendly states, which is what the Vanunu affair shows every sign of doing. The matter cannot rest where it is unless the Israeli authorities can show that neither their embassy nor their secret service in Britain was involved in Mr. Vanunu's transportation to an unidentified prison to face a secret trial. And, as enforced white spaces [censored articles] proliferate across Israeli newspapers, and the furore grows, that is going to take some doing.

Thatcher, her home secretary under pressure to investigate the entire episode, was also growing wary of the true story. Unconcerned about the details of the Mossad's plans when Peres called, the prime minister now wanted to know if the Israelis had violated their pledge and seized Vanunu on British soil, and she needed the information before it surfaced in the newspapers or in Parliament.

The British made sure Israel understood the Cabinet statement wasn't satisfactory. Hours after Rubenstein made the announcement, the Foreign Office merely took note of Israel's denial of a "kidnap" in Britain—a surprisingly cautious reaction that was quickly interpreted as a sign that London did not necessarily believe the Israeli assertion. In case anyone missed the point, the Foreign Office went one step farther, instructing its ambassador in Tel Aviv, William Squire, to seek a meeting with Israeli officials to discuss the Vanunu matter. Squire was also told to contact Vanunu's lawyer about the circumstances surrounding Vanunu's return. The highly unusual instruction was a clear affront to Israel and another sign that London was not content with Jerusalem's official explanation.

Squire's inquiries met with little success. Bypassing normal diplomatic channels, the ambassador directly approached the political director-general of the Foreign Ministry, Yossi Beilin, Peres' closest advisor. But Beilin agreed only to relay the British request to the appropriate officials.

Zichroni would not even meet with the envoy, telling Squire on the telephone that without the permission of the government, he was bound by his secrecy agreement not to discuss the case with anyone, including the ambassador.

Still stewing over having to say anything at all about Vanunu, Shamir was in no mood to be more forthcoming. "What do they want?" he angrily demanded during a meeting with his senior advisors the day after Squire's request was received. "We have said there was no British involvement. Now we have to say exactly how it was done? They will only call that a lie and demand more."

"No," he insisted, "this is the end of it."

In public, Shamir was just as resolute, if somewhat less strident. "If we show restraint and don't tell everything, we have our reasons," he told an interviewer. "In good time we'll tell the public what it needs to know."

The prime minister also contended there would be no rift with Britain. "After all, we have informed the British government that we did not do anything that violated British laws," he said. Asked if that meant Vanunu had not been captured in Britain, Shamir replied, "I didn't say anything about that. I said British laws were not broken."

During the same interview, Shamir also denied reports that Israel had supplied arms to Iran on behalf of the United States as part of a deal to win the release of American hostages in Lebanon.

But Shamir's obstinacy broke a few days after the November 9 announcement when Thatcher sent a blistering message to him, through the Israeli Embassy in London, that accused the Israeli government of misleading her and undermining her position by refusing to disclose to Britain's satisfaction just what had occurred in London on September 30, the day Vanunu disappeared. The British leader demanded some answers before an upcoming House of Commons debate.

Thatcher's vehemence caught the Israelis by surprise. "We really believed the British would not pursue the matter," one senior official recalled later. "A few headlines, some strong words in Parliament, but they (the government) could withstand that without our help. Once we stated that no laws were broken (in Britain), that is."

Thatcher was in the United States for meetings with President Reagan when Peres, still in the United States on a private visit, telephoned her in Washington on November 15 to discuss the dispute between their two governments. He insisted that he had not misled Thatcher in September and implored her not to insist on a complete accounting of the Vanunu operation. Neither he nor Shamir were prepared to provide such detailed information.

Thatcher was somewhat mollified by Peres' call, but she still wanted something more. Israel, she told Peres, must at least tell her how Vanunu had left Britain. What happened to him after that was Israel's business.

The irony was inescapable. Vanunu had hoped Israel's allies, unnerved by his disclosures about the true extent of the Jewish state's nuclear arsenal, would force a halt to Israel's nuclear adventurism. But Thatcher, like the rest of the allies, didn't seem to care. She didn't ask Peres whether the story in the *Sunday Times* was true. The British leader was only concerned about the possibility that British laws might have been violated.

To Peres, Thatcher's request for reassurance about the Vanunu operation was an acceptable compromise, and Shamir reluctantly agreed. Later that day, Yehuda Avner, Israel's ambassador in London, delivered a confidential explanation about the British end of the capture mission.

The message to Whitehall was simple and direct. Vanunu had left London voluntarily, lured out of the country by a woman, an Israeli secret service agent.

Chapter 44

The Israeli explanation satisfied Thatcher. If the truth should come out, there would be no question that British law had not been violated. If anything, the Israelis would be shown to have gone out of their way to avoid infringing on British sovereignty.

The dispute settled, Britain and Israel danced a delicate diplomatic waltz for the benefit of the public. In Jerusalem, the Foreign Ministry issued a formal response to the British request for clarifications: "Mr. Vanunu left Britain of his own volition and through normal departure procedures. His departure from Britain involved no violation of British law."

The message was relayed to London, and Tim Renton, a Foreign Office minister, assured the House of Commons that the government had no evidence of Israeli misdeeds in England. "In those circumstances, we have no further comment to make on the present position," a Foreign Office spokesman said.

"I hope there won't be any more bother with this matter," Shamir told Israel Radio.

On November 16, Shamir briefed the Cabinet on the Vanunu affair. After the meeting, a spokesman said Israel considered the case "as closed."

To ensure an end to the public campaign for details, British officials leaked portions of the Israeli explanation to the news media, and they were rewarded with a spate of headlines in London and Israel. The *Sunday Times*, which had been working for six weeks on a story about Vanunu's disappearance, again led the pack with an Insight report headlined, "Mossad's Tender Trap," which asserted that "Cindy" had in fact been a Mossad agent, sent to capture Vanunu. The lengthy article was accompanied by an artist's rendering of the woman, based on descriptions provided by reporters Prangnell and Connett, and a photograph of Vanunu, captioned "The Target." After recounting the events that led to Vanunu's disappearance, the *Sunday Times* concluded, "The assumption must be that Vanunu was somehow lured offshore by 'Cindy.' Insight has established that there were three Israeli ships in northern European waters at the relevant time which could have taken Vanunu on board."

Pro-Arab members of Parliament drummed up a feeble debate on the Vanunu issue the next week, and the government sent a Home Office minister to the floor to criticize Israel's official silence on the matter of Vanunu's capture. But the din of voices demanding answers died down. The onus was off Thatcher. Whatever had happened to Vanunu, it appeared that Britain was not involved.

Behind bars, Vanunu was getting the "Prisoner X" treatment. He had spent his first month in the hands of the Shin Bet, in complete isolation at Gadera prison. Many prisoners did not fare too well in the hands of the Shin Bet, an agency with a reputation for physically abusing suspects, especially Arabs, to obtain confessions. A joke that made the rounds told of a competition between agents from the CIA, the Soviet KGB and the Shin Bet to see who could most quickly capture a deer in the wild. The CIA agent entered the forest and returned three days later with a deer on a leash. The KGB agent came back after two days carrying bloody pieces of a dismembered deer. The Shin Bet agent was in and out of the forest in an hour, bringing with him a rabbit that showed signs of having been beaten. When the American and the Russian protested that the object of the exercise had been to capture a deer, the Israeli pointed at the rabbit, and said, "The rabbit confessed. He *is* a deer."

The Shin Bet's treatment of prisoners took on a much more ominous tone in late 1987 when an official investigation concluded that Shin Bet agents for sixteen years had routinely used physical pressure to force confessions, then lied about it to Israeli courts. Agents beat suspects, urinated on them, placed them in cold showers and then in front of air conditioners, denied them food and sleep, and forced them to wear hoods to disorient them.

Vanunu was spared such punishment. The government knew what he had done, and he wasn't denying it. His interrogators were primarily interested in learning whether he had passed secrets to anyone else, particularly hostile sources such as Palestinian groups or Arab countries, while he was working at Dimona or after he left the country. Vanunu's stopover in Moscow on his way to the Far East was of particular concern, but he heatedly denied any plan to sell the Dimona photographs to the Soviets. The flight through Moscow was merely convenient and inexpensive, Vanunu protested. The questioning lasted only a few days.

Twice during his stay at Gadera, Vanunu appeared at secret hearings before a judge who formally extended the order under which he was being held, and after a month Vanunu was moved to the Prison Services top-security facility at Ashkelon. He was registered under the name of "David Anoush" and was refused a razor, forcing him to grow a beard to alter his appearance. Prison officials required him to wear a hat and sunglasses any time he was moved from his cell. Only one guard and the jail commandant knew his true identity. No one else was to know that Vanunu was being held in the Ashkelon prison.

It was a miserable existence. Vanunu spent twenty-two hours a day in a small twelve-foot-long cell with white plastered stone walls. Inside were a bed, two tables, a chair, a cupboard with book shelves, eating utensils and a device for heating water. A shower and a toilet stood behind a stone partition. Outside exercise was allowed between 11 A.M. and 1 P.M. Natural light peeked through a small, barred window in the steel door, and a fluorescent bulb was left on twenty-four hours a day. A television camera mounted in a corner of the ceiling monitored Vanunu's movements around the clock to make sure Vanunu didn't attempt suicide.

The prisoner's only contact with the outside world was Zichroni. The case was like a shot of adrenalin for the lawyer. Hearing on his car radio of the Cabinet announcement that Vanunu was in custody, Zichroni had rushed back to the office and spent the rest of the day giving interviews to a seemingly endless string of journalists. And in the days that followed, he was surrounded by the media. Zichroni's performance greatly amused other attorneys.

One lawyer who needed to consult with Zichroni about a case in which they were both representing defendants spent an entire afternoon in Zichroni's office, listening to him field calls from journalists. Each time, Zichroni told them he had nothing to say about the Vanunu affair. When the lawyer asked why he didn't simply tell his secretary to inform journalists that he had no comment, Zichroni stared at his colleague incredulously, then slowly shook his head.

Zichroni was on the front page again. There were profiles of Vanunu's lawyer in newspapers and magazines, and invitations to appear on television news programs flooded in. Few were rejected. A film company approached Zichroni with an offer to buy the rights to Vanunu's story, but the negotiations eventually fell apart.

Concerned about his client's psychological state, Zichroni still found time to visit the prison three times a week. Vanunu was bearing up well, considering his isolation, in good health mentally and physically. In conversation, Zichroni found him funny, pleasant and exceedingly polite, with a good grasp of the legal issues involved in his case.

The long hours of confinement were brutal, and Zichroni did what he could to improve the conditions. Immediately after the government announcement about his arrest, authorities granted Vanunu's request for daily newspapers and a vegetarian diet. To help pass the time, Zichroni brought Vanunu a Walkman and classical music tapes, and made regular deliveries of books. Vanunu's literary tastes were eclectic, and Zichroni supplied a little of everything—philosophy, a collection of O. Henry short stories, a copy of the New Testament, and politics, including a book about the Knesset written by the lawyer and a volume about the Arab-Israeli conflict penned by Avneri, Zichroni's long-time friend and political cohort. Many of the books were written in English, part of Vanunu's effort to improve his command of the language.

Some of Zichroni's offerings puzzled Vanunu. Although he enjoyed mysteries and thrillers, he was baffled by one batch of espionage novels. At the conclusion of each of the books, the spy was killed, and Vanunu began to wonder if his lawyer was sending him some kind of message.

Prison officials balked at providing the prisoner with a radio. They did not want Vanunu to discover through the BBC or other foreign radio broadcasts how much attention his case was receiving. In addition, forcing Vanunu to listen to music only with a set of headphones increased his sense of isolation.

The almost daily barrage of disparaging stories in the newspapers also left Vanunu in despair, and he pleaded with Zichroni to do something to stop it. The government was not easing up. A story in *Yediot Ahronot* was too much even for Andrew Neil, the *Sunday Times* editor, who had maintained a public silence on the case. The story, supplied by official sources, reported that Vanunu had hoped to sell his Dimona information to the Soviet Union. But Neil issued a statement saying his newspaper had looked into the possibility and concluded Vanunu had never contacted Moscow. Neil also criticized the Israeli media coverage, calling it "full of distortions and disinformation."

Zichroni publicly decried the venomous media campaign, but there was little he could do about it. Faced with a hostile press, Vanunu began writing letters to newspapers and his small band of friends and supporters in Israel and abroad, trying to explain his side of the story. "I did not rise up to save humanity and don't see myself as a world hero," one letter stated.

I just saw an important issue which must be made clear to everyone and which affects world peace. I carried out my duty, which is the duty of every citizen, not to obey orders blindly. Those who founded this state think only about the Holocaust of the Jewish people in Europe. But you can't cause a world holocaust because of that, or cause another people to suffer a holocaust. There is no doubt that if the Israeli government uses its nuclear bomb, it will cause a holocaust for another people.

Chapter 45

The suitcase sat unattended on the curb outside the Christmas Hotel in Arab east Jerusalem for the better part of an hour before one of the soldiers guarding the courthouse across the street spotted it. An assault rifle bouncing at his side, the soldier walked uncertainly into Ali Ibn Abi Taleb Street and stared for a moment at the bag. It was nothing much to speak of, just a scuffed grey Pullman with a few torn airline tags and a long piece of white string dangling from the handle. But in a country like Israel, in a city like Jerusalem, there are rules about how to handle an unattended bag. And the first thing to do is assume the suitcase is a bomb.

The soldier looked around for some sign of its owner. Then he turned toward the corner, shouted at three policemen in the intersection to close the street, and ran inside the courthouse compound for help.

The owner of the suitcase, an Arab merchant, was finally located in the lobby of the hotel. He had been waiting for a ride, and had come inside to make a quick telephone call. Then he decided to have a coffee, and forgot about the bag. The soldiers forced the businessman to go outside and open his suitcase, while they watched from the doorway. When it didn't explode, they ordered him to unpack his belongings and spread them on the sidewalk, wet from a morning of drizzle. Two soldiers briefly poked through the clothes with their gun barrels, then told the Arab to pick up his things and leave the area.

A false alarm. But in Israel a suitcase is not always a suitcase. Living in a country that is constantly in a state of war with enemies abroad and enemies within, Israelis can never be too careful.

Even so, what was happening around the Jerusalem District

Courthouse that day, November 30, 1986, was extraordinary. It began early. Snipers ringed the roof of the building, and Border Police troops were stationed along the streets outside at intervals of a few yards. Inside, courthouse guards and Shin Bet internal security agents in plain clothes roamed the hallways. Two officers took up positions inside the dank basement cafeteria, whose lone window afforded a glimpse only of the shoes of people climbing a rear staircase. Agents were posted in the bathrooms.

Outside, a crowd of about forty reporters, photographers and television cameramen had been standing in the streets and lining nearby rooftops since early morning. It was not an easy assignment. It was chilly, rainy, and they were not allowed inside the courthouse. "We received an order to shoot anyone who tries to come in," one policeman warned a reporter who strayed too close to the building.

The object of all this attention was Mordechai Vanunu. He was about to make his first appearance in public since the day he vanished from London exactly two months earlier. As the troops and police swirled around the Jerusalem courthouse and the photographers jockeyed for the best camera angles, Vanunu was finishing lunch in his jail cell at Ashkelon prison. After eating, he climbed into an unmarked white van and began the two-hour journey to Jerusalem.

Israel had made it clear that Vanunu would be tried behind closed doors, and secrecy reigned inside the Jerusalem courthouse. Vanunu's name did not even appear in the 200-page red clothbound ledger lying on the counter in the court clerk's office. The case was there, Number 461, in the middle of page 117, sandwiched between an illegal possession of a weapon and a murder. Scrawled in ink was "28/11/86," the date the charges were formally filed, and an entry that began, "State of Israel v . . ." But the rest of the line was blank. No details of the charges, no courtroom number and no name for the defendant.

By early afternoon, security at the courthouse was tightened another notch. Guards began turning away lawyers and defendants and others with business inside, and court workers were ordered to remain at their desks. The media horde outside sensed the increased tension, and when Judge Zvi Cohen, who was rumored to be the man presiding over the first hearing, drove his Renault sedan out of the courthouse compound at 1:45 P.M., reporters and photographers knocked each other over in a mad dash for their cars. The judge was going to hold the hearing elsewhere, they believed. The courthouse security was just a ruse.

Cohen, it turned out, was only going home to eat lunch, and the long watch continued.

At 2:45 P.M., Zichroni drove up in an old Chevrolet and parked outside the courthouse. Zichroni had handled many sensitive security cases during his salad days as Israel's preeminent human-rights attorney in Israel, and he had come to expect, even enjoy, the circus-like atmosphere. But even he was startled by the scene unfolding at the Jerusalem courthouse.

"What the hell is all this for?" he muttered to himself as he got out of the car. "Who do they think they have, Arafat?"

The lawyer brushed past the reporters who circled him, waving off their questions but walking slowly enough to make sure they were asked, and headed inside to talk with Uzi Hasson, the prosecutor. After a brief meeting, Zichroni left the building, got into his car and drove off with a cryptic "See you soon."

The courthouse closed exactly at 3 P.M. The building was checked thoroughly to make sure no journalists were hiding inside. Something was happening now, and the cameramen checked their lenses and jockeyed one last time for position.

Zichroni returned shortly before 4 P.M. A few minutes later, the main event began. At 4:03 P.M., a white Ford Transit van and a white passenger sedan, both unmarked and both bearing civilian license plates, turned right off Nablus Road. Traffic was halted on Salahadin Street as the mini-convoy drove two blocks the wrong way up the one-way street, made a left on Ali Ibn Abi Taleb Street, crawled slowly past the Barclay's bank, an Audi sales office, the Christmas Hotel, and pulled up at the gate leading to an alley at the rear of the courthouse.

Inside the van, sitting next to the window on the left side of the middle seat, directly behind the driver, was Vanunu. On his right was a lone guard, police inspector Isaiah Sobelman. His head lowered, Vanunu looked out at the crowd surging toward the van. He smiled weakly, lifted his left hand and waved to the photographers as the vehicle edged through the crowd into the courthouse complex.

He had changed a little since the last time he appeared in public. The sullen man in the newspaper pictures now sported a thick beard. His black hair was cut short, exposing the balding patch at the top of his head, and he had lost some weight. He wore a khaki overcoat, blue jeans and a red T-shirt.

The van entered the courtyard slowly and the gate closed behind it. With jittery Border Police guards carrying automatic weapons hovering around him, Vanunu was hustled out of the vehicle and shoved up a small flight of stairs into the courthouse. Looking tense, he turned briefly and mumbled something to the crowd of reporters and photographers watching him from the gate, but they were too far away to make out what he said. And then, in a flash, he was gone, pushed forward into the building by his guards.

Vanunu was taken by elevator to a second-floor courtroom. After he was inside, the door was padlocked and two policemen armed with Uzi submachine guns took up positions just outside while four Shin Bet agents with machine pistols roamed the corridor. Only the judge, the lawyers, the prisoner and his guards, and a technician operating a battery of recording devices were permitted to attend the court session, a routine hearing on the prosecution's request to keep the prisoner behind bars until his trial. As the session began about 4:30 P.M. Zichroni asked that the proceedings be opened to the public. Judge Cohen denied the request. So Zichroni asked for a postponement to give him more time to review the evidence and prepare his case. That request was granted.

Vanunu was given a copy of the four-page charge sheet outlining the state's case against him. Zichroni received a thick packet of transcripts of Vanunu's interrogation by the Shin Bet and of interviews with people who had know Vanunu and had spoken with the authorities about him. The lawyer and his client huddled briefly to discuss the charges.

After thirty minutes, the hearing was over. Vanunu was hustled down a rear staircase to the alley behind the courthouse and loaded into the white van. At 5:05 P.M., the van and the white security chase car drove slowly out the gate of the courthouse compound. Police tried to move the photographers back, but they converged on the vehicle anyway.

Vanunu was sitting in the same position, and the cameramen pounced. As the driver turned into the street and tried to thread through the crowd of journalists shouting questions in three languages, Vanunu stared out the window, apparently dazed by the chaos surrounding him. He smiled at one point, then shielded his face from the flash units exploding in front of him, and finally bent over, out of sight, as the van broke through the throng and sped away.

It was 5:17 P.M. Now it was certain. Mordechai Vanunu had come home.

The indictment in "State of Israel versus Mordechai, son of Shlomo, Vanunu" was prepared by Justice Ministry officials in consultation with Peres and Shamir. Details of the charges were kept secret; the Justice Ministry announced only that Vanunu had been charged in the Jerusalem District Court under Israel's treason and espionage statutes, and that the court had been asked to keep Vanunu in prison until his trial.

In an outline accompanying the charge sheet but not released to the public, the government laid out its case against Vanunu. The document described the technician's employment at Dimona and noted that after signing a secrecy agreement he "collected, prepared, copied and held secret information—all without authorization to do so, and with the intent to harm state security." The information Vanunu obtained was said to concern the "physical and organizational structure" of the plant, "classified developments" and "classified work methods and production processes." The document traced Vanunu's travels after he left Israel in January 1986, and his dealings with Guerrero and the *Sunday Times* that resulted in the publication of the disclosures.

What the court was not told was that Israel could have stopped Vanunu—and chose not to.

Chapter 46

Although the government decided against seeking the death penalty in Vanunu's case—Nazi war criminal Adolph Eichmann and an Israeli army captain wrongly convicted of spying for the British during the War of Independence are the only individuals ever executed in Israel—he still faced severe punishment. A life sentence in non-murder cases in Israel generally means twenty years behind bars, so the combined charges carried a maximum sentence of fifty-five years in prison. And the likelihood of an early parole for Vanunu was less than remote. An horrendous future lay ahead if he were convicted.

But it was rapidly becoming evident that, aside from his family and a handful of peace activists in Israel and elsewhere, no one cared much about the fate of Mordechai Vanunu. His first appearance in public was a one-day story. There was an occasional report about the latest rumor regarding his capture—the *Financial Times*, quoting Israeli intelligence sources, claimed Vanunu had been smuggled back to Israel aboard a jetliner—but no one was digging anymore. After the "Cindy" story, the *Sunday Times'* appetite had also vastly diminished. With Vanunu in jail and awaiting trial, there was little on the surface that could be done, and Neil in particular was not interested in pursuing any other leads. Never enthusiastic about Vanunu's revelations, he was even more reluctant to commit his resources to the untold story of Vanunu's capture.

From his conversations with Hounam and Morgan, Vanunu had been persuaded that the *Sunday Times* would always be an active ally. Repeatedly, he had been assured that the newspaper would carry the banner if anything were to happen to him. But, as far as Neil was concerned, it was not to be. "We've just got to go to the next story. That was yesterday's story. Readers would be bored with any more," he told his staff when the subject of Vanunu arose.

Morgan believed more should be done, and he asked Neil several times to allow Insight to stay on the story. Morgan was incensed by Israel's action. It was obscene. Vanunu wasn't Eichmann. All he had tried to do was give Israelis some vital information that could affect their future, information that was being withheld by their government. The kidnapping and prosecution of Vanunu, and the government's manipulation of the media in its anti-Vanunu campaign, cemented doubts Morgan had always held about Israel's commitment to democracy.

What Morgan had in mind was no less than a *Sunday Times* investigation of Israel itself. He wanted to send an Insight team to Israel for as long as a year with the mandate to "expose the undemocratic nature" of the country. Each week, the newspaper would focus on an aspect of Israeli life that Morgan believed would belie the country's claims of democracy. The team would probably have been thrown out of the country, he acknowledged, but that too would have proved the point.

At home, the newspaper would uncover the Israeli conspiracy that led to the kidnapping of Vanunu. And Morgan wanted to play tough—identify the Mossad station chief in London, agents in other capitals, and publish their pictures. Israel would be forced to withdraw the agents for their own safety.

Hounam was also unhappy about the newspaper's loss of interest, and lobbied to keep the pressure on the British government to find out exactly what had happened to Vanunu. The reporter was sure British or international law must have been broken when Israel went after Vanunu, and he urged Neil to editorially commit the newspaper to finding out.

But Neil wasn't interested in a crusade. The editor was unyielding: no more Vanunu. If something comes along, we will follow it up. But the story was not going to become anyone's full-time occupation.

Vanunu was old news. If he wanted the world to know what had happened to him, he would have to tell the story himself.

The journalists who had been kept at bay by police and soldiers during Vanunu's first public appearance in late November were better prepared when he made his second appearance three weeks later, on December 21.

As the small convoy of police vehicles approached the court complex, photographers clustered around the white van. The prisoner, pale and drawn, now beardless and clad in drab prison-issue jeans and a beige coat, could be seen sitting in the rear window. The convoy rolled to a halt in the street outside the rear entrance and there was a momentary delay while guards wrestled with locks and swung open the gate to the alley behind the building.

That was all the time Vanunu needed. As the van began moving again, crawling slowly past the Christmas Hotel, he slapped his left palm flat against the glass. A message written in ink was clearly visible on the skin:

> Vanunu M.
> was hijacked
> in Rome ITL
> 30.9.86 2100
> came to Rome
> by BA fly 504

Vanunu was claiming that on September 30, 1986, the day he had disappeared from London, he had flown to Rome aboard British Airways Flight 504. At 9 P.M.—2100 hours—he had been kidnapped. He didn't have to say by whom.

Photographers scrambled for a shot of Vanunu's hand and reporters shouted questions at him. The van quickly pulled into the court complex, and guards rushed Vanunu inside for a three-hour closed-door hearing, where a judge approved a prosecution request to keep him behind bars until trial. By the time Vanunu left, the message had been washed off his palm.

As the van slowly pushed through the crowd after the hearing, guards kept Vanunu's handcuffed arms pinned to his sides. But when a reporter asked in Hebrew where he had been seized, Vanunu shouted, "Italy."

A police officer quickly clapped a hand over Vanunu's mouth, but the damage was done. The man who spilled the secrets had done it again.

Chapter 47

Israel slapped a censorship order on photographs of the palm message and news accounts of the incident, but the ban was lifted a day later after the message appeared in the foreign press. It wasn't worth worrying about. The government had more immediate problems.

For the second time in two months, Israel was embroiled in a diplomatic flap with a European country. Vanunu's message created a furor in Rome. Like Thatcher before him, Bettino Craxi, Italy's Socialist prime minister, was placed in a tenuous position. If true, Israel had mounted a secret intelligence operation on friendly soil without the knowledge of its ally and with complete disregard for Italian law. It could not be ignored.

Italian intelligence and the country's top anti-terrorism investigator were ordered to look into the Vanunu allegations, and the Foreign Ministry summoned newly arrived Israeli Ambassador Mordechai Drory and demanded an explanation. But Drory, like his counterpart in London two months earlier, had no information on the matter. All he could do, he told his annoyed hosts, was pass on the request to his superiors.

Jerusalem was doing what by now came naturally. Shamir refused to comment, Peres insisted that Israel had done nothing to infringe on Italian sovereignty, and other officials went out of their way to downplay the significance of the issue. Drory was instructed to release a statement designed to soothe Italy's hurt feelings. Israel, the ambassador said, "has noted the Italian request for explanation of the case of Mordechai Vanunu and reiterates that both historically and at the present moment relations with Italy are valued of great importance so that Israel cannot in any way be suspected of damaging Italy or its interests."

But Craxi, buffeted by protests from across the political spectrum, was in no mood to play word games. He told reporters he was not satisfied with Israel's explanations, and indicated he believed some sort of operation involving Vanunu had been carried out on Italian soil without the knowledge or consent of his government. Vanunu "would seem to have had no reason to lie." Craxi said.

Nonsense, Israel replied. Peres aide Yossi Beilin urged the world not to take Vanunu too seriously. "Tomorrow," the foreign ministry's political director-general insisted, "he might say he came (via) Tanganyika."

The leaks and the disinformation campaign had worked for a time. But the message printed on Vanunu's palm shattered the carefully constructed maze. Now Israel faced the prospect of an Italian investigation into the Vanunu affair. Jerusalem was confident the probe could be contained, but it was one more messy problem.

PART V

What Atomic Bombs?

Chapter 48

The toughest prison in Israel stands in the middle of a drab, joyless industrial area on the outskirts of the coastal city of Ashkelon. A twenty-foot-high sandstone and cement wall crowned with coils of razor-sharp barbed wire snakes around the facility, which is flanked by a garden nursery, an auto repair shop and a building supply store. Soldiers with automatic weapons swinging from their shoulders slouch in watchtowers along the perimeter, gazing down with evident disinterest at the traffic along Industry Boulevard. From the street, a blue-and-white Israeli flag fluttering from a pole and several rooftops are all that can be seen of the inside of the maximum-security compound, which covers about two city blocks.

It was in a cell at Ashkelon in late January 1987 that Meir Vanunu saw his brother for the first time in two years. Meir hadn't wanted to make the trip. As the vitriolic campaign against Mordechai escalated through the autumn of 1986, Meir remained in Boston, following his brother's plight through news accounts and telephone conversations with his parents. The reports of Motti's situation were increasingly bleak, but Meir recoiled in frustration and anger at the thought of returning to Israel to stand beside him. He had closed that door when he left in 1985, and under no circumstances did he intend to reopen it.

Still, as the weeks passed, Meir could not shake the nagging sense of duty to family instilled long ago in the Vanunu children by their parents. And in early January, he received a letter from his brother that forced his hand.

"My prison conditions have been very difficult up until now," Motti wrote. "Complete isolation. One hour walking outside the cell in a small room. They prevent me from writing my thoughts and ideas to myself. They treat me like State Enemy No. 1. Here I am in jail. If you want, I would like you to come and help me, continue what I've started. I've got no right to ask you to do anything, and I don't know how you feel about what I did. You do whatever you think is right. It's up to you. But I could use your help."

Perhaps better than the rest of his family, Meir realized the hopelessness of Motti's predicament. His brother would have no chance to defend himself in a closed-door trial run by the security forces. In addition, with his mail censored and visits limited to his lawyer and his confused and frightened family, with the government restricting news coverage of the case, there would also be no opportunity to explain his motives to the Israeli people. Motti's fate was sealed: a show trial followed by a long jail sentence.

Meir reluctantly concluded that he would have to become his brother's spokesman, "Mordechai on the outside," raising the issues that Motti could not address from his jail cell. A few days after receiving the letter, Meir packed his bags and flew to Israel.

The meeting with his brother was a warm, emotional moment. Motti was in good spirits, overjoyed to see both Meir and his brother, Danny, who also made the trip up from Beersheba. But the reunion did little to raise Meir's hopes. He quickly discovered the authorities were deadly serious. Before they were even allowed to talk with their brother, Meir and Danny were required to sign secrecy agreements and were threatened with prison if they violated the pledge. To make sure no more secrets were passed, a Shin Bet agent attended the meeting.

In a bizarre example of bureaucratic efficiency, the government had mailed to Vanunu's home a claim form for unemployment compensation owed to him after his layoff from the Dimona plant. The money was urgently needed to pay legal fees, and the brothers brought the application with them.

One question required Vanunu to disclose the amount of time he had spent in Israel since leaving work. "In order to fill this out, we need to know the date of your return to Israel," Danny told Mordechai as the three brothers sat around a wooden table.

"Well, I came on the seventh of October, tied, chained up like Kunta Kinte," Mordechai replied with a laugh, referring to the slave hero of *Roots*.

At the mention of Vanunu's return date, the Shin Bet agent shouted, "Stop that! Stop that right now, or I'll end this meeting! You can't talk about things like that."

The brothers moved on to less sensitive questions, and the agent allowed the meeting to proceed. But the incident was a chilling reminder of the hopelessness of Vanunu's case.

Even with the constant presence of eavesdropping security agents, Meir was able to glean some information about his brother's capture during a dozen meetings over the next six months. When the frequently bored monitors were momentarily distracted, Vanunu would quietly pass along other details, including accounts of how he met Cindy and a description of the assault in the Rome apartment. On one occasion, an agent sat and listened for several minutes as Motti asked Meir to go to Rome to prod the Italian government into investigating the kidnapping. Only after the visit was over did the agent remind Meir that he had signed the secrecy pledge.

Despite public assurances that a Dimona-style security foulup could never happen again, it seemed the Shin Bet still had not learned its lesson.

Heeding his brother's request, Meir flew to Rome in mid-March to seek a meeting with Domenico Sica, a veteran anti-terrorism investigator know as "The Fox" who had been assigned to look into Vanunu's allegations. After a brief flurry of activity and official bluster, the Italian inquiry had largely ground to a halt, stalled by Israel's refusal to cooperate and an enervating political dispute between pro- and anti-Israeli factions within the Italian government. After his initial demands for information met with silence from Jerusalem, Prime Minister Craxi was more than willing to let the Vanunu matter fade from the headlines.

Sica appeared intent on pursuing the case, but the preliminary results of his investigation were discouraging. Vanunu's name was found on the passenger manifest for British Airways Flight 504, and the airline confirmed he had boarded in London with one piece of luggage and an open return ticket. Investigators initially theorized that if Vanunu had indeed been kidnapped in Rome by the Mossad, he might have been flown back to Israel on the next flight to Tel Aviv, which left Fiumicino shortly before 1 P.M. on the day after Vanunu arrived. But airport workers had noticed nothing unusual about any of the passengers or cargo aboard the aircraft, and airport security officials contended no one could have been kidnapped or forced to leave the country without attracting the attention of security patrols. Investigators also found no evidence that Vanunu had checked into a hotel or rented a car in Rome, as a visitor might have done.

Sica's suspicions shifted to the possibility that Vanunu had been smuggled out of the country on an Israeli ship, the *Tapuz*, that briefly docked at the northern Italian port of La Spezia on October 4. The ship, property of the Israeli-owned Zim shipping line, was supposed to have sailed for Marseilles, France, but it instead headed back to Israel, arriving at Ashdod on October 9. Sica also discovered a junior official at the Israeli Embassy in Rome had rented a van during the week after Vanunu disappeared. The van was returned with about 540 miles on the odometer; the round-trip drive between La Spezia and Rome is approximately 510 miles. But when Israeli officials refused to discuss the ship or the van, the trail went cold. By the time Meir arrived in Rome, Sica was still vowing to unravel the mystery, but warning it might take a while.

Meir's meeting with Sica at the investigator's heavily guarded office not far from Vatican City was a rocky one. Meir, who showed up without an appointment, was ushered into a meeting room and told to wait. Sica strode in about thirty minutes later, flanked by two plainclothes police officers. He wasted little time on pleasantries.

"Tell me what you know," the investigator demanded.

Meir was caught off-guard. He didn't want to talk about what he knew. In fact, he couldn't discuss anything he had learned about the case. If the Israelis found out, he would face legal problems.

"I came to express my family's concern about this matter," Meir told Sica. "We would appreciate a thorough investigation by your office. It's really our only hope. We'd like to know what you have learned."

Sica sat down in a chair facing Meir, spread his palms on the table, and glared at the young Israeli. "You are not here to ask questions," he barked. "You are here to answer them."

The magistrate's attitude shook Meir. It was as if Meir were somehow responsible for his brother's kidnapping. "I'm not ready to answer anything," he protested angrily. "I just want to know what's happening here, in Italy."

But Sica, who harbored some suspicions about Vanunu's claims, was adamant. Pointing a finger at Meir, he warned, "If you don't cooperate, you're going to jail. It's against the law here not to cooperate with us."

Meir couldn't believe what he was hearing. He had come to Rome trying to find out what the authorities knew about his brother's disappearance, and now they were threatening to lock him up. Had Sica, he wondered, been as tough on Israeli officials?

Then another thought occurred to him. A few days in an Italian prison would certainly attract some media attention, which would only help his effort to put the Vanunu case back in the headlines. "Well, okay," he said finally. "Put me in jail then."

After several minutes of threats, Sica backed down, and the meeting ended. As Meir got up to leave, Sica handed him his business card. "If you think of anything, give me a call," he said.

Some investigation, Meir thought.

Accompanied by his brother, Asher, who had come down from Holland for the meeting with Sica, Meir next flew to London to talk with the *Sunday Times*. Money was becoming a serious problem. The brothers and sisters had raised a few thousand dollars, and Meir had withdrawn some cash from Motti's bank account in Boston. But the legal case and the public relations campaign would require much more substantial financing. Perhaps the newspaper would help.

The *Sunday Times* had certainly promised to lend a hand. In discussions with Mordechai, the newspaper had pledged $100,000 for Vanunu's legal defense in the event he was arrested, and for support to his family. But now officials were not particularly forthcoming. Alistair Brett, the newspaper's attorney, agreed to contribute $5,000 to the legal fund, but cautioned that any additional support could only be provided through the sale of a book about Vanunu's case— the project for which Vanunu was to have signed a contract the week he disappeared. And to write a book, the lawyer added, the *Sunday Times* staff would have to learn more about how Vanunu was returned to Israel.

To Meir, Brett's comments sounded like blackmail and he resented it. Motti had already earned some support. The newspaper had done very well with his story. Wasn't that worth something? Meir bitterly recalled the statement that Neil had released in late November, a few days after Vanunu appeared in public for the first time since his arrest. "We recognize that we have a moral commitment to assist Vanunu and his family, which we are anxious to discharge in whatever way we can," the statement read. "We are urgently exploring how this can best be achieved." Meir was convinced the *Sunday Times* did not plan to honor its pledge.

Meir's requests for financial help were icily rejected in the newsroom as well. Within Neil's strict guidelines, the Insight team was eager to learn how Vanunu was captured. It was, after all, a legitimate news story. But the staff had no interest in bankrolling Meir's defense efforts, and accepted no responsibility for Motti's mounting legal bills. Meir had expected some expression of regret or even guilt that the newspaper hadn't done more to protect Motti. Instead, the *Sunday Times* appeared to have simply written his brother off. Some of the reporters even voiced anger at Motti himself for wandering out of London. "Their attitude was, 'He knew what he was doing. Let him pay the price for what he did. It's too bad, but that's the way it goes,' " Meir said. Only Peter Hounam, the one reporter who had developed any kind of a personal relationship with Vanunu, expressed remorse about Motti's fate, and even Hounam was piqued by his decision to leave the city.

Meir resented the newspaper's apparent lack of concern, but Mordechai didn't share Meir's rancor. Pleased with the way the story had appeared in print, Vanunu waved aside his brother's complaints and insisted that Meir maintain good relations with the *Sunday Times*.

The newspaper had legitimate reasons for maintaining an arm's length relationship with both Vanunus. Any direct financial involvement would have heightened suspicions in Israel that Vanunu had indeed sold his country's secrets. The question of money was already receiving prominent play in the Israeli media. Reports alleged the *Sunday Times* had paid Vanunu as much as $300,000 for his information. Neil and Morgan denied the stories, downplaying the discussions about a book contract and saying Vanunu had received only expenses, which the newspaper would pay any important source. But prosecutors had a major stake in the secrets-for-cash angle. The idea that Vanunu had sold out his country stacked public opinion even more heavily against him.

Seen in that light, Meir's grandiose scheme to generate public sympathy for his brother also aroused some suspicions in London. Somewhat unfairly, the *Sunday Times* concluded that Meir was motivated more by self-interest than by any genuine concern for Motti. A defense campaign would provide him with an income and a spotlighted stage from which to advance his own career goals. And he wanted the newspaper to finance it, regardless of the perception that might create in Israel.

"When we balked, he accused us of not caring," one reporter said. "Maybe he was the one who didn't care so much."

The newspaper would pursue the story in a normal fashion. Neil did agree to permit his reporters to testify on behalf of Vanunu, primarily to make sure the court understood Vanunu acted out of political, not financial, concerns. But the *Sunday Times* felt no special obligation to its source.

Among themselves, however, the reporters and editors were openly agonizing over whether the newspaper had done enough to protect its source. Losing Vanunu had been a major embarrassment. Few thought the *Sunday Times* could have prevented Vanunu's kidnapping if Israel was intent on capturing him, but there were second thoughts about the way the story had been handled and the questions filtered through the newsroom.

- Why hadn't the newspaper pushed Vanunu to seek political asylum in London? Placing Vanunu under the protection of Britain might have dissuaded the Mossad from snatching him. The move had been planned, but nobody took the time to take care of it.

- Why hadn't the newspaper been more discreet in Israel? The early inquiries had tipped the Israelis that Vanunu was talking.

- Why hadn't Vanunu been kept away from Wapping? It was more comfortable to talk with him there, but it made it easier for the Israelis to track him down.

- And, most importantly, why hadn't someone sat down with Vanunu at the outset and firmly told him that the newspaper would not take another step until he agreed, in writing, to around-the-clock protection? That proposal had also been considered and quickly abandoned. Nobody wanted him to walk away. The story was simply too good to lose.

Chapter 49

Whatever the misgivings about Meir, Vanunu's palm message in December had rekindled interest in the story at the *Sunday Times*, and the discovery of an airline ticket sold to a "C. Hanin" who sat next to Vanunu on British Airways Flight 504 gave the newspaper a lead. If Cindy had been telling Vanunu the truth, she might very well have lived in Florida. And if she had returned home, she might be able to shed some light on his disappearance.

A search of Florida telephone directories uncovered a Cynthia Ann Hanin in Orlando who worked as an assistant beautician. But in September the woman was preparing for her wedding to a man named Randy Hanin and never left the United States. She could not have been the woman Vanunu met in London.

The coincidence, however, was striking. Hounam and the other reporters quickly concluded that Vanunu's friend Cindy must be someone who knew Cynthia Ann Hanin and "borrowed" her identity. Assisted by a private investigator, the newspaper soon stumbled on the fact that Cynthia Ann Hanin had a sister-in-law, Cheryl, who had moved to Israel. A high-school graduation photograph of Cheryl and pictures of Cheryl at her brother's wedding were shown to Connett and Prangnell, and both reporters were confident she was the woman they had seen with Vanunu. Their confidence growing, the Insight staffers dug deeper into Cheryl's background, tracing her life through high school in Orlando to Israel where she had married Ofer Bentov. The couple was now living in the beach resort city of Netanya, north of Tel Aviv.

It was too much to be a coincidence. Cheryl Hanin Bentov had to be the woman who lured Vanunu to his capture.

In July 1987 Hounam and Connett were dispatched to Israel to track her down. Posing as a tourist, Connett bought a tour package that included a few nights in Netanya. On his first day in Israel, the reporter staked out the Bentov bungalow, on a quiet street not far from the beach. There was no sign of life at the house. No one came or went. The shutters were closed. The front lawn needed mowing. Wearing short pants in the midsummer sun, Connett developed a severe case of sunburn as he whiled away the afternoon staring at the empty house.

Hounam, who was staying in a hotel in Tel Aviv, joined him at dusk and the two went for dinner in Netanya. As they drove past the house later that night, a light was on inside and from the street the reporters spotted a woman unpacking a suitcase. Connett crept up to the house for a closer look. Peering through the window, there was no doubt in his mind: the woman inside was the same one he had seen with Vanunu that night in Leicester Square.

Hounam and Connett decided to maintain the stakeout until they were sure Bentov was alone. For two days, they watched the house, waiting for their opportunity. One afternoon, Hounam followed Bentov's husband down to the beach where he played volleyball with friends for about an hour. At lunchtime, Bentov was joined by his wife and an older woman, who Hounam determined was Cheryl's mother. The three later returned to the bungalow.

The next day, July 13, Bentov drove off about 4 P.M., leaving Cheryl and her mother sitting in the small garden in the rear of the house. With Connett beside him, Hounam walked up to the front door and rang the doorbell. As he had hoped, Cheryl came to the door alone. She was dressed in a sleeveless blouse and shorts, and smiled quizzically at her visitors.

"Hello," Hounam began. "Are you Cheryl Hanin?"

"Yes. What can I do for you," she answered pleasantly in English. Hounam was struck by her broad American accent.

"I'm from the *London Sunday Times*. I've come to see you about something, and I think you probably know what it's about," Hounam said.

Cheryl appeared shocked. She stared at the two men for a moment, then stood aside and said briskly, "You better come in."

Paydirt. If this woman was not Cindy, she never would have understood Hounam's reference, and by no means would she have invited two strangers talking nonsense into her home.

Without another word, Bentov led the reporters to the dining room, then darted through a set of French doors leading into the garden where she engaged in a brief but animated conversation with her mother. After a few minutes, the two women walked inside.

"What can I do for you?" Cheryl asked.

Hounam outlined the story the newspaper planned to write about her role in the Vanunu affair. There was no question of her identity, he stressed. The reporters had flown to Israel only to obtain her side of the story.

"And you're going to *publish* this?" Bentov said finally, for the first time showing signs of strain.

She asked to see Hounam's *Sunday Times* identification. As she examined the card, Hounam sat down on a sofa and produced a small tape recorder, preparing to begin a formal interview. Suddenly, Bentov's mother, alarmed by the sight of the recorder, screamed, "Don't say anything! Don't say anything! He's got a tape recorder!"

Hounam tried to calm the woman. "Look, if the tape recorder is any problem, I'll turn it off. But only if you agree to talk," he said.

"Turn it off!" Cheryl snapped as she sat in a chair across the room.

The reporter clicked off the machine. Leaning forward on the sofa, he tried to persuade Cheryl that there was no longer any way to prevent the story and that her cooperation was essential if the story was to be accurate and balanced. "I've pointed out to you that you are the woman who did it, who broke the law. You have committed an offense in Italy. You have lured a man back to Israel and, you know, he's now in very serious danger. And I've pointed this out to you and you haven't denied it," he said.

At that, Cheryl jumped to her feet and shouted, "I deny it. I deny what you are saying."

Hounam switched the tape recorder back on and tried again. "We know it's you," he said. "You've just sat here. You haven't asked me any questions about the whole affair. You know exactly why I'm here. You didn't need any explanations as to who Vanunu was, was the *Sunday Times* involved, why we're following this up. You have reacted just as I would expect someone who was involved."

Cheryl turned and began to leave the room. Hounam had a camera strapped to his neck, and he snapped three photographs before she snatched a piece of paper from a table and hid her face behind it. Still clutching the paper shield, Cheryl bolted into the bedroom and locked the door behind her, leaving her mother in a state of near-hysteria. When the older woman had calmed down, Hounam and Connett asked if she could persuade her daughter to sit for a brief interview.

"She won't talk to you," the mother said firmly. "Maybe if you could come back later when her husband is here."

With considerable reluctance, the reporters agreed to leave, saying they would call later to set up an appointment. When Hounam telephoned the house that evening, Ofer Bentov answered. He politely rejected a request for an interview and laughed off Hounam's efforts to draw him out on his intelligence background, claiming he was a driver for a plastics company.

Hounam and Connett drove back to the house the next morning. The shutters were closed again, and the family car was missing. Neighbors reported the Hanins had left.

For the next few days, Hounam called the house at regular intervals, never receiving an answer. One morning a week later, a woman speaking English with an Israeli accent picked up the telephone. She was housesitting for Cheryl, the woman explained. Cheryl wouldn't be back for some time. She'd gone on a safari with her mother.

Chapter 50

Meir's problems with Sica and the *Sunday Times* paled in comparison to his relationship with Amnon Zichroni. The lawyer was at loggerheads with his client's brother from the day they met. The two men had sharply divergent views on the best approach to take in the case. Meir, pessimistic about Vanunu's chances in court, saw the legal effort as simply one arm of his campaign to highlight the political nature of the prosecution, and he insisted on the right to approve Zichroni's strategy. The attorney secretly shared Meir's feeling that the courtroom battle was already lost, but he adamantly refused to politicize the proceedings. Vanunu's best chance, in his estimation, was a plea bargain. Zichroni was urging his client to enter a guilty plea in exchange for a prison sentence of eight years, and he was convinced that Meir's attempt to highlight the nuclear issue and further publicize the case would only hinder his efforts to broker a deal with the government.

The relationship between the two men deteriorated rapidly, and it was not long before Meir began to openly question the depth of Zichroni's commitment to his brother. Perhaps, he speculated, Zichroni approved of the state's plan to keep the case under wraps, and was merely going through the motions to move the matter along. Meir concluded that Zichroni couldn't be trusted. There was nothing concrete, but he became convinced Zichroni was cooperating in some way with the Shin Bet, perhaps agreeing to the government's terms in this case to receive favorable treatment in another.

It didn't take much to turn Mordechai against Zichroni. The steady harassment by prison officials and the weeks of solitary confinement were making him increasingly suspicious of nearly everyone. "It isn't enough that I've been imprisoned pending trial before being convicted—they are also trying to restrict me more and more by way of isolation," he wrote to his brother after a visit on March 1. "I'm totally cut off from any possibility of contact with people. And I've been in this situation for about five months and I don't know what exactly they want to do or how long my isolation will last."

He complained about being kept in his cell for twenty-two hours a day, with two hours alone in a small courtyard for exercise and only one thirty-minute visit from his family every two weeks. He staged a thirty-three day hunger strike, refusing all sustenance except water, to protest the conditions of his confinement. He angrily lashed out at the "slander" campaign against him in the media, including the publication of his diaries.

Jail authorities defended the restrictions as a means of preventing Vanunu from revealing still more secrets, but the prisoner contended the government only wanted "to take revenge upon me and harm me in the hope that I will emerge from prison a broken man."

All the stories about protecting state secrets don't hold because I was taken to prison directly from abroad where I had been for nine months. So if there are any secrets I know, either I gave them away or I didn't. It seems to me that the manner in which they're holding me and everything related to it—such as preventing contacts with others, an excessively severe charge sheet which is out of proportion to the crimes I am suspected of—are all being used to bolster some government policy. Mordechai Vanunu has become the fall guy for political deceptions. And all of this is being done in the light of day in a democratic state. The question is: how long will solitary confinement last and will I have a fair trial?

Under Meir's prodding, Vanunu eventually blamed Zichroni for his predicament. "What is surprising is that the lawyer didn't do anything about the matter and I didn't know what my rights were," he wrote to Meir.

Mordechai was apoplectic about Zichroni's apparent inability to arrange visitation privileges for Judy Zimmet, who had arrived in Israel to help her boyfriend. Vanunu balked at the government's requirement that he talk with Judy only through a glass barrier, and he demanded that Zichroni seek a removal of the restriction. At a hearing in late January, prosecutor Uzi Hasson argued against face-to-face meetings between Vanunu and Zimmet. For the first time, the government contended in court papers that Vanunu's disclosures had seriously damaged national security. The episode with the palm message was evidence he would do it again, if given the chance, Hasson told the court. Vanunu had promised "to refrain from talking about state secrets" during meetings with visitors and asked authorities to "put this promise to the test." But Hasson said Vanunu could pass on more secrets to Zimmet—primarily about the way in which he was returned to Israel—and the woman might try to spread the information once she left the country.

Zichroni said Zimmet would do no such thing. The woman is Jewish, he reminded the judges. "But Vanunu isn't Jewish," Hasson noted. The restriction was allowed to stand.

Zichroni didn't help matters by leading Vanunu to believe he was representing him without charge out of concern for the apparent violation of his civil rights ("I may have forgotten to discuss money with him, I don't know," Zichroni explained later) and by failing to inform him that his testimony at trial would be severely limited.

Vanunu had weathered the arduous conditions of his imprisonment in the belief that he would eventually have an opportunity to tell his story in court. When Meir corrected Motti's misunderstanding, Vanunu angrily blamed Zichroni. The brothers decided to find another lawyer. At the very least, Meir believed, a switch would delay the trial, affording him more time to fire up the publicity campaign.

In early March, Meir approached Avigdor Feldman, an attorney with a widely known reputation in the civil rights movement in Israel, and asked him whether he would be interested in taking over the case.

It was an ironic choice. Feldman began his career in Zichroni's office and worked there for eleven years before leaving in 1985, disenchanted with Zichroni's move away from civil rights toward the business world. Feldman had long been regarded as the brains behind the bluster at Zichroni's firm. In legal circles it was generally assumed that Feldman did all the work on a case—conducting the research, preparing the motions, even appearing in court—while Zichroni went on "Mabat," an evening television news program, to discuss the verdict. Such an arrangement between a lawyer and one of his assistants was not unheard of, but Feldman tired of it and left. He spent a year studying for a master's degree at American University in Washington, D.C., under a program sponsored by the Association for Civil Rights in Israel, then returned to set up a litigation center for the association in Tel Aviv.

At thirty-eight, Feldman was regarded as something of a legal rebel. He was a short, pudgy man with bushy, greying hair whose impish demeanor, bemused smile and casual, almost sloppy style of dress masked a sharp intellect. Feldman had never shied away from attacking the legal establishment. In a newspaper article a few months earlier, he had written a blistering attack on a prominent Tel Aviv lawyer for representing both sides in legal disputes.

Writing was Feldman's passion, and he derived enormous pleasure from using his writing skills as a legal tool. His written arguments were regarded as literary and imaginative, and he regularly contributed legal analyses to newspapers.

A proudly secular Jew with an intense dislike for the stifling religious atmosphere in the holy city of Jerusalem, Feldman liked to describe himself as an "undoctrinated, uneducated" socialist.

He was fascinated by the Vanunu case. Shortly after Vanunu's arrest, he had written an article for the newspaper *Hadashot* outlining possible defense strategies, including a challenge to the legality of nuclear weapons. "I was very intrigued by the person behind the issue and by the legal issues involved. I thought from the beginning it would be a hell of a job of translating this issue into a certain legal discourse or legal justification," he recalled. "Was I for or against Vanunu? I thought that if he really did it out of ideological motives to reveal the nuclear issue, then he has my sympathy."

When Meir called him, Feldman was in the process of winding up his work for the civil rights group and planning to start a private practice—a move that strained relations with his mentor. But as much as he was interested in the Vanunu affair, Feldman was not about to wade into murky ethical waters. At their first meeting, he urged Meir to work out his problems with Zichroni. But when Meir approached Feldman a second time, saying the chasm was insurmountable, Feldman agreed to take the case, provided Zichroni dropped out and if Vanunu agreed with his strategy. And his services wouldn't come cheaply. Fifty thousand dollars was the fee Feldman wanted from the very first client of his brand-new business.

After tentatively securing Feldman's services, Meir went to Zichroni's office one afternoon and demanded to speak with him privately.

"Listen," Meir began, "I kind of see this case as like a little boat. And in this boat are you and Mordechai and the secret service, the judges, the government. This boat is floating quietly on a very dark lake. And everybody's comfortable with the ride. Everybody just wants the boat to sail along the lake, to the other side and disappear into the darkness. And nobody will know anything else about it."

"I want to shake up the boat," Meir said. "I want to make waves. I want the boat to sail into the spotlight. I want to make sure everybody knows what's going on. Not matter what the outcome, at least I want them to know what's going on."

Zichroni puffed quietly on his cigar for several moments. "How do you do that?" he asked finally.

"Well, for example," Meir said quietly, "we could change the defense attorney."

Zichroni never changed his expression. "And how would that help?" he asked.

Meir explained a new lawyer might be more receptive to his approach. In addition, the change would allow more time to work the media, to get the true story out.

Zichroni dismissed the second argument. The case wasn't that complicated, he said. A new attorney wouldn't need much time to familiarize himself with it, a week or two at most. Anyway, he concluded dismissively, who would take the case? Meir didn't mention Feldman.

Zichroni urged Meir to reconsider his decision, and Meir agreed to discuss it one more time with Mordechai. As he left the office, Meir turned and asked Zichroni, "Is there something you're doing that I don't know about? Something that would make me change my mind about how you're handling this?"

"No. Nothing at all," Zichroni said.

Meir's report about the meeting with Zichroni left Mordechai convinced that he needed a new lawyer. On Friday, March 6, 1987, he signed the necessary court documents and Meir announced Zichroni's ouster to the news media. Zichroni and an associate went to the prison two days later to make sure their client approved of the move. Vanunu was polite and slightly embarrassed by the dispute, but it was clear the decision had been his.

That night, Zichroni was once again on television, shrugging off his dismissal. And for months afterward, he was a much sought after speaker at international conferences on nuclear proliferation.

Chapter 51

Because of other commitments, Feldman did not officially take the case for two more months, which did give Meir more time for his media campaign. And he needed it. The effort to sway public opinion in Israel was going nowhere and the attempts to win support overseas were only slightly less disheartening.

The worldwide protests and demonstrations that Meir expected never materialized, despite his frequent trips abroad in search of allies. Frontline anti-nuclear and human rights groups shunned his pleas for assistance because of misgivings about Vanunu's motives. Small community peace groups and religious organizations in various countries were somewhat more willing to take a stand. Defense committees were formed in the United States, France and Scandinavia; in England, writer Graham Greene and three other authors publicly called for Vanunu's release. But the impact of this grass-roots campaign was negligible. The Israeli government, confident the tumult would soon die down, largely ignored the calls for better treatment of Vanunu and an open trial. Authorities also pointed contemptuously at some of the fringe political organizations that sorted through Vanunu's explanations of his motives to find a position they could support. In the United States, for example, the anti-Zionist Spartacist League decided Vanunu had struck a blow for the "international working class," and his plight was featured at a forum entitled "For International Class-Struggle Defense."

Meir's bid for the support of foreign governments fared even worse. He had been confident that American officials would be forced to confront Israel over the Vanunu disclosures, and he traveled to the United States to roil the waters. But there was little interest. A news conference in Washington drew only a reporter for a religious newspaper interested in Vanunu's conversion, and both the Reagan administration and Congress shunned the subject. Massachusetts Congressman Joseph P. Kennedy, responding to requests from constituent Judy Zimmet, did query the Israeli ambassador in Washington for information about Vanunu's case, and was politely assured Vanunu would receive a fair trial. Americans, Meir soon came to believe, were too close to Israel to get involved.

There was one notable international success. Nine Australian senators and the British-based Bertrand Russell Peace Foundation, joined by thirty-six members of the British Parliament, nominated Vanunu for the 1987 Nobel Peace Prize.

"Vanunu's revelations serve to uphold the non-proliferation regime throughout the world, and are clearly a matter of conscience, quite unsuitable for criminal reprisals," the foundation's nomination letter stated. "It is our opinion that the Nobel Committee can make a powerful contribution to justice and peace by publicly considering Mr. Vanunu for an award which he has richly earned."

The Australians were even more direct:

"We believe that Moredechai (sic) Vanunu's action in revealing details of Israel's nuclear weapons arsenal to the world was motivated by a great and long standing desire for world peace, and we believe that he deserves the world's recognition for his selfless action. The award of the Nobel Peace Prize to him would be a timely and appropriate expression of such recognition."

The letters, however, were purely cosmetic. The February deadline for 1987 nominations had long since passed.

In October, Vanunu did win the Right Livelihood Award, a prize created in 1980 to honor work in the areas of the environment, world poverty and nuclear disarmament. "Vanunu is awarded the prize for his courage and for placing loyalty toward mankind first, despite great personal risks," said Jakob von Uekkull, a Swedish-German writer who created the award, which is presented by the Swedish Parliament in Stockholm the day before the Nobel Prizes are announced. One of four recipients, Vanunu was awarded a $25,000 share of the $100,000 prize. Through his brother, he announced he would use the money to establish a U.S.-based lobby for a nuclear-free Middle East. But no plan was ever submitted to the awards committee, which refused to release the money without one.

Meir's efforts flopped in Israel. He quickly realized there was no hope of changing public opinion. No one seemed to be listening. No one was interested in the larger questions posed by Vanunu's actions. The Israeli people were like a monolithic "wall of hostility," Meir complained, either too stupid or too brainwashed to deal with the issue properly.

The response from the few Knesset members willing to listen was equally frustrating. "Don't get involved in this too deeply," one told Meir ominously. "There's more to it than you know."

Mordechai was dismayed by the lack of public support. "The question I'm asking is why are there not more people who take this path for the sake of the community of the whole when they see that those responsible are not acting right?" he wrote in a letter. "How is it that those people who are capable of contributing and fighting are evading responsibility?"

From the start, Meir had understood that asking Israelis to condone Vanunu's actions would be futile. Instead, he attempted to win public support for an open trial in the hope that what the people heard would spark a serious domestic debate on the nuclear question. With the help of Yael Lotan, a writer and leading leftist, he formed The Committee for an Open Trial for Vanunu, a small band of left-wing activists whose support for Vanunu actually served to further poison public opinion. The group held news conferences and took out newspaper advertisements to draw attention to the cause, but even that approach failed miserably.

Lotan, a writer with an unquenchable enthusiasm for ideas and philosophical debate, was a native Israeli, born during the British Mandate, and was well aware that her strident views on everything from religion to the Palestinian question were out of step with prevailing public opinion. But to her amazement, not even her colleagues on the left were willing to get involved in this cause. The committee circulated a petition that argued the presence of nuclear weapons in the volatile Middle East was "especially dangerous."

"As citizens of Israel, we have a right to know what our government is developing in the nuclear installation at Dimona, where Mordechai Vanunu worked," the petition read. "While Israel refused to endorse the Nuclear Non-proliferation Treaty or submit its installations to international supervision, we believe that it is our duty to demand urgent public debate on this issue."

Even without a single word about Vanunu's action, the petition garnered only 160 signatures, almost exclusively from the academic and artistic communities. "Everyone we approached had some reason for not signing it," Lotan said. "And these were people who would sign almost any petition. It was, 'Well, he did it for money,' or, 'He's crazy,' or, 'We don't know the rights and wrongs of it.' "

"Quite a few of them said, 'Well, the nuclear issue is really terribly important and it should be discussed and really we should be opposed to it. But he went about it the wrong way. He broke the law. He shouldn't have violated state secrets.' " They might have been willing to take up the subject of nuclear arms, but not if it involved Vanunu. People would say to us, 'Yes, he made tremendous sacrifices. But don't ask me to sign your petition because I'm about to be appointed professor or because my wife's about to be appointed professor or I'll be kicked out of my job.' "

Vanunu's conversion to Christianity was a major roadblock. It made Israelis uncomfortable if not angry. "It is strange. The idea of Zionism was to create an ordinary nation, to give Jews a normal place in history," Lotan said. "But in the last few years, this sense of exclusivity, this sense of 'we the Jews against the whole world' has come back again strongly. And people saw the conversion as Vanunu siding with the whole world."

From his jail cell, Vanunu remained defiant about his conversion. "[I]n this state they force us to observe the religious law even if you don't believe in it, such as eating Matzot and fasting on Yom Kippur and circumcising the children and religious marriage, et cetera," he wrote to a supporter. "I am proud of my independent thinking and the ability which I developed to cross all these barriers and to apply my own faith and values. To me, the Christian religion is above all a system of human values, and only after that a religion. The belief in

Jesus and his salvation is part of the way of life which I have adopted. And I believe it is a great example which helps people to live a better life. I do know that there are other religions, and it is everybody's right to adopt the religion that they believe in. I'm an independent man. I've chosen my way. I am not accountable to anyone."

In rambling, sometimes confusing letters to newspapers and supporters around the world, Vanunu did what he could to explain his decision to reveal the secrets of Dimona. Whatever uncertainties or confusion had stalked him since his departure from Israel had been cleared up. His explanation of his motives had been honed to a sheen by McKnight's anti-nuclear workshops in Australia and his efforts to explain himself in London.

"An action like mine teaches citizens that their own reasoning, the reasoning of the individual, is no less important than that of the leaders. Don't follow them blindly in important and crucial issues, such as nuclear weapons," he wrote in a July 1987 to Lotan:

I maintain that the Israeli policy in the matter of the atom is dangerous—they don't admit the existence of nuclear arms, and on the other hand they hint at its existence but do not allow the international bodies to inspect the Dimona reactor. The danger is that, assuming there are nuclear weapons in Israel, and the citizens don't know about it, they cannot express their opinions in this matter. Nor can they prepare for the threat of nuclear disaster.

Later:

A good way to start protecting yourself from the nuclear threat is to know about it, to organize against the outcome of nuclear disaster and, above all, to try in every possible way to prevent it.

To conclude—a society which does not see the immediate danger to the physical survival of mankind and fails to take steps to defend itself is a psychologically unhealthy society. It doesn't matter if we ignore the danger—it will always hang over us and its menace is evidence of an unhealthy society. Ignoring it is the cause of the disease. A society which can live with such a threat develops social and psychological dangers. And this is only what happens before the nuclear weapons are actually used. So that the existence of the nuclear bomb, not to say its deployment, is very bad for all mankind—and who can foresee the outcome!

By April 1987, seven months after his brother's abduction and five months after Vanunu first appeared in custody, the strain of failure had become more than Meir could bear. He was living in a tiny apartment, traveling around the country by bus and covering most of the costs out of his own pocket. He had soured on the open-trial committee members, who seemed to be interested only in using the case to further their own highly unpopular political agenda. Their involvement was so damaging to Vanunu's prospects that at times Meir wondered if some of them were actually government agents.

The rest of the Vanunu family was doing what it could to help. Even Solomon had recovered sufficiently from the psychic blow of his son's conversion to appeal publicly for Israelis to stop vilifying Mordechai and give him his day in court. "My son is not a traitor," the father told a newspaper. "Mordechai was sincere in his belief that it was his moral duty to tell these things. I want people to know that I support my son. I want to see he has a fair trial. If people go on like this, they will drive him mad before he gets to court."

Through this tragedy, the strong sense of family survived intact. No matter what Motti had done, his brothers and sisters decided, the family would stand by him. His sister Miriam told a television reporter, who seemed surprised that the Vanunus would not abandon Mordechai, "He's our brother, even though he did what he did. I know that what he did is wrong. (But) I'm not going to sever contacts with him. We're going to encourage him, and we'll go to visit him whenever we can."

Even with his family's backing, however, Meir felt isolated, leading a lonely crusade that attracted few followers. The lack of support had rekindled his resentment toward Israel. It was time to leave. During a visit to the prison in June 1987, Meir outlined his problems to Motti. "I just don't think I can keep it up physically and emotionally in Israel," he said. "I'll move out of here and carry on the campaign. Nothing will change here anyway."

Mordechai didn't object. Meir moved to London and intensified his efforts to spark global interest, mounting a campaign that would take him to twenty countries in the next eighteen months, financed by Vanunu's Boston savings and contributions from supporters.

From the start, Meir was careful to confine his pleas for help to what was already publicly known about the Vanunu case. He was ever mindful of the warnings from the Israeli security services that he too would face prosecution for revealing anything about how Mordechai was returned to Israel—in fact, anything that might portray Vanunu in a sympathetic light.

In early August, however, despairing of ever winning public support for his brother, Meir decided to reveal some of the details his brother had leaked to him during their jailhouse conversations. Mordechai had urged him to release the information—it would expose Israel's "treachery," he believed—and Meir was finally willing to comply. He gave the information to the *Sunday Times*, which was about to publish a story about Vanunu's capture that focused on the discovery of "Cindy's" true identity.

The article, with Meir's recollections, appeared August 9 under the front-page headline, "How Israeli agents snatched Vanunu," and Meir followed up the story with a news conference at which he called on Britain to reopen its investigation into Vanunu's disappearance.

Israel dismissed the latest disclosures with a smile. "The allegations sound like the basis for a film script," a Foreign Ministry spokesman said.

But once again a Vanunu had unwittingly played into Israel's hands. The idea that Mordechai Vanunu was still spilling secrets, this time from his jail cell, further outraged many Israelis and effectively killed any fleeting hopes of garnering public support for an open trial. And Meir's involvement in the revelations provided the government with an opportunity to turn off the spigot of pro-Vanunu publicity at the source. After the *Sunday Times* story was reprised in Israeli newspapers, authorities quickly issued a warrant for Meir's arrest on charges of violating security laws. With a fifteen-year prison sentence dangling over his head, Israel was now off-limits to the man leading Mordechai's public defense efforts.

Even government legal experts conceded the case against Meir was flimsy. But the Vanunu prosecution was now in the hands of the security forces who wanted to make sure Meir would not be in Israel, trying to kick up a public storm, once the trial began. The move against his brother was also one more blow to Vanunu's deteriorating mental state. Meir was one of the few people he trusted. Now, only weeks before he was to go on trial, Vanunu had lost another anchor.

Meir had hoped the revelations might spur Italian and British investigators to look more closely at Israel's involvement in his brother's disappearance. He was sadly mistaken. In Rome, Sica had already largely abandoned his probe, and the new disclosures did little to stimulate his interest. British authorities also refused to reopen their inquiry. Britain was no longer interested in the Vanunu case. Senior officials still believed some acts of illegality might have been committed on British soil. But it was old news. The Vanunu matter was closed. "We keep hearing of new evidence, and growing evidence, but the fact is that there has been no evidence whatsoever to back up Meir Vanunu's claim," a Foreign Office spokesman said. "His version of events, as detailed in the newspapers on Sunday, quite frankly adds nothing to the sum of human knowledge."

Vanunu and his family were crushed by the Italian and British reactions. Now, the trial was their only remaining hope of exposing the illegal means by which Mordechai was brought back to Israel. But Israel was not about to let the truth come out in court.

Chapter 52

Israel had reached a crossroads in the fall of 1987, squirming uncomfortably into middle age as it approached its fortieth birthday. The country was on edge, uneasy about the past and uncertain about the future, and the view in both directions was unsettling. Orthodox Jews fought their secular brothers in the streets of Jerusalem over the right to watch movies on the Sabbath. The government canceled plans to build a new fighter jet; thousands of workers faced unemployment and the country wondered if it could afford to defend itself. An accused Nazi war criminal went on trial, stoking the painful, frightening embers of the flames of the Holocaust. Palestinian blood stained the West Bank and the Gaza Strip even as Israelis reveled in the memory of the triumph of the 1967 war. The past seemed poised to catch the future, and nothing good could come of that. It was no time for a messenger with unpleasant news.

After firing Zichroni, Vanunu's hopes had again risen that the court proceedings would be more than simply a stage for his sentencing. He believed the trial would be a chance to force Israel to listen to his arguments. Despite Feldman's candid, pessimistic assessments of the upcoming trial, Vanunu confidently boasted that he would expose the Israeli nuclear program in open court.

As he plotted his trial strategy in his basement office in Tel Aviv, Feldman realized he had nothing to lose by going for broke. His client was all but convicted of being a traitor. In Feldman's view, this was absurd. Vanunu's aim, the lawyer believed, was not to harm the state but merely to warn its citizens of the nuclear threat they faced. He had not given his information to a foreign power but to a newspaper in hopes of reaching millions of people.

But to make his case, Feldman would have to invent a legal

framework for Vanunu's defense. What he came up with was a two-pronged strategy that would effectively place Israel in the dock. First, he intended to argue that Israel's abduction of Vanunu was illegal under the Universal Declaration of Human Rights, which had been incorporated in the country's legal system. Israel, Feldman believed, should have followed accepted legal procedures, such as a request for extradition, in seeking to arrest him. And because British courts might easily have viewed Vanunu's act as political, there was some question about whether he would have been handed over.

The argument was not without risk. It was bound to make many Israelis recall the 1960 abduction of Nazi war criminal Adolph Eichmann from Argentina. Eichmann had also challenged the legality of his return to Israel and the courts had rejected his claim. But the issue was fuzzy. In Eichmann, the courts based their decision on Argentina's waiver of its extradition rights. Israel could not claim that Britain, or any other country, had done the same in Vanunu.

Feldman's second line of defense would make Israelis even more uncomfortable. He intended to argue that Israel's nuclear weapons program violated both international law and the country's democratic traditions. Therefore, Vanunu had a moral right, indeed a moral responsibility, to pierce the veil of secrecy surrounding the program. This argument had formed the foundation of the prosecution of Nazi war criminals at Nuremberg after World War II. The Allied powers had successfully contended that the Nazis had a duty to disobey illegal orders or to refuse involvement in the illegal activities of their government. Conjuring up memories of Nazis, Feldman knew, could paint Vanunu as a kind of war criminal. But if the court agreed with even part of his arguments, Vanunu might at least receive a reduced sentence. And if he succeeded, Vanunu could very easily go free.

But there would be no room for that sort of philosophical inquiry at the Jerusalem District Courthouse. And even if there were, no one outside the sealed doors of the courtroom would hear it. Israel was at last playing again on familiar turf. Before the trial opened, Defense Minister Rabin quickly issued a secret order closing the proceedings to the public and barring any evidence or testimony regarding the nature of the Dimona facility, Vanunu's work at the plant, or, perhaps most importantly, the circumstances surrounding Vanunu's return to Israel. Under the order, no one in the courtroom—not the prosecutor, not the defense attorney, not even the three judges assigned to hear the case—would be given any information about those subjects. The court would decide only whether Vanunu had violated the terms of his secrecy oath by giving his story to the *Sunday Times*. What his motives were and whether any of the information was true were immaterial. Israel would not have to prove that Vanunu's revelations had actually harmed state security. The judges would start with the assumption that any abridgement of the secrecy oath was illegal.

Vanunu was going to stand trial not for what he revealed, but for merely opening his mouth. If, after signing a secrecy oath, he had told the *Sunday Times* that Israel didn't have nuclear weapons, that it was secretly publishing cookbooks at Dimona, he would have faced the same penalty.

The government's strategy was brilliant. Going to the trouble of a trial behind closed doors would underscore the gravity of Vanunu's actions. Israel would convince any remaining doubters in the Arab world that Vanunu was not part of an elaborate Mossad ruse, and that his allegations were true. His sentence would have the added advantage of sending a warning signal to other potential whistleblowers. And testimony and evidence about how Vanunu was captured would be barred from the proceedings. Israel's decision to allow Vanunu to tell his story would remain a state secret.

Feldman challenged the Rabin order, and an appeals court eased the restrictions to allow Vanunu to testify about the manner in which he was captured, the conditions under which he was held, and his emotional state at the time of his arrest and interrogation. But he was prevented from discussing anything he knew about the operation that led to his capture, including the name of the country where the abduction occurred. Testimony about the names of the prison where he was held and of any of the people involved in his capture and incarceration was also prohibited.

There would be no chance to cross-examine "Cindy," or Oscar Guerrero, or any of the Mossad agents who kidnapped Vanunu, or even Shimon Peres on the background of the case. Feldman, who harbored some suspicions about the extent of the government's involvement in the matter, would not even be given a chance to look at all the evidence. Only one person, the judge who had heard the appeal, had seen the evidence. The restrictions meant Feldman, in the presence of the prosecutor, would have to outline his strategy for the judge and ask him whether there was anything in the sealed record that might be of assistance to the defense. There was no recourse if the judge said no.

The case, in effect, was closed. The trial of Mordechai Vanunu was a formality, a polite nod in the direction of democracy. Rabin's order meant it was essentially over before it began.

Even the prosecutor, Uzi Hasson, a veteran government lawyer who headed the state attorney's tax unit, realized he didn't have to do much to guarantee a conviction. Hasson didn't even leave his post in the tax office to handle the Vanunu case. He spent one morning flipping through the handful of documents in the file. He spent a few hours preparing the formal charge sheet. And he showed up in court a few times to argue against Feldman's efforts to improve Vanunu's prison conditions. But to prosecute the man accused of spilling the country's most important secrets, Uzi Hasson didn't even need an assistant.

Chapter 53

The trial of Mordechai Vanunu opened on August 30, 1987, in Room 105 of the three-story sandstone Jerusalem court building. The government made no official announcement about the start of the proceedings—"It's a secret investigation. We don't say anything. Not about Vanunu, not about the investigation, not about the trial," one Justice Ministry official scolded a reporter without the slightest trace of irony. But word leaked anyway and shortly after dawn dozens of reporters and photographers began arriving at the courthouse, hoping for a glimpse of the defendant.

Vanunu left Ashkelon prison between 5 A.M. and 5:30 A.M. in an unmarked Ford van with its windows painted white and a curtain between the front and back seats to prevent anyone from spotting the prisoner through the windshield. The van was part of a four-vehicle convoy that included a decoy vehicle identical to Vanunu's and Border Police jeeps at the front and rear. On some days, an unmarked white Ford Escort sedan carrying Shin Bet agents also tagged along.

Vanunu slept and recited Christian prayers during the long ride to Jerusalem. About 8 A.M., the convoy arrived at the courthouse and drove through a twelve-foot-high gate topped with barbed wire into the alley behind the building. Anxious to avert a repeat of the palm incident, security had been tightened to unprecedented proportions. Not even accused Nazi war criminal John Demjanjuk, standing trial in an auditorium across town, was subjected to the kind of precautions that Vanunu faced. Shrouded from view by a canvas curtain, Vanunu emerged in handcuffs and was whisked inside without incident.

There were other safeguards as well. Security agents stood ready

279

to turn on a loud siren to prevent him from shouting to reporters or supporters, and on some days he was forced to wear a motorcycle helmet to keep quiet, prompting jokes about "the man in the iron mask." On the second day of testimony, Vanunu managed to tear off the helmet, but guards subdued him after a brief scuffle and switched on the deafening siren before he could open his mouth.

Inside the courthouse, the corridors through which Vanunu passed had been cleared, and the doors to courtrooms along the route were closed and locked. Employees were ordered to remain inside their offices. In the basement cafeteria, a plywood board was placed in a tiny window high on the wall to prevent a view of Vanunu's legs as he walked up a flight of stairs leading to the courtroom. Corridor doors, some built especially for the Vanunu case to cut off access to the courtroom, slammed shut behind the prisoner as he walked through. Uniformed police and plainclothes Shin Bet agents hugged the grey walls along the route, and others loitered outside a command post set up next to the courtroom.

The guards were primed. Standing outside the courtroom one afternoon, awaiting a court-approved glimpse of his brother, Asher Vanunu popped open a soft drink can. The corridor quickly flooded with Uzi-toting agents.

In the corridor outside the courtroom, three hallway windows that faced an air shaft were boarded up, and the windows in the bathroom set aside for the prisoner were covered with opaque plastic sheets.

The three judges hearing the case—District Court Vice President Eliahu Noam, Zvi Tal and Shalom Brenner—normally sat in a larger courtroom on the second floor, but security officials were concerned about its proximity to the roofs of Arab homes across the street. So the case was heard in courtroom 105 on the first floor, a smaller room with tiled floors that was lighted by flourescent bulbs and cooled by two ceiling fans. After Vanunu entered, the double doors to the courtroom were locked, and armed guards were posted just outside.

The judges, in black robes, sat behind a raised bench with their backs to the windows, which were covered with heavy curtains. In front of them were the defense and prosecution tables and three rows of spectator seats, which remained empty throughout the trial. Vanunu sat to their left, flanked by two Shin Bet agents. In the well were a stenographer and an audio technician who tape-recorded the proceedings. Every few days, the command post was cleared and locked, and two security agents carrying submachine guns took up positions outside the door. Inside, a female typist with top-secret security clearance would sit by herself for hours in front of a personal computer, transcribing the tape. When she was finished, court workers carried the tapes and the transcripts under guard to the Justice Ministry across the street. There, the material was locked in a safe in a room in the corner of the first floor. If Feldman or Hasson wanted to study the transcripts or examine the evidence, they could do it only in the safe room. Only the judges were allowed to study the evidence in their chambers and even then guards were stationed outside while they read.

The Shin Bet had wanted to build a special courtroom in Ashkelon prison to avoid the headache of transporting Vanunu and the evidence to court every day. But the suggestion outraged court officials. "There must be some minimum level of respect for the court process," the chief judge of the district court said in rejecting the proposal.

Feldman thought the unprecedented security was ridiculous—"you get the feeling that when Mr. Vanunu is brought to court, the H-bomb itself is arriving"—and further undermined his client's chances of a fair trial. All the concern over Vanunu revealing more secrets was nonsense, the lawyer believed. Vanunu had already revealed what he knew about his capture. What else was there for him to say? "The secret which should have been held in a cage has already sprouted wings and flown the coop," Feldman pointed out.

The first phase of the closed-door trial lasted little more than a week. Hasson presented his case—seven security officials and investigators who testified about Vanunu's confession and the security pledge he had signed at Dimona, and portrayed Vanunu as an opportunist who sold out his country for money. On the third day of the trial, with a dozen protesters carrying signs reading, "Let My People Know" parading outside the courthouse, Vanunu himself took the stand to claim he was brought home illegally and against his will. Wearing an open-neck shirt and standing without guards in the witness box, Vanunu testified for almost four hours, but was not permitted to identify the country where he was kidnapped or how he was brought back to Israel.

Despite his outbursts outside the courthouse, Vanunu was an exemplary witness, talking in a normal tone of voice that occasionally dropped so low the judges asked him to speak up.

After the first week, one of the judges suffered a heart attack and the trial was halted for almost two months. During the delay, the state made one more attempt to end the charade. Hasson proposed another plea bargain, but it was considerably tougher than the arrangement Zichroni had worked out a year earlier. Under the new offer, prosecutors would have dropped an aggravated espionage charge and allowed Vanunu to plead guilty to two other treason and espionage counts in exchange for a reduced sentence. But Feldman would only deal if the aggravated espionage and treason indictments were dismissed, leaving Vanunu to face a fifteen-year sentence. Vanunu would never plead guilty to treason. In his mind, he was not a traitor.

When the trial resumed December 1, 1987, the judges turned down Feldman's motion to dismiss the charges on grounds the state had not proved its case. Vanunu took the stand the next day but, angered by the court's ruling, initially refused to speak. Feldman eventually coaxed him into two additional days of testimony about his background and a limited explanation of his motives.

Feldman's challenges to the legality of Vanunu's arrest and his appeal for an open trial had also slowed the pace of the proceedings. Anxious to wrap up the matter, the court held hearings on his arguments, and rejected them, as the main trial moved along. But despite the adverse rulings, Feldman would not quit. He called Frank Barnaby, the British nuclear weapons expert who had debriefed Vanunu for the *Sunday Times*, and George Quester, a University of Maryland professor, to discuss the effect of Vanunu's actions and to point out that the world had long assumed Israel had a nuclear capability. Quester testified that the revelations quite possibly strengthened Israel's security by portraying the country as a nuclear power, and served to buttress the series of official hints dating back to 1974.

Feldman also forced appearances by Peres and Knesset member and former foreign minister Abba Eban in what he knew would be a vain attempt to make his case about the illegality of Israel's nuclear program. Peres showed up in court on January 6 armed with an order from Prime Minister Shamir that effectively barred him from testifying about anything except general observations concerning the damage to national security caused by Vanunu's revelations.

Peres, who was permitted to bring his media advisor and two bodyguards into court with him, barely acknowledged Vanunu's presence as he walked to the witness box. He told a television interviewer later that he felt "sorrow and shame" when he glanced over at Vanunu.

Feldman and Peres dueled politely over the limits of the foreign minister's testimony. Peres maintained that Vanunu's disclosures had in fact harmed Israel's security, but when Feldman respectfully pressed him for details, the minister fell back on the Shamir and Rabin orders and said he was not permitted to answer the questions. Frustrated, Feldman ended his examination after ninety minutes.

In an effort to counter the state's claim that Vanunu had acted for profit, Feldman also asked Peter Hounam to testify. The reporter had met repeatedly with Feldman during the summer and fall, both as a journalist and a potential witness.

The night before the journalist testified, Feldman, displaying his playful sense of humor, took Hounam for dinner at a Tel Aviv restaurant frequented by Shin Bet officials and other government employees. The restaurant filled quickly as the two men dined and customers crowded the entrance, waiting for a table. Feldman spotted a man waiting in the line with a woman, and waved him over to the table. A sly grin on his face, the lawyer introduced his dinner guest, saying Hounam was in town to testify at the Vanunu trial.

The man nodded politely at Hounam, then turned to Feldman and began chatting in Hebrew. After several minutes, Hounam jumped in.

"Avigdor, you haven't told me who your friend works for," he said.

"Oh, he's a lawyer like me," Feldman answered, grinning broadly in anticipation.

Hounam asked Feldman's friend where he worked. The man replied he was employed by the government, and swiftly changed the subject. After a few minutes of small talk, the man abruptly leaned across the table and whispered to Hounam, "I'd just like to say, you did a very good job in the Vanunu affair."

Surprised, Hounam stammered his thanks for the compliment, and the conversation shifted to other subjects. A short time later, Hounam and Feldman finished their meal and left.

"And we're walking along the road," Hounam recalled, "and I said, 'Who was that bloke?' Feldman said, 'He works for Shin Bet.' "

"And I go into court the following day and who's sitting behind Hasson? This guy. He was a legal advisor for Shin Bet."

In fact, the man had also been one of the security officials who questioned Vanunu about his political activities while he was still employed at Dimona.

The next morning, after security agents carefully searched him for notes or tape recorders, Hounam was ushered into Courtroom 105. It was a difficult moment. For the first time since London, he was face-to-face with the news source who he had come to regard as a friend. Vanunu, dressed in jeans and a plain shirt, smiled weakly, his eyes moist. He appeared healthy, albeit much thinner after more than a year in prison. Hounam felt helpless. Seeing Vanunu in court, surrounded by guards, cut off from any support, Hounam realized there was little he could do for him. No number of newspaper stories was going to improve this situation.

He tried to smile reassuringly, then walked to the witness box and glanced around, soaking up the scene. Hounam was immediately struck by the lack of paper. He was used to British or American courtrooms, where the desks in front of lawyers are usually littered with papers, documents, pieces of evidence, law books. In Court-room 105, all that was missing. A small pile of document sat on the judges' bench. But on the table in front of Hasson was only a pad of paper and a pencil. Feldman had just a single notebook.

Hounam's appearance stretched through the morning session and into the afternoon as Feldman walked him through an account of how he had met Vanunu and the nature of their discussions, then turned to the question of Vanunu's motives. Hounam stressed that Vanunu had received no money for his story, although he acknowl-edged that a book deal had been discussed. He pointed out that Vanunu had even tried to have the story published without his name. Vanunu, Hounam testified, was simply interested in ridding the Middle East of nuclear weapons.

Almost deferentially, Hasson cross-examined Hounam about Vanunu's decision to supply the *Sunday Times* with details about the layout of Dimona and the names of people who worked there. Why would Vanunu have disclosed that sort of information unless he was interested in harming the state? he asked.

Vanunu hadn't volunteered the information, Hounam explained patiently. The newspaper had demanded the information as a means of confirming Vanunu's story. And Vanunu had resolutely refused to compile a list of names of employees precisely because he was con-cerned about jeopardizing their safety.

Hasson switched gears. His tone of voice hardening, he suggested that Hounam must have known Vanunu was betraying his country when he discovered the Israeli had abandoned his religion. "You knew that he had renounced Judaism and converted to Christianity," Hasson contended. "Therefore, you knew that he had renounced his country and his family, didn't you?"

Hounam was irritated by the prosecutor's conclusion. "That is ridiculous," he retorted hotly. "No English person would ever think that just because you've changed your religion, that somehow you've turned into a traitor and that you've abandoned all your links with your family."

Turning to the judges, he added, "I find the question offensive."

At that, Hasson moved on to other subjects. But he had made his point. By converting, Vanunu had committed the ultimate act of treachery.

Aside from the skirmish on the religion question, Hounam received a polite reception in court. He had expected a chillier response; after all, Hounam had encouraged Vanunu to reveal Israel's nuclear secrets to the world. But the judges were exceedingly courteous and appeared genuinely interested in his remarks. They permitted him to finish his answers when Hasson attempted to cut him off, and interrupted the proceedings on several occasions to ask Hounam to clarify some points of his testimony. Even the reporter's passing comments about the "outrageous" way in which Vanunu had been brought back to Israel elicited nothing but smiles from the judges, the prosecutor and the other government officials in the courtroom.

As he left the courtroom at the conclusion of his testimony, Hounam walked directly to Vanunu's bench to say goodby. With tears in their eyes, they briefly embraced.

"Keep your spirits up and best of luck," Hounam said quietly.

"Thank you very much," Vanunu replied.

The guards moved in to gently separate the two men, and Hounam was led from the courtroom. Later, Hounam received a letter from Vanunu. "I can't thank you enough for what you've done," Vanunu told the reporter.

Chapter 54

As the trial progressed, Vanunu's mental state became a matter of growing concern to his attorney and his supporters. He was battered by the frustration of failure in court and the prospect of a lengthy imprisonment and many more years of solitary confinement. The acts of extremism that had marked Vanunu's last years of freedom now guided his life behind bars. He bucked prison regulations at every turn, claiming his refusal to cooperate was his only means of exercising a free will. He would not be examined by prison physicians, refused to leave his cell for his daily exercise period, and balked at body searches on his way to and from court. Disturbed by the around-the-clock monitoring of his cell, Vanunu smeared shaving cream on the lens of the television camera installed on the ceiling. In early 1987, he went on another monthlong hunger strike, ending it only after deciding that he needed to gain strength to stage other hunger strikes in the future. Vanunu began comparing himself to Mohandas K. Gandhi, the Indian leader whose non-violent campaign for change frequently included hunger strikes, and to Jesus Christ and Socrates.

Instead of improving his plight, Vanunu's gestures of defiance prompted even tougher measures from prison authorities. His radio and books were confiscated, his mail was withheld, and the disruptions were used against him in court as reasons for denying Feldman's frequent appeals for less restrictive jailhouse conditions.

More so than most prisoners, Vanunu was living in a world of his own, and the long hours of solitude fueled a growing paranoia. Yael Lotan first noticed the signs in early October as Vanunu entered his second year of incarceration. The letters from prison were becoming less focused. Vanunu's thoughts appeared fragmented and unconnected, and his suspicions were deepening. In one note, Vanunu complained about the defense committee and warned Lotan that "among you are some double agents whose business is to undermine your work."

In the ensuing weeks, Vanunu accused a committee leader of attempting to steal $10,000 of his Right-Livelihood prize, and demanded the removal of the wife of a man who had once been jailed for attempting to talk with Palestinian leaders in Syria. In another letter to Lotan, he complained that only leftists were backing him and wondered again whether they were in fact agents of the security services.

Lotan attempted to calm his fears by vouching for the integrity of her colleagues, some of whom had spent time in prison or saw their careers suffer as a consequence of their beliefs. "You have to face the facts," she wrote. "You have no allies except in the left because only the left is capable of taking up this nuclear issue. These are your only allies and if you now start to disqualify them because they're leftists, you're going to be left without any supporters. And you need the people outside."

In December 1987, Vanunu turned on Judy Zimmet, who had spent the year raising almost $20,000 for his defense and trying to drum up media interest in the case in the United States and Israel. Twice she had flown to Israel to see Vanunu but prison officials denied her requests. Despite her efforts, however, Vanunu was entertaining doubts about Judy. At best, she was using his case to advance leftist causes that he didn't support. At worst, she too was an Israeli agent.

Without personal contact, her communication limited to heavily censored letters, Judy had no way of knowing what her erstwhile boyfriend was thinking. When the trial resumed in early December, Judy flew to Tel Aviv to testify on his behalf. Feldman met her at the airport and, aware of Vanunu's growing disillusionment with the woman, hinted strongly on the drive to Jerusalem that it might be better if she did not take the stand.

The break came after Vanunu, on his way to court, saw Zimmet standing in the rain holding a placard with the words, "Free My

Fiance" written in seven languages. He angrily told Feldman that
he never wanted to see Zimmet again and instructed him to pass
along a message that he had never cared for her and wanted nothing
else to do with her. He sent back her letters, pictures and presents.
Feldman tried to sugarcoat the bombshell, assuring Zimmet that
Vanunu's explosion was only the result of his lengthy imprisonment. But the woman was devastated, and quickly flew home.

In long overseas telephone calls to Feldman, Zimmet tried to
make sense of the turn of events. "I have letters from Motti saying
he wanted to get married and have a family with me when he was
released," she wailed to the lawyer. "Why did he do this?"

With no answers, Feldman urged her to go ahead with her life.

It wasn't long before Lotan got the ax. On Christmas Day 1987,
Vanunu wrote to her saying he was now convinced that all of his
supporters were agents of the Mossad and Shin Bet.

This is to tell you that I have no doubt, no shadow of a doubt,
that I do not trust you or your friends. I'm asking you and the
others to stop acting in my name and for me, not to publish
any letters or anything. You played a bad game. I want you to
send all the letters back, you and all the others, and to stop
bothering my brothers and my lawyer. The trial will end soon.
You can stop acting. I don't need a committee. This is my last
letter to you and your friends. Every game has an end. End.
That's all.

Chapter 55

On March 24, 1988, a warm, sunny day in Jerusalem, the verdict came in: guilty as charged. Vanunu sat quietly, occasionally shaking his head, as the judges issued their ruling during a five-minute hearing. Only one sentence of their sixty-page decision was released, but it was the only one that mattered—"We decided the defendant is guilty on all three counts."

About 10 A.M., Vanunu headed back to prison in his van, its siren wailing as it pushed through the throngs of photographers outside the rear gates of the courthouse. In front of the building, Feldman vowed to appeal.

"The way we approached the case was that nuclear weapons put the society and the individual in a very big dilemma, and require, maybe, a different kind of obligation," the lawyer told reporters. "An obligation to the public in general, more than to where you work. It requires you to act on your conscience. We said that Vanunu did act on his conscience and undertook this social process."

"And that's the reason he did what he did. But the court didn't accept it."

In London, the *Sunday Times* released a statement that seemed as much an attempt to defend its actions as an expression of support for Vanunu. Governments have a right to protect secrets, the newspaper stated, but the existence of Israel's nuclear arsenal and Vanunu's story were of interest to the world. Vanunu "was primarily motivated by a desire to inform the people of Israel that their country was also a nuclear power—something which has hitherto been kept secret from them."

The *Sunday Times* also used the opportunity to point out it had warned Vanunu about the risks he faced, and would "always regret that he did not take our warnings seriously enough, with the tragic consequences of his abduction which followed. We remained concerned about the manner in which he was removed from British soil by agents of the Israeli security service."

No one from the *Sunday Times* was on hand for the verdict.

Vanunu's brother, Asher, said he was shocked by the outcome of the trial, and pledged an "international campaign" to win his brother's freedom. Meir Vanunu called the verdict "a sad day for all of us, and for justice in general," and vowed to hold "an alternative Vanunu trial" in the United States or Britain.

That night, Vanunu's conviction wasn't even the main story on the television news in Israel. The Palestinian uprising in the West Bank and Gaza Strip had pushed him to the sidelines.

At a hearing three days later, Vanunu was sentenced to eighteen years in prison. Feldman pleaded for leniency, saying Vanunu had acted out of ideological, not criminal motives, and presented the court with an appeal signed by twenty scientists from around the world, including a dozen Nobel Prize laureates and American astronomer Carl Sagan, who called Vanunu "a man of conscience."

"No greater regard can be shown by the court for the decent opinion of humankind than by acknowledging the lonely courage of Mordechai Vanunu, who has acted from considerations of conscience," the petition read.

But the court swept aside Feldman's arguments. "We informed the defense in the course of his argument that some of the worst crimes in human history—from the Middle Ages until today—were committed for ideological reasons," the judges said in a brief statement announcing the sentence.

The judges also maintained it was irrelevant whether the information was correct; simply releasing it was wrong.

Hasson had asked for one full life sentence, which amounts to twenty years in Israel in cases not involving murder, but the judges trimmed two years from the request because Vanunu had cooperated with authorities and had shown "signs of regret in recent remarks over the path that he chose." In addition, the court noted, Vanunu was likely to serve the entire sentence in solitary confinement.

The day of the sentencing, Sica announced plans to fly to Israel to interview Vanunu. "I'm not concerned with whether or not Vanunu has been found guilty," the investigator said. "What has to be cleared up is how he ended up in Israel."

The news was greeted cooly by Israeli officials, who warned the Italian would not be allowed to see the prisoner. "If Dr. Sica comes," one Foreign Ministry official said, "it would be very, very embarrassing for our government."

Epilogue

By the summer of 1989, two years into his sentence, Vanunu was struggling to survive the rigors of solitary confinement.

The paranoia he exhibited during his trial had deepened. Desperate for companionship, he occasionally talked aloud to imaginary friends, concluding the "conversations" by flashing the V-shaped sign of peace with his fingers. Living in a world of his own, Vanunu had created a bewildering set of precepts that he wrote on pieces of paper and taped to the wall of his cell to guide his struggle to survive. "Don't answer when you are talked to," one stated. "Don't get angry," another read. In an effort to exert some control over his existence, he arbitrarily alternated between accepting privileges like exercise and refusing to leave his cell.

Christianity and his Australian friends had become Vanunu's only anchors. Adopting his Christian baptismal name, Vanunu now called himself "John Motti." He drew a large cross on a piece of cardboard and prominently displayed it on the wall of his cell, and prayed every day, using an Anglican missal and taped religious services sent to him by the parishioners of St. John's Church in Sydney.

When he wasn't praying, Vanunu, isolated from the rest of the Ashkelon prison population, whiled away the time by reading, watching television, listening to the radio, and wading through the mail he had received from supporters around the world. For the first six months, the lights in his tiny cell were left on around the clock and the television camera on the ceiling continued to monitor his activities. The security watch ended only after Vanunu signed a letter promising not to hurt himself, a document that appeared designed to absolve the government of any responsibility if the prisoner committed suicide.

Angered by the prison's refusal to permit face-to-face meetings, Vanunu had ordered his family to end their visits, which in any case had been cut back from once every two weeks to one hour a month. Feldman, busy with his thriving practice, seldom called on his first client. There was little else to discuss after the filing of the appeal, which was still undecided in March 1990.

As a result, the only human being in regular, daily contact with Vanunu was the guard who brought his meals.

To keep his spirits high, Vanunu thought about the future. He planned to move to Australia and rejoin the Sydney church community that had so warmly embraced him. Under Israeli law, Vanunu could be released after serving two-thirds of his sentence, or twelve years. He will be eligible for parole in the year 2000. If he can weather the psychological strain of confinement, Vanunu will be forty-five years old.

Feldman doesn't believe his client will serve his entire sentence in solitary, but the Shin Bet is expected to insist. Even with Vanunu behind bars, the security forces have not eased up on their campaign of vilification. In mid-1989 the Justice Ministry drafted a response to overseas inquiries about the Vanunu case. The three-page form letter blamed Vanunu for a 1988 Palestinian bus hijacking in the Negev region that claimed the lives of three Dimona workers.

Vanunu "could not have been unaware of the fact that every intelligence service, including those of countries that maintain a state of war with Israel, would benefit" from his disclosures, the letter stated.

"Anyone who reads the articles in the *Sunday Times* will see that Mr. Vanunu provided information which he claimed to be true, concerning the security arrangements for the reactor, procedures for hiring personnel, the route that employees take to work every morning, and the exact place where workers are picked up by buses," the letter went on.

"These details have no connection whatsoever to the political views which Mr. Vanunu now alleges to have been his motivation for supplying the information for publication. While he, and many of his supporters, claims he acted solely in opposition to the development of nuclear weapons in the world, and in Israel in particular, the details he chose to reveal had the effect of setting-up the reactor and its workers for military or terrorist attack. Following the *Sunday Times* publication of Mr. Vanunu's article, on 7 March, 1988, a group of PLO terrorists hijacked a bus transporting workers to the reactor and three of these workers (Miriam Ben-Yair, Rina Shiratzki and Victor Ram) were killed. Eight other women employees of the reactor were wounded. It is logical to conclude that the terrorists who murdered these workers were aided by information revealed by Mr. Vanunu. Clearly, Mr. Vanunu's actions, apart from any information he may have passed on about Israel's alleged nuclear capacity, have damaged the security of the state," the letter stated.

The attempt to link Vanunu to a PLO attack was another bid to stir up public resentment against the prisoner. As the government surely knew, the Dimona bus routes, pickup points and hiring procedures have long been common knowledge. Vanunu provided no information about the defenses of the plant. Most importantly, the "terrorist attack" wasn't even aimed at the plant or its employees. The army itself concluded that the terrorists had slipped across the Egyptian border intent on staging any kind of attack. They had stumbled on an army patrol and eventually hijacked two cars and the bus in an attempt to escape. Vanunu's information had nothing to do with the tragedy that ensued, but authorities callously chose to make him an accomplice in the deaths as part of their campaign to justify the government's treatment of him.

Uzi Hasson, the prosecutor, acknowledges Israel is intent upon making sure Vanunu doesn't reveal anything else about his case, even if the information is nothing but a source of embarrassment to the Israeli government.

"Everything that is embarrassing to Israel is in a way causing damage to our security," Hasson contended.

And are there any other secrets left for Vanunu to spill?

"When you will interview Vanunu, you will ask him," Hasson said with a sly grin.

In late 1988, the Italian inquiry into Vanunu's allegations was closed on the strength of a seven-page confidential final report filed by Domenico Sica that suggested the Vanunu affair was in fact a carefully planned Mossad operation from the start. Sica stated he had found no evidence "that the Israeli was really kidnapped and that the kidnapping itself occurred in Rome or in any way on state territory."

Sica's report was clearly a political document, designed to give the Italian government a convenient excuse not to confront Israel over the Vanunu affair. If the Vanunu disclosures were part of an official Israeli disinformation campaign, and if Vanunu was actually a Mossad agent, then no crimes had been committed in Rome, or London, for that matter. Italian officials readily acknowledge that Sica was talking tough in public and trying to dump the case in private. A veteran of Italy's political wars, Sica understood that political pressures would leave him open to attack no matter what his conclusion.

In any event, Israel's refusal to cooperate with the Italian probe hindered any serious efforts by Sica, and he was loathe to press the point. His ties to Israeli intelligence, with whom he had worked closely during terrorism investigations in the 1970s, dampened his enthusiasm. The magistrate was a welcome guest at the Israeli Embassy during and after the Vanunu episode. Israel couldn't have been happier with his report.

Britain also fell into line. Two days after Vanunu was sentenced, Home Secretary Douglas Hurd said the Thatcher government planned no further action on the matter. "Following Mr. Vanunu's disappearance and later arrival in Israel in 1986 the Israeli government issued a statement that Mr. Vanunu left Britain of his own volition through normal departure procedures and that his departure from Britain involved no violation of British law," Hurd wrote in a letter to opposition foreign affairs spokesman George Robertson. "There is no evidence to the contrary."

There is no doubt that Israeli agents violated the laws of both Britain and Italy to carry out the Vanunu abduction. Regardless of whether Vanunu voluntarily agreed to leave London with Cheryl

Hanin Bentov, the scheme to kidnap him was hatched on British soil. And the Mossad's actions in Rome were blatantly illegal. But officials in the two countries concluded that Vanunu's legal rights were of less significance than diplomatic relationships with Israel.

The Vanunu family is attempting to put the nightmare behind them. Solomon has returned to his stall on the edge of the Beersheba central market. He and his wife, Mazal, are again part of the community in the Dalet neighborhood, where residents seem willing to forgive the parents for the sins of their son. Mordechai's younger brothers are attending university and his sisters have settled back into obscurity with their husbands and children. If anything, life has improved somewhat. The Vanunus' apartment house was repaired and painted, one of the first targets of a government building rehabilitation program in Beersheba.

But the tight family circle that Solomon struggled to defend through the arduous early years in Israel has been irrevocably broken. His three eldest sons—the jewels in the family crown—are gone and seem unlikely to return. Mordechai, of course, is in prison. Disillusioned with life in Israel, Albert, the oldest son, abandoned his carpentry business and moved his family to Canada in mid-1989. "I'm leaving now for a long time and if you can tell Motti, I won't be back for quite a long time," he told Avigdor Feldman in a telephone call just before he left.

Meir is truly a man without a country. The warrant for his arrest remains in effect in Israel and Britain has spurned his applications for political asylum. "You have applied for asylum on the grounds that you have a well-founded fear of persecution in Israel for reasons of race, religion, nationality, membership of a particular social group or political opinion," the government informed Meir in a letter in late 1987. "However, the secretary of state considers that your fear is more one of prosecution than persecution.

"You signed an acknowledgment when visiting your brother that you recognized you would be in breach of national security and liable to prosecution if you were to disclose details of your brother's case. This warning was repeated on numerous occasions, yet you decided to disclose these details."

Meir has been permitted to remain in London temporarily, but is barred from working. He shares a small house in a working-class area of north London with several roommates, supporting himself with some of the funds raised through the organization he established to win Mordechai's release, "The International Campaign to Free Mordechai Vanunu and for a Nuclear Free Middle East."

The public relations effort, never a very powerful force, is barely surviving, although Meir drummed up some support for a petition campaign aimed at securing Mordechai's release. In late 1988 members of the European Parliament nominated Vanunu for its Andrei Sakharov Award for "his courage (and) his selfless determination to make public Israel's work on nuclear technology with martial capabilities." Other nominees included former Soviet Jewish dissident Natan Scharansky and South African black nationalist leader Nelson Mandela. In 1989 Vanunu was again nominated for the Nobel Peace Prize, which was eventually awarded to the Dalai Lama.

As he sits in his prison cell, Mordechai Vanunu has few regrets.

"I don't see myself as someone who descended from the moon in order to save mankind," he wrote to a supporter. "But I do see myself as a hero because I succeeded in freeing myself of the suffocating, security-minded mentality and doing something which would contribute to stopping and restraining the proliferation of nuclear arms in the area. This was my contribution to raising this subject to the consciousness of all the people in the region, because if we don't stop now, it will be too late. A small step today may prevent a major catastrophe, and may be a large step for the future of mankind."

In a speech written for the Right-Livelihood Award ceremonies in 1987, Vanunu said he hoped the open acknowledgment of the dangers of nuclear war would push forward the peace process:

Israel has attained the summit of its military might. (censored). But there is still no peace. There is still a state of war.

Men, women and children are being killed. All this military might has not produced a life of peace and security. So we have no choice but to proceed to invest more in the effort to achieve peace. War only leads to war and then another war. Eventually they may lead to a nuclear disaster. But perhaps the danger of nuclear disaster will drive the people in the region to take a chance on peace. Forty years of war in our region are more than enough. There is a limit to what people can stand. Now they are weary of war and want to live in peace, to feel that there is no more danger, that their children are not destined to be soldiers, that children are brought into this world to live in it, not to fight.

Unquestionably, Vanunu raised an extremely important issue. The existence of a powerful and sophisticated nuclear arsenal in an always contentious region such as the Middle East is a threat to world security that must be dealt with openly, particularly at a time when the superpowers are searching for ways to stand down from the nuclear stalemate that has dominated global affairs since the end of World War II. The paramount problem with a nuclearized Middle East is not so much the bombs Israel has buried beneath the desert sands, but the judgments Israel's enemies have made about the purpose of the weapons. Vanunu's belief that the world, and especially the Israeli people, must address that subject was entirely legitimate.

As so often happens in history, however, this vital message was delivered by the wrong man, acting largely on the wrong motives. Mordechai Vanunu was a naive misfit, truly a restless rebel searching for some cause out of an almost childish pique, who saw in the Dimona revelations an opportunity to strike back at a country that had shunted him aside. In a very real sense, the Dimona secrets were a vehicle for attacking a system that had ignored him. As his loathing and bitterness toward Israel deepened, Vanunu came to see Israel's bomb program as a metaphor for the policies and attitudes that had prevented him from joining the mainstream of Israeli society. With his fragile mental state deteriorating under the strain of loneliness and rejection, Vanunu seized upon Dimona as his chance to exact a measure of revenge. And from the outset, he knew his actions represented a betrayal of Israel for which he could pay a steep price.

Vanunu's crime was far more serious than espionage or treason. He had broken faith with his country. The Holocaust experience, which tinges every aspect of Israeli society, has left most Israelis uncomfortable with the knowledge that they could inflict such a monstrous horror on another people. But the nightmare of the death camps is also a compelling reason for ensuring their ultimate survival, even if that requires a nuclear arsenal. Israelis were relieved of the grim task of reconciling their conflicting emotions by the government's policy of ambiguity, which allowed them to simply ignore the nuclear issue. For most, it was enough to assume the bomb was in the basement. There was no reason to go down to look at it. But Mordechai Vanunu not only turned on the lights, he invited the world over for a peek. In a state where security and secrecy are a way of life, Mordechai Vanunu talked.

In the minds of many Israelis, Vanunu had threatened the very existence of the Jewish state. The long, tragic history of the Jewish people is a bloody tale of unimaginable persecution that appeared to have climaxed in the gas chambers of Nazi Germany and finally ended in 1948 where it began, in the land of Canaan, with the establishment of a parliamentary democracy strongly influenced by religious authority. To give up the land of Israel now, after thousands of years of struggle, is inconceivable. And that the man who imperiled the security of the state was a Jew who had renounced his religion was the consummate irony of the Vanunu affair.

Vanunu had committed the most heinous form of betrayal possible in Israel. The conversion was a sign to many Israelis that Vanunu was mentally unstable. At the very least, it was a searing comment on his character. Even leftist Israelis, who might have been expected to sympathize with Vanunu politically, could not abide his decision to give up Judaism. One leading Israeli leftist, angered by the conversion, called Vanunu the "scum of the earth."

A headline over a *Jerusalem Post* story tracing Vanunu's life best summed up national opinion: "Mordechai Vanunu's drift from the fold."

By talking about the bomb and converting to Christianity, Vanunu had rubbed raw two extremely sensitive social nerves. It was virtually impossible for Israelis to even try to understand his decision.

With the Holocaust and Israeli fears of annihilation serving as a blood-drenched backdrop, Israelis eagerly accepted the government's portrait of Vanunu as an unmitigated villain and overwhelmingly supported its decision to stage a severely restricted trial behind closed doors. Asked to choose between a perceived threat to their security, however tenuous, and the defense of civil liberties, Israelis frequently endorse without question the official abrogation of rights considered basic in modern democracies. The siege mentality that pervades Israeli society—perhaps the single most cohesive strand in the country's social fabric—ensured that the government's handling of the Vanunu case and the secrecy surrounding it would receive absolute public approval.

That the Peres government was faced with a disaster of enormous proportions is undeniable. Its decision to allow Vanunu to tell his story and send a message to the world about Israel's nuclear strength was perhaps the best of the available options. There was certainly a hint of ironic brilliance to it: the man who betrayed Israel became its unwitting ally.

Whatever its motives, however, Israel's actions cannot be excused. The decision to circumvent established procedures of international law—a not uncommon choice by the country in its often overzealous, singleminded pursuit of security—flew in the face of acceptable behavior of democratic nations. The kidnapping called into question the legality of Vanunu's trial and his subsequent imprisonment, as well as Israel's commitment to human rights. Moreover, the government's public contention that Vanunu damaged national security pales in the light of the secret agenda of the "prime ministers' club." With that background, Vanunu's life sentence, with a strong likelihood of years of solitary confinement, was a particularly callous and cynical act. To allow Vanunu to spill the secrets of Dimona and then punish him for doing it was unconscionable.

There was, however, no serious condemnation of Israel's actions from other countries. Vanunu's bizarre behavior and the shaky moral foundation of his stated motives allowed the world to once again look the other way. In the end, Israel's problem was not what Vanunu told the world. Instead, the challenge to Jerusalem was masking its violation of the laws of sovereign nations in seizing him.

Vanunu's message has been largely lost on the world. As long as Israel does not officially flaunt its power, countries like the United States are willing to pretend the bomb does not exist. To confront Israel on this issue would be a losing proposition that could upset the balance of power in the Middle East.

Israel has played its U.S. gambit with sangfroid. It has a unique security relationship with the United States, frequently acting in the past as a surrogate for U.S. power in the Middle East. In return, the United States has allowed Israel to operate with little or no restraint.

Still, Israel's intransigence on the nuclear issue—its refusal to submit to international nuclear non-proliferation treaties or to allow international inspection of its facilities—should be a source of greater concern to the United States. Other potential nuclear states already see an element of hypocrisy in U.S. calls for non-proliferation while Washington ignores the burgeoning nuclear capability of its close ally.

There are signs the United States is becoming somewhat more critical of Israel's nuclear buildup. U.S. officials took the extraordinary step of restricting the access of Israeli scientists to American nuclear weapons laboratories after discovering the Israelis had been given classified information on nuclear technology. The Bush administration was also wrestling in 1989 with the problem of whether to allow Israel and other countries believed to be developing nuclear programs to purchase U.S.-built supercomputers, which permit the accurate simulation of the effect of nuclear explosions and missile trajectories without the need for testing. Israel managed to build an entire strategic nuclear program with little or no testing, using computer simulations. A supercomputer would permit even more sophisticated tests on a new generation of weapons.

But none of this appears to have slowed the Israeli nuclear juggernaut. In the three years after the Vanunu affair, the Israeli nuclear program reached new heights, even as the government continued to deny its existence. In 1987 Israel test-fired a Jericho II missile capable of carrying an atomic payload. U.S. intelligence experts believe Israel has between forty-five and sixty-five Jerichos, with a range of almost 900 miles—a distance that would make every Arab capital and Soviet naval bases on the Black Sea potential Israeli targets. In the fall of 1988 Israel successfully launched a three-stage rocket carrying a space satellite. U.S. experts concluded Israel had the capability of launching a ballistic missile that could travel more than 2,800 miles and carry a one-ton payload.

In September 1989 Israel tested the Jericho intermediate range missile again. The missile flew more than 800 miles before splashing down in the Mediterranean, 250 miles north of Benghazi, Libya. One month later, there were reports the Israelis had shared advanced missile technology with South Africa in exchange for uranium supplies needed to build nuclear weapons.

The reports about the South African connection coincided with a visit to Washington by Prime Minister Yitzhak Shamir for talks on the Middle East peace process. Following a meeting with President George Bush on November 15, Shamir appeared on the Public Broadcasting System's "McNeil-Lehrer News Hour." At the end of the interview, the prime minister was asked about the military relationship between South Africa and Israel. Shamir acknowledged "some ties" between the two countries in the past, but assured host Jim Lehrer that any "existing contracts" would expire in a few years.

"Do some of these contracts involve nuclear missiles, nuclear weapons?" Lehrer persisted.

The prime minister responded with practiced dismay.

"Oh, God forbid, Israel doesn't have any nuclear arms," Shamir said. "It is our policy not to introduce nuclear arms in the Middle East, not to be the first to introduce any nuclear arms in our region, and we will not do it. We will not be the first to do it and we will not transfer any technologies of such kind to other countries."

"Did President Bush raise this with you in your meeting today?" Lehrer inquired.

"He asked me about it and I gave him the same answer," Shamir said.

"Just what you just told me?" Lehrer asked.

"Yes," the Israeli leader calmly replied. "Yes."

Source Notes

At the outset, I must note that I was unable to interview Mordechai Vanunu. Israeli prison authorities refused several requests for meetings. In addition, I made four attempts to contact Vanunu by mail, but he either never received the letters or chose not to answer them.

Likewise, several requests for interviews with the three principal government ministers involved in the Vanunu affair - Shimon Peres, Yitzhak Shamir and Yitzhak Rabin - were also denied.

The book is based on interviews with more than 120 people in five countries—Israel, Britain, Italy, the United States, and Australia—with direct and detailed indirect knowledge of various aspects of the case. For personal and professional reasons, many of the sources, particularly individuals still connected with the government of Israel, preferred to remain anonymous, and I respected their wishes. But most of the information supplied by these individuals was confirmed with at least one, and frequently more, sources.

In a few cases, an account of a particular event is based solely on one source. This practice was employed only when the source had convinced me beyond reasonable doubt of his or her veracity, usually by supplying other information that subsequently proved to be accurate.

The book includes a number of direct quotations from conversations at which I obviously was not present. They are instead drawn from the recollections of participants or individuals who were given detailed accounts of the conversations by participants soon after they occurred. In a few cases, the conversations are taken from notes kept by participants. I was careful to use quotations from only those sources who I came to trust implicitly.

Prologue

Vanunu's explanation of his motives is taken from interviews with Peter Hounam, Meir Vanunu and Avigdor Feldman, and letters written by Mordechai Vanunu to friends and supporters.

The information regarding the Dimona plant and the employees' routine is drawn from Vanunu's recollections and confidential interviews with three Dimona workers employed at the plant in the summer of 1989 and a former technician who left his job in 1987.

Part I

Chapter 1

The brief history of Beersheba and the post-1948 development of the Negev is drawn from interviews with several Beersheba residents and accounts in various books about Israel's early years and David Ben-Gurion.

Chapter 2-3

The account of Vanunu's early years and the family's life in Israel is based on the written and oral recollections of Mordechai Vanunu, Meir Vanunu and other family members.

A fuller account of the Mossad's secret Moroccan emigration network is provided in *The Imperfect Spies* by Yossi Melman and Dan Raviv (London: Sidgwick & Jackson Limited, 1989).

Chapter 4-6

The description of the Dimona training program, Vanunu's first years at the plant, and his early university days are based on recollections he provided to the London Sunday Times, as well as interviews with Meir Vanunu and other friends and family members.

Chapter 7-10

Vanunu's changing political and philosophical outlooks are drawn from his diaries, interviews with Meir Vanunu and other family members, interviews with Chaim Marantz and two other professors, at least five students who attended Ben-Gurion University with Vanunu, and Israeli media reports that followed his capture.

The discussion of the Shin Bet's troubles in identifying Vanunu as a security risk is based on interviews with three current Shin Bet officials and two former officials, who cooperated with the author on condition of anonymity.

The May 1985 meeting between Vanunu and security officials in Tel Aviv is reconstructed from Vanunu's recollections of the session.

Chapter 11
Vanunu provided a detailed account of his photographic efforts inside Dimona to the *Sunday Times*, and to three other individuals who requested anonymity.

Chapter 12
The information about Vanunu's last days at Dimona and his final months in Israel is drawn from accounts he provided to several *Sunday Times* staffers, and the author's interviews with Meir Vanunu, Chaim Marantz, Judy Zimmet, two Israeli friends and one Arab acquaintance.

Part II

Chapter 13
Vanunu's travels in Asia and his relationship with the church in Sydney are reconstructed from his written recollections, letters and postcards to Judy Zimmet, various newspaper and television interviews with John McKnight, and the author's interviews with David Smith and other St. John's parishioners.

Chapter 14-16
The information on Oscar Guerrero's background is based on the author's interviews with Peter Hounam, Portugese journalists and the recollections of a number of individuals who encountered Guerrero, as well as Interpol records.

The dealings between Vanunu and Guerrero are drawn from Vanunu's recollections.

The information regarding Guerrero's initial contact with the Mossad is based on the author's confidential interviews with three Israeli intelligence officials and one Israeli government official, all of whom were directly involved in the case.

Chapter 17-18

The nature of Guerrero's involvement with the Sunday Times and the newspaper's handling of the story are drawn from the author's interviews with Peter Hounam, Wendy Robbins, Robin Morgan, and more than a dozen other current and former *Sunday Times* staff members.

A fuller account of the Hitler diaries scandal can be found in *Selling Hitler* by Robert Harris (London: Faber and Faber, 1986).

The description of the Wapping dispute is taken from British newspaper coverage of the conflict, and interviews by the author.

Chapter 19

The description of problems within the Israeli intelligence community is based on the author's interviews with current and former Israeli government officials, Israeli media reports and several books about Israeli intelligence, including *The Imperfect Spies* by Yossi Melman and Dan Raviv (London: Sidgwick & Jackson Limited, 1989).

Information about the history of Israel's nuclear program is taken from books and media reports on the subject, the author's interviews with Shai Feldman and Avner Cohen of Tel Aviv University, and Israeli officials.

Chapter 20-21

The descriptions of the deliberations of the Vanunu working group as well as Prime Minister Shimon Peres' analysis are based on the recollections of three participants in the meetings, two individuals who were directly involved in the planning, and three other individuals who were intimately familiar with the case. Because of possible criminal and political liabilities, all eight agreed to cooperate with the author only on condition of anonymity.

Chapter 22

The account of Vanunu's last days in Australia is based on the author's interviews with Peter Hounam.

Part III

Chapter 23-25

The information about Vanunu's involvement with the *Sunday Times* in London is drawn from the author's interviews with several *Sunday Times* staff members and with Meir Vanunu.

The background about the *Sunday Times* and the Insight team was provided by current and former *Sunday Times* staff members.

Vanunu's meeting with Yoram Bazak was described by Wendy Robbins, who was present at the dinner.

Chapter 26

The activities of the Mossad were reconstructed through the author's interviews with Israeli intelligence sources involved in the operation.

Chapter 27-29

Vanunu's dealings with the *Sunday Times* were described by several current and former *Sunday Times* staff members.

Guerrero's activities in London were reconstructed through interviews in London by the author, and *Sunday Mirror* accounts.

Hirsh Goodman provided the account of his meeting with the two Peres aides.

Chapter 30

The information about the discussion between Shimon Peres and Margaret Thatcher was drawn from the author's interviews with official sources in Israel and Britain.

The account of the editor's committee meeting comes from two participants and one other Israeli journalist who did not attend the meeting but discussed the session with participants shortly afterwards.

Vanunu's meeting with "Cindy" is based on his conversations with the *Sunday Times*.

Chapter 31-32

The information about the Mossad operation came from Israeli intelligence sources.

Background on Cheryl Hanin was obtained from sources in the United States.

Chapter 33

Vanunu's final days in London and the *Sunday Times'* deliberations were reconstructed through the author's interviews with *Sunday Times* staff members and Vanunu's own account, as described to Meir Vanunu and others.

Chapter 34

The description of the kidnapping in Rome is based on Vanunu's own recollections and information provided by both Israeli and Italian official sources.

Chapter 35

The activities of the *Sunday Times* and the reactions to the Dimona story are drawn from the author's interviews with the participants and various media reports.

Vanunu described his return to Israel to several individuals, who were interviewed by the author.

Part IV

Chapter 36-40

The various aspects of the search for Vanunu were drawn from the author's interviews with participants.

Chapter 41

The Israeli government's handling of the media furor was described by Israeli government officials familiar with the case.

Chapter 42
The information about U.S. State Department inquiries regarding the Vanunu case and the assessment by the U.S. Embassy in London was contained in documents obtained by the author under the Freedom of Information Act.

The account of the November 9 meeting and the deliberations leading to it was provided by government officials familiar with the process.

Chapter 43
The contacts between the Israeli and British governments were outlined by Israel, British and U.S. officials.

Chapter 44-47
The accounts of Vanunu's incarceration and court appearances are drawn from the author's interviews with participants and Israeli media reports.

Part V

Chapter 48
The account, of Meir Vanunu's jailhouse meetings with his brother and Meir's negotiations with Sica and the *Sunday Times* was provided by Meir Vanunu and *Sunday Times* staffers

Chapter 49
The meeting between Peter Hounam and David Connett and Cheryl Hanin Bentov is based on the recollections of Hounam, who tape-recorded much of the discussion.

Chapter 50
Meir Vanunu's dealings with Amnon Zichroni and Avigdor Feldman were described by all three men.

Chapter 51

Meir Vanunu's attempts to drum up public support for his brother were outlined by Meir Vanunu and Yael Lotan.

The account of Meir's legal problems following his disclosure of additional details about his brother's case was drawn from interviews with Meir Vanunu and Israel Justice Ministry officials.

Chapter 52

Avigdor Feldman's legal strategy and the government's reaction were outlined by the lawyer and Israeli officials involved in the case.

Chapter 53

The account of Vanunu's trial was based on the recollections of Israeli journalists, individuals who attended the trial and Peter Hounam.

Chapter 54

Mordechai Vanunu's deteriorating mental state was described by Yael Lotan and other supporters, as well as Avigdor Feldman and Judy Zimmet.

Chapter 55

The account of Vanunu's conviction and sentencing was drawn from newspaper coverage and interviews with Avigdor Feldman.

Index